THE OFFICIAL

DESSERTS COOKBOOK

Remembering 101 Sweet Delicious Disney Recipes

THE OFFICIAL

Disney Parks
DESSERTS COOKBOOK

Remembering 101 Sweet Delicious Disney Recipes

PAM BRANDON & THE DISNEY CHEFS

EDITIONS

Los Angeles • New York

EDITOR'S NOTE: Please remember that the Disney parks are constantly changing and growing, and the printed recipes you hold in your hands are our best effort at accuracy at the time of printing. If given an opportunity to update this book at a future date, we will refine and expand our materials to even better enhance your experience.

These recipes have been converted from a larger quantity in the restaurants' kitchens. The flavor profiles may vary from the restaurants' versions.

Always use caution when handling sharp objects and hot contents, and please supervise children who are helping or are nearby.

All recipes are the property of Walt Disney Parks and Resorts U.S., Inc., and may not be reproduced without express permission.

Thank you, and enjoy!

Published by Disney Editions, an imprint of Buena Vista Books, Inc. No part of this book may be reproduced or transmitted in any form or by any means, electronic or mechanical, including photocopying, recording, or by any information storage and retrieval system, without written permission from the publisher.

For information address Disney Editions, 7 Hudson Square, New York, New York 10013.

Editorial Director: Wendy Lefkon
Senior Editor: Jennifer Eastwood
Senior Designer: Lindsay Broderick
Managing Editor: Monica Vasquez

ISBN 978-1-368-10619-1
FAC-025393-25093
Printed in China
First Hardcover Edition, October 2025

1 3 5 7 9 10 8 6 4 2
Visit www.disneybooks.com

D23
THE OFFICIAL DISNEY FAN CLUB

THIS PAGE: Greetings from Goofy, Mickey Mouse, Minnie Mouse, Donald Duck, and Pluto in front of Cinderella Castle in the Magic Kingdom at the Walt Disney World Resort

CONTENTS

INTRODUCTION
Delicious Disney Desserts

EAT DESSERT FIRST. I'm not sure that's really about dessert; maybe it's more about doing the things you love first or doing things out of order, like my preference for heading to the Canada pavilion instead of the fan-recommended Mexico pavilion at EPCOT to start my stroll around World Showcase. Whatever the reason, we say eat dessert first, especially on vacation.

I've swooned over hundreds of Disney desserts. But my sweetest memory is the crisp, chewy oatmeal cookie from the kitchen of Master Pastry Chef Erich Herbitschek at Disney's Grand Floridian Resort & Spa that I first tasted way back in 1995 when he joined the culinary team at The Grand. Chef Erich turned out legendary wedding cakes and the most gorgeous sweets, but it was his humble oatmeal cookie with molasses and a splash of rum that I dreamed about and for which I begged the recipe. (You can find it these days on page 163 of *The Official Disney Parks Cookbook: 101 Magical Recipes from the Delicious Disney Vault*.) Chef Erich is long retired, but that recipe is one I still make for school bake sales, or potlucks, or just to stash at home for a snack with a glass of ice-cold milk.

Speaking of fond flashbacks, we collected a hundred and one sweet things from the Disneyland Resort; the Walt Disney World Resort; Aulani, A Disney Resort & Spa; and the Disney Cruise Line ships—and put them all in *this* book. We go back decades to share the flaky Stilton Cheesecake from Victoria & Alberts, the rich Piña Colada Bread Pudding from a Disney Cruise Line ship, and one of my longtime favorites from the EPCOT International Food & Wine Festival, the Peanut Butter–White Chocolate Mousse (from *The Chew*). And we've got new favorites, like the unusually delicious vegan Plant-Based Lavender Donut from the California Grill at Disney's Contemporary Resort and the sweet, tart Lemon Tea Cake from Disney's one hundredth anniversary celebration.

Every recipe is tested in a home kitchen. We test each recipe up to three times, and if they just aren't working in our kitchen, we toss them out, even though they might work perfectly in a professional Disney kitchen. Some of these recipes use fun shortcuts, like store-bought cake mix or cookie dough. Some take a lot of patience, and as baking is a science, measurements are more important than when you're making a savory dish. We recommend reading a recipe before beginning, and lining up your ingredients just to make it easier. Take your time and have fun re-creating a Disney memory.

Then gather your family or friends around the kitchen table for a delicious meal, and end on a high note with one of the desserts from this book. Or make these sweets an anytime treat!

—Pam Brandon
Summer 2025

OPPOSITE: Guests enjoying ice cream from the Anandapur Ice Cream Truck in Asia at Disney's Animal Kingdom Theme Park, 2021

CHAPTER ONE
Cookies & Bars

THE AROMA OF THESE freshly baked cookies will take your mind on a journey to happy times at the Disney parks and resorts. Bite into a Meyer Lemon Macaron to be transported back to memories of a Disney California Adventure Food & Wine Festival paying tribute to the citrus groves of the Golden State. Or savor every bite of an Italian classic with a twist from Trattoria al Forno at Disney's BoardWalk Inn & Villas.

MEYER LEMON MACARONS
WITH BLUEBERRY PRESERVES & HOMEMADE BUTTERCREAM

FESTIVAL DEBUT: 2017 · LEMON GROVE/CITRUS GROVE FESTIVAL MARKETPLACE

A favorite from the Disney California Adventure Food & Wine Festival, this lemony macaron has a surprise in the middle—blueberry preserves. Delicious with a late-harvest Riesling.

MAKES ABOUT 24 MACARONS

FROM THE DISNEYLAND RESORT

FRENCH MACARON SHELLS

6 large egg whites, at room temperature

1 teaspoon cream of tartar

1⅓ cups sugar, divided

1¼ cups powdered sugar

1¼ cups almond flour

Zest of 4 large Meyer lemons, divided

12 drops yellow food coloring, plus more if desired

Favorite blueberry preserves (for assembly)

FOR FRENCH MACARON SHELLS

1. Preheat oven to 300°F. Place two large baking sheets in oven during preheat. Place silicone mats on top of two additional large baking sheets and set aside.

2. Combine egg whites and cream of tartar in mixing bowl of standing mixer. Using wire whisk attachment, whip on medium speed until foaming, about 2 to 3 minutes.

3. Add ⅔ cup sugar and whip on medium speed until thick. Then add another ⅓ cup sugar and mix until soft peaks form.

4. Add remaining ⅓ cup sugar, mix, then whip until very stiff peaks form. Scrape down bowl and whisk. Replace whisk with paddle attachment.

5. In a separate bowl, combine powdered sugar and almond flour, sifting 3 times. Mixture should be very fine.

6. Add a third of the flour mixture to egg whites, mixing until just combined. Repeat twice, mixing after every addition. Batter should be stiff but not overmixed.

7. Mix in half of lemon zest and food coloring to batter; add more food coloring, if desired, as color fades during baking.

8 Fit plastic piping bag with small round tip. Fill bag with macaron batter. Pipe macarons onto reserved baking sheets/silicone mats, keeping size uniform at about 1½ inches in diameter per cookie. (A printable piping template is available online and may be helpful for consistent sizing. Just remember to remove template before baking.) Leave space between macarons as batter may spread slightly. Using balance of Meyer lemon zest, quickly sprinkle small amount of zest onto half of piped shells. These will be the macaron tops.

9 Let macarons stand for about 30 minutes to develop film before baking. Then remove baking sheets from oven and carefully transfer one silicone mat with cookies onto each sheet. Bake, one sheet at a time, for about 15 minutes. Macarons are done when they release from mat.

10 Remove from oven and cool on wire rack. Set aside.

RECIPE CONTINUES ON NEXT PAGE

MEYER LEMON MACARONS
WITH BLUEBERRY PRESERVES & HOMEMADE BUTTERCREAM

(CONTINUED)

FOR MEYER LEMON PURÉE

1. Peel skin off Meyer lemons with vegetable peeler, scraping away any white pith from the peels with paring knife. Then juice lemons and strain. Set juice aside.

2. Place Meyer lemon peels, honey, and water in saucepot. Bring to boil and reduce heat to simmer until peels are tender, about 30 minutes, adding more water if needed.

3. Transfer mixture to blender. Add reserved lemon juice and salt, and purée until smooth. Set aside.

FOR HOMEMADE BUTTERCREAM

1. Add sugar and water to large pot over low to medium heat, stirring gently. Be careful not to get sugar on sides of pot so that sugar crystals do not form during cooking.

2. When sugar mixture reaches about 120°F and while it continues to heat, add egg whites to bowl of standing mixer with wire whisk attachment. Whisk until egg whites are firm.

3. Once sugar mixture has reached 240°F (make sure sugar is completely dissolved), remove from heat and let sit for about 1 minute. Turn mixer to low speed and slowly pour hot sugar mixture into bowl containing egg whites, keeping stream toward outer edge of bowl and away from whisk to avoid creating chunks.

4. After all sugar has been added to mixer, turn to high speed and mix for 15 to 20 minutes or until bowl is cool to touch. Mix will have shiny appearance.

MEYER LEMON PURÉE

2 Meyer lemons

2 tablespoons honey

½ cup water

⅛ teaspoon salt

HOMEMADE BUTTERCREAM

1 cup sugar

4 tablespoons water

3 large pasteurized egg whites, at room temperature

1½ cups plus 3 tablespoons unsalted butter, cubed

¾ teaspoon vanilla extract

5   While mixer is running, remove cubed butter from refrigerator, allowing it to warm up a bit. Once mixing bowl is cool to touch, slow mixer down to medium speed and add softened butter in batches.

6   Whip until buttercream is smooth and stiff, then stir in vanilla extract. Remove from mixing bowl and place into another container, or, if moving directly to the Meyer Lemon Purée–Marshmallow Filling steps, then leave buttercream in mixing bowl, remove whisk attachment from the mixer, and replace with a paddle attachment before proceeding.

MEYER LEMON PURÉE–MARSHMALLOW FILLING

1   Add Homemade Buttercream to mixing bowl of standing mixer with paddle attachment. Soften with mixer until smooth.

2   Add lemon zest to Meyer Lemon Purée. Slowly add purée-zest mixture to buttercream in mixing bowl, and then gently fold in marshmallow creme.

TO ASSEMBLE & SERVE

1   Place cooled French Macaron Shells on parchment paper, matching up in pairs—one lemon-zested top alongside each bottom half.

2   Fit plastic piping bag with small round piping tip and fill bag with Meyer Lemon Purée–Marshmallow Filling.

3   Pipe filling in ring along the edge of each bottom French Macaron Shell, leaving spot in middle for the blueberry preserves.

4   With small spoon, fill center of each macaron bottom with blueberry preserves. Then gently pat macaron top onto bottom.

MEYER LEMON PURÉE–MARSHMALLOW FILLING

½ cup Homemade Buttercream

Zest of ¼ Meyer lemon

2½ tablespoons Meyer Lemon Purée

½ cup favorite marshmallow creme

ABOVE: Pixar Pal-A-Round, located at Pixar Pier, is a memorable backdrop of the annual Disney California Adventure Food & Wine Festival.

SNICKERDOODLE COOKIES
WITH SNICKERS® BAR PIECES

The cinnamon-sugar cookie known as a snickerdoodle has been around in some form or fashion since the late 1800s. This version from the EPCOT International Festival of the Holidays adds a little Disney magic with a topping made from SNICKERS® bars. (Note if you're working in a warm or humid environment, place the candy bars in a refrigerator before chopping to keep the chocolate from melting.)

MAKES 24 COOKIES

FROM THE WALT DISNEY WORLD RESORT

2¾ cups all-purpose flour

1 teaspoon baking soda

2 teaspoons cream of tartar

½ teaspoon salt

1 cup shortening

1½ cups plus 2 tablespoons sugar, divided

2 large eggs

2 teaspoons ground cinnamon

2 cups roughly chopped SNICKERS® bar pieces

½ cup semisweet chocolate chips, melted

1   Preheat oven to 350°F. Line a baking sheet with parchment paper or silicone baking mat. Then sift flour, baking soda, cream of tartar, and salt in a medium bowl and set aside.

2   Cream shortening and 1½ cups sugar in the bowl of an electric mixer fitted with a paddle attachment until fluffy. Reduce speed to medium and add eggs, one at a time, until combined. Add reserved flour mixture, one cup at a time, scraping bowl as needed.

3   Beat on medium speed until just combined. Then roll dough into 24 balls using a 1½-inch cookie scoop and refrigerate for 15 to 20 minutes.

4   Combine remaining 2 tablespoons sugar and ground cinnamon in a small bowl, and set aside. Place chopped SNICKERS® bar pieces in a medium bowl, and set aside in a cool area.

OPPOSITE, BOTTOM: Guests listening to storytellers during EPCOT International Festival of the Holidays

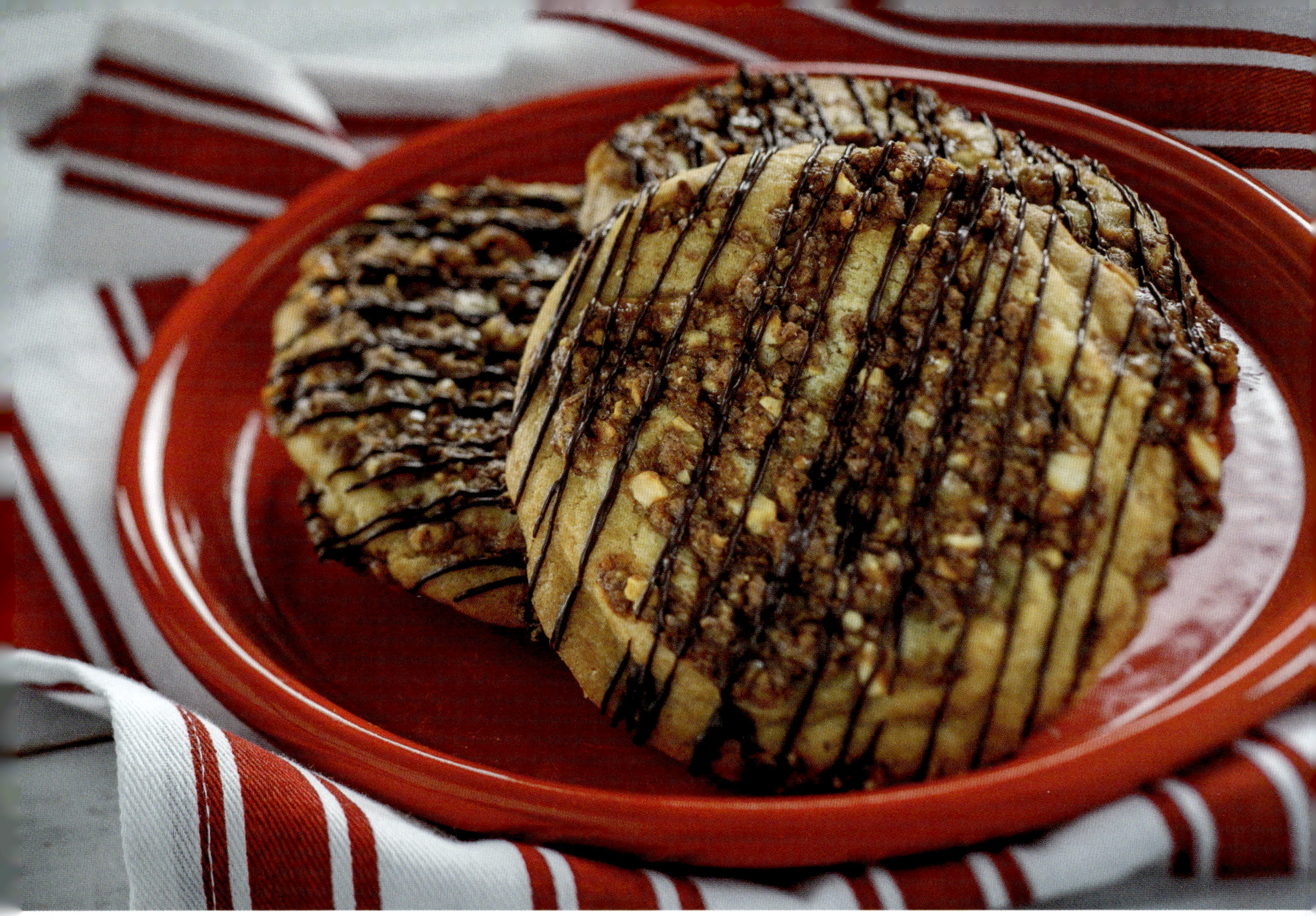

5　Remove 12 of the chilled dough balls from refrigerator, roll them in the cinnamon-sugar mix, and place on prepared baking pan. Bake for 8 minutes. Carefully remove from oven and sprinkle 1 tablespoon chopped SNICKERS® bars on top of each cookie.

6　Return cookies to oven and bake for an additional 5 to 8 minutes, until edges begin to brown. Cool on pan for 2 minutes before moving to wire racks, and then drizzle with desired amount of melted dark chocolate. When ready, repeat with remaining 12 chilled dough balls.

PEANUT BUTTER BROWNIES

FESTIVAL DEBUT: 2012 · PARTY FOR THE SENSES GLOBAL MARKETPLACE

There's nothing better than a scratch brownie, especially this version with a creamy peanut butter filling and silky ganache icing. You could stop right there, but the Toffee Pretzel Crunch and homemade ice cream take it to the next level. (Note an electric ice cream freezer is used to make the homemade ice cream, so store-bought ice cream could stand in if you don't have that on hand.) For grown-ups, add an aged tawny port, the perfect pairing.

SERVES 6-8   **FROM THE WALT DISNEY WORLD RESORT**

FOR BROWNIE BASE

1 Preheat oven to 350°F. Lightly grease 8½-inch-square pan; line bottom with parchment paper. Combine chocolate and butter in a medium heat-safe bowl. Set bowl over a small saucepan of simmering water. Do not let bowl touch water. Stir chocolate and butter until completely melted, and set aside.

2 Combine eggs, sugar, and vanilla extract in a large bowl; using an electric mixer, beat until eggs have doubled in volume and mixture is pale yellow. Stir in chocolate-butter mixture. Fold in flour and salt using a rubber spatula until just combined; do not overmix.

3 Transfer batter to prepared pan and bake for 20 to 25 minutes, until a wooden pick inserted in center is moist but not gooey. Then cool brownies in pan on a wire rack. Once cool, flip brownies upside down onto a parchment paper–lined baking sheet.

BROWNIE BASE

4 (1-ounce) squares unsweetened chocolate, chopped

1 cup unsalted butter, cubed

4 large eggs

1½ cups sugar

1 teaspoon vanilla extract

1 cup unbleached all-purpose flour, sifted

½ teaspoon salt

FOR PEANUT BUTTER FILLING

1 Whisk heavy cream in a medium bowl until it forms soft peaks. Transfer whipped cream to a small bowl, and set aside. Then whisk together cream cheese and sugar until well combined in same medium bowl, using an electric mixer. Add peanut butter and mix until evenly combined.

2 Gently fold whipped cream into peanut butter mixture. Spread the Peanut Butter Filling in an even layer over top surface of the Brownie Base, and then place pan in refrigerator to let the Peanut Butter Filling set.

FOR CHOCOLATE GANACHE

1 Place chocolate in a medium heatproof bowl and set aside. Then heat heavy cream in a small saucepan over medium heat until just simmering.

2 Pour hot cream over chocolate, stirring until chocolate is melted and mixture is smooth. Add butter, stirring until completely melted and combined.

3 Remove the Brownie Base from refrigerator and place it on a wire cooling rack set over the parchment paper–lined baking sheet.

4 Pour ganache over brownie. Lightly shake cooling rack to level out ganache. Then place brownie back into refrigerator to allow ganache to set.

FOR TOFFEE PRETZEL CRUNCH

1 Line bottom of a 9 × 5-inch baking pan with parchment paper and then with pretzels. You may not use all the pretzels. Then melt butter in a small saucepan over medium heat. Add brown sugar and increase heat to high. Boil, stirring constantly, until mixture reaches 300°F on a candy thermometer, about 10 to 13 minutes.

2 Pour mixture over pretzels, and set aside to cool. Place chocolate in a medium heat-safe bowl. Set bowl over a small saucepan of simmering water. Do not let bowl touch water. Stir chocolate until completely melted.

PEANUT BUTTER FILLING

4 tablespoons heavy cream

4 ounces cream cheese, softened

4 tablespoons sugar

½ cup creamy peanut butter

CHOCOLATE GANACHE

8 (1-ounce) squares semisweet chocolate, chopped

1 cup heavy cream

1 tablespoon unsalted butter, softened

TOFFEE PRETZEL CRUNCH

18–22 mini pretzel twists

½ cup unsalted butter

½ cup light brown sugar

6 (1-ounce) squares semisweet chocolate, chopped

RECIPE CONTINUES ON NEXT PAGE

PEANUT BUTTER BROWNIES

3 Spread melted chocolate evenly over surface of toffee, and refrigerate until set. Once set, toffee can be stored at room temperature.

FOR VANILLA BEAN ICE CREAM

1 Combine heavy cream and milk in a medium saucepan. Cut vanilla bean in half lengthwise. Using back of a butter knife, scrape seeds out of vanilla bean. Place seeds and vanilla bean in pan with cream and milk. Bring mixture to a simmer over medium heat.

2 Whisk egg yolks and sugar in a medium bowl until light and fluffy. Slowly drizzle half of cream-and-milk mixture into the eggs, whisking constantly.

3 Pour cream-egg mixture back into saucepan and reduce heat to medium-low. Cook, whisking constantly, until it coats back of a wooden spoon.

4 Pour mixture through a fine-mesh sieve into a medium bowl. Place this bowl in a larger bowl filled with ice water; stir mixture until cool.

5 Freeze in an electric ice cream freezer according to manufacturer's instructions. Once frozen, place ice cream in freezer until firm.

TO ASSEMBLE & SERVE

1 Remove Brownie Base from refrigerator. Dip a knife into a glass of hot water. Then cut brownies into 6 to 8 pieces and place on serving plates.

2 Break Toffee Pretzel Crunch into ½-inch pieces. Sprinkle crunch beside each brownie. Then place a scoop of Vanilla Bean Ice Cream on top of the crunch.

VANILLA BEAN ICE CREAM

1½ cups heavy cream

¾ cup milk

1 vanilla bean

4 large pasteurized egg yolks

6 tablespoons sugar

MADELEINES

REMEMBERED FROM LES CHEFS DE FRANCE

The madeleine is a traditional French sponge cake with a distinctive scallop-shell shape, so you will need a madeleine mold, sold at cookware stores. The little cakes are best served warm, but you can prepare the mix, place in mold, refrigerate, then bake just before serving. At Les Chefs de France, madeleines accompany the crème brûlée. Bon appétit!

MAKES 20 MADELEINES

FROM THE WALT DISNEY WORLD RESORT

½ cup unsalted butter

3 large eggs

¾ cup sugar

4 tablespoons whole or 2 percent milk

1 teaspoon vanilla extract

Zest of 1 orange

Pinch salt

1⅔ cups all-purpose flour, sifted, plus more for dusting pan

1½ teaspoons baking powder

1. Melt butter over low heat in a small saucepan. Separate 1 tablespoon melted butter and use to lightly brush madeleine molds, then dust molds with flour, shaking off excess. Refrigerate pan. Keep leftover butter at room temperature.

2. Beat eggs and sugar with an electric mixer in a large bowl until just blended. Beat in milk, vanilla extract, orange zest, and salt.

3. Stir in flour and baking powder with a spatula until just combined. Gradually add cooled melted butter in a steady stream, beating until just blended.

4. Refrigerate at least 2 hours. (You can make the day before and refrigerate overnight.)

5. When ready to serve, preheat oven to 475°F. Fill each indentation in pan with 1 tablespoon mix. Place in oven and reduce heat to 375°F. Bake for 10 to 12 minutes, or until golden around the edges and puffed. Cool 5 minutes. Gently remove from pan, and serve immediately. Repeat process, buttering and flouring pan before each batch.

S'MORES

This super-easy version goes all the way back to 2006 when these cookies were first served at 50's Prime Time Café in Disney's Hollywood Studios. The treat is an example of delicious simplicity, and you only need four ingredients to re-create this childhood favorite.

SERVES 1-2   **FROM THE WALT DISNEY WORLD RESORT**

2 graham crackers

2 chocolate bars

12 marshmallows

4 tablespoons chocolate syrup

1 Preheat oven on broil. Then lay graham crackers on a baking sheet side-by-side. Cover each graham cracker with a chocolate bar.

2 Broil for a few seconds to soften chocolate. Put 6 marshmallows on each chocolate-covered cracker, and broil until browned. Drizzle chocolate syrup over the top, and serve.

LEFT: The waiting area of 50's Prime Time Café

DISNEY'S RIVIERA RESORT SIGNATURE COOKIE

REMEMBERED FROM PRIMO PIATTO

For Primo Piatto at Disney's Riviera Resort, these are a version of a "kitchen sink cookie." Each cookie has a crunch from walnuts and pistachios and a tart sweetness from cherries—and a finish of sea salt intensifies the flavor.

MAKES 18-24 COOKIES

FROM THE WALT DISNEY WORLD RESORT

- 2 cups all-purpose flour
- 1 teaspoon coarse salt
- ¾ teaspoon baking soda
- ½ teaspoon baking powder
- 2¼ cups oats, ground
- ¾ cup mini semisweet chocolate chips, ground
- 1 cup unsalted butter, at room temperature
- 1¼ cups brown sugar
- 1 cup sugar
- 1 tablespoon molasses
- 2 large eggs
- 1 teaspoon vanilla extract
- 1 cup walnuts, finely chopped
- 1¼ cups pistachios, finely chopped
- 1¼ cups dried cherries, finely chopped
- 1¼ cups mini semisweet chocolate chips
- Sea salt flakes, to taste

1. Preheat oven to 350°F. Line a baking sheet with a silicone baking mat or parchment paper, and set aside. Sift flour, salt, baking soda, and baking powder in a large mixing bowl. Stir in ground oats and ground chocolate chips, and set aside.

2. Cream butter, both sugars, and molasses in the bowl of an electric mixer fitted with a paddle attachment until fluffy. Then add eggs, one at a time, and beat on low speed until fully incorporated.

3. Add vanilla and beat, scraping the bowl as needed, for 1 minute. Then add one-third of the flour mixture and beat on low speed until just mixed. Continue with remaining flour. Add walnuts, pistachios, dried cherries, and mini chocolate chips and mix on low speed until fully incorporated into dough.

4. Place six balls of dough (about 4 tablespoons per ball) on baking sheet. Flatten slightly, and top with desired amount of sea salt flakes. Bake for 12 minutes, and cool for 2 minutes before moving to wire rack. Repeat with remaining dough.

PIZZELLE CANNOLI

REMEMBERED FROM TRATTORIA AL FORNO

A classic Italian treat with a fun twist: the filling is cannoli cream, but the shell is a crunchy waffle-like pizzelle—easier and lighter than the traditional deep-fried pastry dough.

MAKES 10 CANNOLI

FROM THE WALT DISNEY WORLD RESORT

PIZZELLE

¾ cup all-purpose flour

½ teaspoon lemon zest

4 tablespoons sugar

2 large eggs

4 tablespoons unsalted butter, melted

½ teaspoon vanilla extract

FOR PIZZELLE

1 Combine flour and lemon zest in a small bowl, and set aside.

2 Beat sugar and eggs with an electric mixer on medium speed for 1 to 2 minutes until mixture is pale yellow and smooth. Slowly add in butter while mixer is on low speed, and mix until combined.

3 Add vanilla, and then stir in flour mixture until batter is smooth. Refrigerate for 1 hour.

4 Preheat and grease a pizzelle pan according to manufacturer's instructions. Then spoon 1 tablespoon batter into the center of each pizzella round. Cook until golden brown.

5 Remove pizzelle one at a time from the pan. Roll each warm pizzella tightly around a dowel rod until the ends meet. Press to seal. Remove dowel and set pizzella on a cooling rack. Repeat with remaining pizzelle.

ABOVE: A 2019 gingerbread display in Disney's BoardWalk Inn & Villas lobby re-created the exterior of Trattoria al Forno and its neighbor Flying Fish.

FOR PISTACHIO RICOTTA-MASCARPONE CREAM

1 Whip heavy cream using an electric mixer on high speed until soft peaks form, and then set aside.

2 Whisk ricotta, mascarpone, and powdered sugar in a medium bowl. Stir in lemon zest and juice. Then add pistachio paste and orange cognac, and stir until combined. Finally, fold in whipped cream until smooth.

TO ASSEMBLE & SERVE:

Place pistachio ricotta-mascarpone cream into a piping bag fitted with a ½-inch-round tip. Pipe filling into each pizzella.

PISTACHIO RICOTTA-MASCARPONE CREAM

½ cup heavy cream

4 tablespoons ricotta

½ cup mascarpone cheese

½ cup powdered sugar

¼ lemon, zested and juiced

2 tablespoons pistachio paste

1 ½ teaspoons orange cognac

COOKIES & CREAM BONBONS

REMEMBERED FROM CAPE MAY CAFE

Start with store-bought cookies for these light mousse-filled bonbons. And give yourself plenty of time for the mousse to freeze before coating in chocolate for this favorite sweet ending from Cape May Cafe at Disney's Beach Club Resort. (For those visiting the resort, notice how the chefs will airbrush the chocolate different colors to match the season. The ones in our photographed dish were sprayed with dark chocolate.)

MAKES 20–24 BONBONS

FROM THE WALT DISNEY WORLD RESORT

COOKIES & CREAM BONBONS

2 (silver) gelatin sheets

8 ounces white chocolate, chopped

1 cup heavy cream, divided

2 tablespoons whole or 2 percent milk

2½ tablespoons pasteurized liquid egg yolks

⅓ cup chocolate cookie crumbs

24 chocolate sandwich cookies

FOR COOKIES & CREAM BONBONS

1 Bloom gelatin sheets in a small bowl of ice water. Place white chocolate in microwave-safe bowl and cook on 50 percent power, stirring every 30 seconds until melted, and set aside.

2 Bring ⅓ cup heavy cream and all the milk to a simmer over medium heat in a small saucepan.

3 Remove gelatin sheets from water and add to simmering heavy cream. Reduce heat to low and whisk until smooth. Pour into melted white chocolate and whisk until smooth.

4 Stir in pasteurized egg yolks and cookie crumbs. Cover with plastic wrap and refrigerate for at least 1 hour.

5 Whip remaining ⅔ cup heavy cream in the bowl of an electric mixer fitted with a whisk attachment until medium peaks form. Gently fold into white chocolate mixture.

6 Fill silicone mini-muffin molds with 2 tablespoons filling. Place a chocolate sandwich cookie on top of each bonbon. Freeze overnight.

ABOVE: Minnie Mouse greets guests of Cape May Cafe, 2022.

FOR CHOCOLATE TOPPING

1 Remove bonbons from freezer and carefully unmold. Place bonbons, cookie side down, on a baking sheet. Return to freezer while preparing chocolate.

2 Place cocoa butter in a microwave-safe bowl and cook on medium heat, stirring every 30 seconds until melted, and set aside. Repeat with white chocolate.

3 Combine cocoa butter and white chocolate and whisk until smooth. Then place a wire rack on top of a baking sheet lined with parchment paper.

4 Remove frozen bonbons from freezer and place on wire rack. Pour warm chocolate topping over each bonbon, making sure to fully cover the top and sides.

FOR WHIPPED CREAM

Whip heavy cream in the bowl of an electric mixer fitted with a whisk attachment until medium peaks form. Then place in a piping bag fitted with a star tip. Pipe desired shape on top of each bonbon.

CHOCOLATE TOPPING

¾ cup cocoa butter, chopped

¾ cup white chocolate, chopped

WHIPPED CREAM

½ cup heavy cream

PLANT-BASED CHOCOLATE CHIP COOKIE FRIES

Similar to biscotti, these are perfect for dunking in a hot beverage or to serve with your favorite dipping sauces. For the latter, we prefer chocolate and strawberry!

MAKES 32 COOKIE FRIES

FROM THE WALT DISNEY WORLD RESORT

1. Combine flour, powdered sugar, and plant-based margarine in the bowl of an electric mixer fitted with a paddle attachment. Beat on medium speed until smooth.

2. In a small bowl, combine warm water and egg substitute. Add water-egg mixture and molasses to mixer. Mix on medium speed until smooth.

3. Fold in chocolate chips. Then place in an 8 × 8–inch pan and refrigerate for 30 minutes.

4. Preheat oven to 325°F. Line two baking sheets with parchment paper or silicone baking mats.

5. Cut dough into a total of 32 strips by dividing pan in half and then dividing each half into strips that are each ½ inch wide and 4 inches long. Place 16 strips on each baking sheet. Bake for 20 to 22 minutes, until crunchy.

2¾ cups all-purpose flour

½ cup plus 1 tablespoon powdered sugar

½ cup plus 1 tablespoon plant-based margarine, softened

7 tablespoons warm water

5 tablespoons liquid egg substitute

1 tablespoon molasses

½ cup dairy-free mini chocolate chips

ABOVE: An ice-cream-cone-shaped light fixture at Beaches & Cream Soda Shop, 2013

S'MORES COOKIES

It's your favorite campfire treat rolled into a cookie with gooey marshmallows, graham crackers, and chocolate chips. Refrigerate for at least 3 hours before baking—or make the dough the day before.

MAKES 18 COOKIES

FROM THE WALT DISNEY WORLD RESORT

1 Whisk flour, graham cracker crumbs, baking powder, baking soda, and coarse salt in a large bowl, and set aside.

2 Cream butter and sugars in the bowl of an electric mixer fitted with a paddle attachment until fluffy. Add vanilla extract and eggs, one at a time. Beat on low speed until combined.

3 Add flour mixture to sugar mixture, one cup at a time, and beat on low speed until combined. Then add marshmallows, chocolate chips, chopped chocolate, and chopped graham crackers. Beat on low speed until mixed.

4 Refrigerate dough for at least 3 hours, up to one day.

5 Preheat oven to 375°F. Line baking sheet with parchment paper or a silicone baking mat. Scoop chilled dough into ¼-cup balls, and place 4 on baking sheet.

6 Bake for 12 to 15 minutes, until edges begin to brown but cookies are still soft. Cool for 5 minutes on baking sheet, then transfer to cooling rack. Repeat with remaining dough balls.

3 cups all-purpose flour

⅔ cup graham cracker crumbs

1 ½ teaspoons baking powder

1 ¼ teaspoons baking soda

1 ½ teaspoons coarse salt

4 tablespoons unsalted butter, at room temperature

1 ⅓ cups brown sugar

1 cup sugar

2 ¼ teaspoons vanilla extract

2 large eggs

1 cup mini marshmallows, cut in half

1 ½ cups semisweet chocolate chips

6 ounces semisweet chocolate, chopped

1 cup coarsely chopped graham crackers

SALTED CARAMEL MAGIC BAR BLONDIE

REMEMBERED FROM CHEF MICKEY'S

The only magic is how quickly these bars will disappear. They take some time, but the payoff is layers of flavors: chocolate, butterscotch, coconut, and pecans in the bars, topped with Salted Caramel Buttercream and a kiss of Chocolate Coffee Ganache.

MAKES 1 (9 × 13-INCH) PAN

FROM THE WALT DISNEY WORLD RESORT

SALTED CARAMEL SAUCE

½ cup sugar

1 teaspoon corn syrup

2 tablespoons water

⅓ cup heavy cream

¼ teaspoon lemon juice

¾ teaspoon sea salt

MAGIC BAR BLONDIE

½ cup unsalted butter, softened

½ teaspoon salt

⅓ cup sugar

⅓ cup brown sugar

3 large eggs

1 teaspoon vanilla extract

1 cup plus 2 tablespoons cake flour

1½ teaspoons baking powder

4 tablespoons mini chocolate chips

4 tablespoons butterscotch chips

4 tablespoons toasted coconut

4 tablespoons pecans

FOR SALTED CARAMEL SAUCE

1 Pour sugar in a small pot with a handle, shaking lightly from side to side to level. Top with corn syrup. Pour water evenly across; do not stir.

2 Cook over medium heat 10 to 12 minutes to a deep amber color; remove from heat. Heat heavy cream in microwave for 20 seconds.

3 Add cream, lemon juice, and sea salt to sugar mixture; carefully stir until combined. (Mixture will bubble when cream is added.) Cool to room temperature. Refrigerate until ready to use.

FOR MAGIC BAR BLONDIE

1 Preheat oven to 300°F. Mix together butter, salt, sugar, and brown sugar on medium speed in the bowl of a stand mixer.

2 Add eggs and vanilla extract, mixing until combined and scraping bowl as necessary. Then add cake flour and baking powder, mixing well.

3 Fold in mini chocolate chips, butterscotch chips, toasted coconut, and pecans, mixing until just combined.

4 Lightly spray a 9 × 13–inch baking dish with cooking spray, then line bottom with parchment paper. Add batter, spreading with an offset spatula until smooth and even.

5 Bake for 25 to 28 minutes, or until a toothpick inserted in the center comes out clean. Then remove from oven, cool, and turn out of pan onto a cutting board so that the bottom is on top.

FOR SALTED CARAMEL BUTTERCREAM

1 With paddle attachment on a stand mixer, beat shortening and butter on medium speed for 3 to 4 minutes, or until light and fluffy.

2 Add powdered sugar and mix on low speed for 1 minute. Add heavy cream and corn syrup, mixing until combined. Turn to medium-high speed and mix for 2 minutes. Scrape sides of bowl and mix for 1 more minute.

3 Turn off mixer and add Salted Caramel Sauce, mixing well.

CHOCOLATE COFFEE GANACHE

Heat cream just to simmering in a heavy pot over low heat. Then add hot cream to chocolate pieces in a small bowl; allow to sit for 1 minute. Whisk in coffee until smooth, and set aside to cool to consistency of peanut butter.

TO ASSEMBLE & SERVE

Spread Salted Caramel Buttercream over each cooled Magic Bar Blondie. Cut to serving size and desired size. Use a piping bag to add 2 small kisses of Chocolate Coffee Ganache to each bar. (Note our photographed dish was topped with chocolate and white crisp pearls for added flair.)

SALTED CARAMEL BUTTERCREAM

⅓ cup shortening

⅓ cup unsalted butter, softened

2½ cups powdered sugar

1 tablespoon plus 2 teaspoons heavy cream

1 tablespoon plus 2 teaspoons corn syrup

4 tablespoons Salted Caramel Sauce

CHOCOLATE COFFEE GANACHE

¾ cup heavy cream

1 cup plus 2 tablespoons dark chocolate, chopped into small pieces

1 teaspoon brewed coffee

WHOLE WHEAT CHOCOLATE CHIP COOKIES

REMEMBERED FROM DISNEY'S CONTEMPORARY RESORT BAKERY

Whole wheat flour adds a mild nuttiness and rich flavor, and the powdered sugar makes them chewier. We like to add one cup of walnuts or pecans for added texture.

MAKES ABOUT 60 COOKIES

FROM THE WALT DISNEY WORLD RESORT

1 cup unsalted butter, softened

1½ cups powdered sugar

1¼ cups brown sugar

2 large eggs, lightly beaten

1 teaspoon vanilla extract

2 cups plus 2 tablespoons whole wheat flour

½ cup all-purpose flour

Pinch salt

1 teaspoon baking soda

1½ cups mini chocolate chips

1   Preheat oven to 350°F. Beat butter, powdered sugar, and brown sugar in a large bowl with an electric mixer until light and fluffy, about 4 to 5 minutes. Add eggs and vanilla, beating well, about 2 minutes more.

2   Whisk together whole wheat flour, all-purpose flour, salt, and baking soda in a large bowl. Slowly add flour mixture to butter mixture, mixing until just combined.

3   Stir in chocolate chips. Refrigerate dough 1 hour. Then drop by rounded tablespoons 2 inches apart onto ungreased baking sheets. Bake for 9 to 12 minutes, or until golden brown. Cool on baking sheets for 5 minutes, then transfer to a cooling rack.

LEFT: Mickey Mouse greets a young guest at Chef Mickey's at Disney's Contemporary Resort.

CHAPTER TWO
Pies, Tarts & Crisps

AFTER SNOW WHITE PROMISES to make a gooseberry pie in the 1937 classic *Snow White and the Seven Dwarfs*, even Grumpy agrees that she can stay. Win friends with these pies, tarts, and crisps—from a classic cobbler to a dense chocolate tart with barbecue potato chip crust—and take dessert from ordinary to extraordinary.

STRAWBERRY TWISTS

REMEMBERED FROM MAURICE'S TREATS

These were a favorite walk-around snack from Maurice's Treats at Disneyland. The treats are best eaten quickly before the puff pastry loses its crispness. If you're in a hurry while making them, substitute ⅓ cup of your favorite strawberry jam instead of making the filling.

MAKES 6 TWISTS

FROM THE DISNEYLAND RESORT

1 cup sliced fresh strawberries

1 cup sugar

4 tablespoons fresh lemon juice

2 sheets frozen puff pastry, thawed (often found in a 17.3-ounce package)

Powdered sugar, for garnish

1 Combine strawberries, sugar, and lemon juice in a small saucepan over medium heat. Mash mixture with a potato masher until the berries are softened and the sugar dissolves.

2 Increase heat to high and bring the mixture to a full rolling boil. Boil, stirring often to prevent mixture from sticking to pan, until thick, about 5 minutes. Cool to room temperature.

3 Place one sheet of puff pastry onto a lightly floured movable flat surface, such as a lightweight cutting board. Dust surface of pastry with flour and roll to smooth creases.

4 Spread pastry sheet with ⅓ cup of the strawberry mixture. (Refrigerate any remaining strawberry mixture for up to 5 days.)

5 Roll second sheet of puff pastry on a lightly floured surface to smooth creases; place on top of first sheet and press down gently.

6 Place filled puff pastry in refrigerator for 15 minutes. Preheat oven to 400°F. Line a baking sheet with parchment paper or a nonstick silicone mat.

BELOW: The Fantasy Faire Snack Wagon sign for Maurice's Treats

FANTASYLAND · DISNEYLAND

7 Using a ruler as a guide, cut pastry into 1½-inch strips. Carefully pick up strips and place on baking sheet, twisting each 3 times before laying them down.

8 Bake for 20 to 22 minutes, or until puffed and golden brown. Cool 10 minutes and finish with a dusting of powdered sugar.

CHOCOLATE MUD PIE-O-RAMA

REMEMBERED FROM FLO'S V8 CAFE

The house-made pies at Flo's Route 66–inspired diner are worth a stop, especially this chocolate-on-chocolate-on-chocolate goody. Give yourself plenty of time; the chocolate filling needs to be refrigerated for twenty-four hours for best results.

MAKES 1 (9-INCH) PIE, OR 8 (4-INCH) MINI PIES

FROM THE DISNEYLAND RESORT

CHOCOLATE MUD FILLING

2 cups unsalted butter

1½ cups semisweet chocolate chips

10 large eggs

½ tablespoon vanilla extract

4 tablespoons all-purpose flour

1 cup sugar

CHOCOLATE PIE DOUGH

2 tablespoons sugar

½ cup unsalted butter, softened

1⅔ cups all-purpose flour

4 tablespoons unsweetened cocoa powder

1½ teaspoons baking powder

1 teaspoon salt

2 large eggs

1½ teaspoons vanilla extract

FOR CHOCOLATE MUD FILLING

1   Melt butter and chocolate chips in a heavy saucepan over low heat, mixing until smooth; take off heat and set aside.

2   Whisk together eggs and vanilla extract in a mixing bowl. In a separate bowl, sift together flour and sugar.

3   Add flour-sugar mixture to egg-vanilla mixture, whisking to combine. Use an immersion blender to thoroughly combine until completely smooth.

4   Add chocolate-butter mixture; using immersion blender, mix until smooth and completely incorporated. Refrigerate, covered, for 24 hours.

FOR CHOCOLATE PIE DOUGH

1   Mix sugar and butter in the bowl of a stand mixer fitted with a paddle attachment.

2   Sift together flour, cocoa powder, baking powder, and salt in a mixing bowl. Add flour mixture to butter-sugar mixture.

3   Slowly add eggs and vanilla extract until dough holds together and is no longer sticky.

4   Dump dough out onto a piece of plastic wrap on the counter; press dough into a rough circle and wrap tightly with plastic wrap. Refrigerate at least 1 hour.

OPPOSITE, TOP: At dusk, the neon lights turn on across Cars Land, including at Flo's V8 Cafe.

FOR COFFEE GANACHE

Place chocolate chips in a medium heatproof bowl. Then bring cream to a simmer in a small saucepan; pour hot cream over chocolate and stir until chocolate is completely melted. Stir in coffee extract.

TO ASSEMBLE & SERVE

1 Preheat oven to 350°F. Then roll Chocolate Pie Dough to ¼-inch thickness. If making mini pies, cut dough into 8 circles.

2 Press dough into 9-inch pie tin, or eight 4-inch pie tins if making mini pies. Each side should reach the outermost part of the lip on the tin.

3 Fill large shell a third full with Chocolate Mud Filling, or scoop ½ cup Chocolate Mud Filling into each mini shell.

4 Bake approximately 40 to 45 minutes for a large pie, or 15 minutes for mini pies.

5 Cool to room temperature. Add about 1 tablespoon Coffee Ganache to centers of pie slices (or mini pies) before serving.

COFFEE GANACHE

1 cup bittersweet chocolate chips

1 cup heavy cream

1 teaspoon coffee extract

MILK CHOCOLATE–ALMOND TARTS

FESTIVAL DEBUT: 2017 · LA STYLE FESTIVAL MARKETPLACE

Start with a store-bought tart shell and build these crunchy tarts with a layer of almond crumble topped with caramel-chocolate ganache and chocolate mousse. Chocolate pearls and pieces are optional, but don't forget the sea salt. Pour a tawny port if you want to be fancy.

MAKES 12 TARTS

FROM THE DISNEYLAND RESORT

DARK CHOCOLATE MOUSSE

1⅔ cups semisweet chocolate chips

4 tablespoons cold water

1 (¼-ounce) package powdered gelatin

3 large pasteurized egg yolks

1½ tablespoons milk

2 cups heavy cream

FOR DARK CHOCOLATE MOUSSE

1 Melt chocolate chips in double boiler and set aside. Combine cold water and gelatin in a small bowl, and set aside. Place egg yolks in a separate small bowl.

2 Heat milk in a small saucepan. Add gelatin mixture, and stir until smooth. Add a small amount of milk-gelatin mixture to egg yolks, stirring constantly. Add another small amount to egg yolks and mix well. Carefully pour entire egg yolk mixture into remaining milk-gelatin mixture. Cook over medium heat, stirring constantly, until mixture reaches 155°F.

3 Add egg yolk mixture to melted chocolate and stir until smooth. Cool in refrigerator for 15 to 20 minutes.

4 Whip heavy cream to soft peaks. Slowly add some of the chocolate mixture to the whipped cream. Add remaining chocolate mixture and whip until combined. Refrigerate for 3 hours, until chilled and set.

FOR ALMOND TOFFEE CRUMBLE

1. Line a baking sheet with a silicone baking mat. Heat sugar, water, and corn syrup in a small saucepan until it reaches 240°F.

2. Add butter and almonds, stirring carefully to fully combine. Carefully spread onto prepared baking sheet. Cool for 2 hours, and then chop into small pieces.

FOR WARM CARAMEL-CHOCOLATE GANACHE

1. Place chocolate chips in medium bowl. Bring heavy cream to a boil in a small saucepan. Pour over chocolate chips. Let cream and chocolate rest for 2 minutes.

2. Stir chocolate in center until melted and cream fully mixed. Stir in caramel sauce. Keep warm until ready to serve.

TO ASSEMBLE & SERVE

1. Evenly divide Almond Toffee Crumble among 12 chocolate tart shells. Pour Warm Caramel-Chocolate Ganache over toffee, filling to the top. Refrigerate 1 hour, or until ganache is set.

2. Add 2 tablespoons of Dark Chocolate Mousse to center of each tart. Then top with chocolate pearls, sea salt, and chocolate pieces

ALMOND TOFFEE CRUMBLE

¾ cup sugar

1 tablespoon light corn syrup

½ cup unsalted butter

1 cup slivered almonds

WARM CARAMEL-CHOCOLATE GANACHE

2 cups milk chocolate chips

1 cup heavy cream

½ cup favorite caramel sauce

SHELL

12 mini rectangular chocolate tart shells

FOR SERVING

Chocolate pearls

Sea salt

Chocolate pieces

RIGHT: Mickey Mouse greets a guest along Buena Vista Street at Disney California Adventure.

BOURBON-CHIPOTLE CHOCOLATE WHOOPIE PIES

FESTIVAL DEBUT: 2018 · I ♥ ARTICHOKES FESTIVAL MARKETPLACE

Make these whoopie pies ahead and give the mousse time to firm up (about an hour or two) before filling and serving. Serve with a chocolate stout for a grown-up pairing.

MAKES 12 WHOOPIE PIES

FROM THE DISNEYLAND RESORT

DARK CHOCOLATE BOURBON MOUSSE

⅓ cup dark chocolate chips

4 (¼-ounce) packages powdered gelatin

⅓ cup water

⅓ cup milk

4 large pasteurized egg yolks

3 tablespoons bourbon

1 ½ cups heavy cream

FOR DARK CHOCOLATE BOURBON MOUSSE

1. Melt dark chocolate chips in microwave-safe bowl, stirring every 30 seconds until smooth, and set aside.

2. Place gelatin in a small bowl with water, and stir to combine. Heat milk over medium heat in a small saucepan until just boiling. Stir in gelatin mixture until smooth.

3. Beat egg yolks in a small bowl until pale. Slowly pour half of hot milk mixture into egg yolks, stirring constantly. Pour entire egg yolk mixture into saucepan with remaining milk mixture and cook over low heat, stirring constantly for 1 to 2 minutes, until it reaches 155°F.

4. Slowly add milk mixture to melted dark chocolate and stir until smooth. Add bourbon and cool for 15 minutes.

5. Whip heavy cream in the bowl of an electric mixer fitted with a whisk attachment until soft peaks form.

6. Slowly fold half of whipped cream into cooled chocolate. Add remaining whipped cream. Refrigerate for 4 hours, or until firm.

FOR CHOCOLATE CAKE ROUNDS

1. Preheat oven to 350°F. Line two half-sheet pans with parchment paper or silicone baking mats.

2. Cream shortening and brown sugar in the bowl of an electric mixer fitted with a paddle attachment until fluffy. Then mix in eggs and vanilla until smooth.

3. Sift flour, salt, baking soda, and cocoa powder into small bowl. Add half of flour mixture to shortening mixture and beat on low speed until blended. Add half of milk. Repeat with remaining flour mixture and milk.

4. Using a 2-tablespoon scoop, drop batter onto prepared sheet pans. There should be 24 scoops of batter, separated 12 per sheet pan. Then bake for 8 to 11 minutes, rotating trays halfway through baking. Cool completely before assembling whoopie pies.

FOR SPICY GANACHE

1. Place chocolate chips in a small heat-safe bowl, and set aside. Then heat cream in a small saucepan over medium heat until hot but not boiling. Pour hot cream over chocolate chips and let sit for 1 minute.

2. Add chipotle pepper and stir until smooth. Cool at room temperature for 30 to 60 minutes.

TO ASSEMBLE & SERVE

1. Allow Dark Chocolate Bourbon Mousse to soften at room temperature for 30 minutes. Place in piping bag fitted with large round tip. Then pipe a circle of mousse on 12 Chocolate Cake Rounds. Place a generous spoonful of Spicy Ganache in the center of each.

2. Top with remaining 12 Chocolate Cake Rounds, and roll sides of the whoopie pie sandwiches in chocolate curls. Then drizzle with melted white chocolate.

CHOCOLATE CAKE ROUNDS

½ cup shortening

1 cup brown sugar

2 large eggs

1 teaspoon vanilla extract

1½ cups all-purpose flour

½ teaspoon salt

1 teaspoon baking soda

½ cup unsweetened cocoa powder

½ cup milk, divided

SPICY GANACHE

1 cup dark chocolate chips

1 cup heavy cream

1 teaspoon ground chipotle pepper

TOPPINGS

1 cup chocolate curls

½ cup white chocolate chips, melted

KUMQUAT MINI PIES

FESTIVAL DEBUT: 2014 · DESSERTS & CHAMPAGNE GLOBAL MARKETPLACE

A kumquat's flavor is distinctly citrusy—slightly sweet but also sour and tangy—and the peel is the sweetest part of the fruit. No peeling, just cook and finely chop. A bubbly, crisp prosecco is a lovely pairing.

MAKES 24 (4-INCH) MINI PIES

FROM THE WALT DISNEY WORLD RESORT

24 (4-inch) frozen puff pastry shells

2 cups kumquats, halved

1 cup sugar, divided

Juice of one large lemon

3 tablespoons cornstarch

1¾ cups water

1 tablespoon unsalted butter

3 large pasteurized eggs, separated, at room temperature

1. Preheat oven to 425°F. Then place puff pastry shells on a baking sheet and bake for 7 to 8 minutes, or until golden. Cool slightly, then remove the baked dough from the center to create a hollow shell. Lower oven temperature to 325°F.

2. Simmer kumquats in a small saucepan of boiling water for 2 to 3 minutes, then drain. Return kumquats to saucepan and add 2 tablespoons sugar plus lemon juice; cook until kumquats are softened slightly and begin to become transparent.

3. Remove from heat and finely chop mixture with an immersion blender or in a food processor, and set aside.

4. Then combine cornstarch and ¾ cup sugar in a medium saucepan. Add water and butter. Slowly bring to a boil while whisking. Once mixture is thick, smooth, and shiny, remove from heat and quickly whisk in egg yolks, one at a time. Stir in chopped kumquats.

5. Spoon 2 tablespoons kumquat filling into each pastry shell. Bake for 7 to 8 minutes. While pies bake, beat reserved egg whites with an electric mixer at high speed until frothy. Add remaining 2 tablespoons sugar. Beat to medium peaks.

6 Remove pies from oven, and set aside to cool to room temperature. Spoon egg white meringue into a zip-top bag. Snip off one corner of bag and pipe meringue onto kumquat pies. Place oven rack to within 3 inches from the top, and preheat broiler. With oven door ajar, place pies in oven and broil until meringue is light brown, about 1 to 2 minutes.

OPPOSITE: The iconic Spaceship Earth and EPCOT entrance fountain

BLUEBERRY-ALMOND TARTS

FESTIVAL DEBUT: 2019 · THE ALPS GLOBAL MARKETPLACE

When fresh blueberries are in season, this is a fancy way to showcase them. With the recipe coming from an EPCOT International Food & Wine Festival, these small tarts are delicious with coffee, for dessert, or with a glass of bubbly. You can always take a shortcut with frozen tart shells.

MAKES 6 TARTS

FROM THE WALT DISNEY WORLD RESORT

TART SHELLS

1½ cups flour

4 tablespoons sugar

⅛ teaspoon salt

10 tablespoons unsalted butter, cut into cubes

1 large egg yolk

2 tablespoons cold water

¼ teaspoon vanilla extract

CRÈME FRAÎCHE TOPPING

4 tablespoons crème fraîche

1½ tablespoons sugar

½ teaspoon vanilla extract

½ cup heavy cream

FOR TART SHELLS

1 Combine flour, sugar, and salt in a food processor, and pulse to combine. Add cold butter and pulse until coarse.

2 Combine egg yolk, cold water, and vanilla in a small bowl. Pour into food processor and pulse until smooth dough forms. Divide dough into 6 balls and refrigerate for 2 hours.

3 Preheat oven to 350°F. Spray 6 (4-inch) tartlet pans with nonstick cooking spray, and set aside. Then roll out each ball of dough and fit inside tartlet pans. Place tartlet pans in freezer for 5 minutes.

4 Poke the bottom of each tart with a fork 2 to 3 times. When ready, bake for 20 to 25 minutes, until light brown. Cool completely before filling.

FOR CRÈME FRAÎCHE TOPPING

1 Whisk crème fraîche, sugar, and vanilla extract in a large bowl until smooth. Then, in the bowl of an electric mixer, whip heavy cream to medium-stiff peaks.

2 Gently fold half of the whipped cream into the crème fraîche using a spatula. Fold in remaining half, and refrigerate until ready to serve. Whisk before serving.

FOR ALMOND FILLING

1. Combine sugar, almond paste, and 1 egg in the bowl of an electric mixer fitted with a paddle attachment on medium until blended. Add butter, vanilla, and lemon zest, and cream until smooth. Add remaining egg, and beat until mixed.

2. In a separate bowl, combine flour, baking powder, and salt. Add to the butter mixture and beat on low speed until just mixed. Cover and refrigerate for 1 hour.

3. Preheat oven to 350°F. Place 3 tablespoons of almond filling in each cooled tart shell. Place blueberries in a circle inside of each tart. Bake for 20 to 25 minutes, until golden brown.

4. Cool and remove from pans before serving. Top with Crème Fraîche Topping.

ALMOND FILLING

6 tablespoons sugar

⅓ cup almond paste

2 large eggs, divided

½ cup unsalted butter, at room temperature

¾ teaspoon vanilla extract

1 teaspoon lemon zest

3 tablespoons all-purpose flour

¼ teaspoon baking powder

¼ teaspoon salt

2 cups blueberries

SPICED CHOCOLATE TART

For fans of salty-sweet and a bit of heat, this oddly delicious, dense chocolate cake has a spicy barbecue potato chip crust and a salted whiskey caramel topping with a hint of smoked sea salt. Just try it.

SERVES 12

FROM THE WALT DISNEY WORLD RESORT

BARBECUE POTATO CHIP CRUST

1 (1-ounce) package barbecue potato chips

12 graham cracker squares

2 tablespoons butter

⅛ teaspoon salt

SPICED CHOCOLATE TART

2 cups bittersweet chocolate chips

4 tablespoons milk chocolate chips

2 cups heavy cream

1 teaspoon corn syrup

1½ tablespoons ground cinnamon

1½ teaspoons ancho chile powder

Barbecue Potato Chip Crust, cooled

FOR BARBECUE POTATO CHIP CRUST

1 Preheat oven to 300°F. Spray an 8 × 8-inch pan with nonstick cooking spray, and set aside. Then place barbecue potato chips and graham cracker squares in a food processor. Pulse until fine powder forms, and set aside.

2 Melt butter in a medium microwave-safe bowl. Add salt and reserved barbecue potato chip powder to bowl, and stir until moist. Then press mixture evenly into prepared pan, and bake for 8 minutes. Cool completely before adding ganache.

FOR SPICED CHOCOLATE TART

1 Place bittersweet and milk chocolate chips in a large bowl, and set aside. Then bring heavy cream, corn syrup, cinnamon, and ancho chile powder to a simmer over medium-low heat, stirring occasionally.

2 Pour over chocolate chips, and let it rest for 3 minutes. Then whisk chocolate chips and heavy cream mixture together until smooth, and promptly pour over cooled Barbecue Potato Chip Crust. Refrigerate tart for at least 6 hours, up to 1 day.

FOR SALTED WHISKEY CARAMEL

Pour dulce de leche into a small bowl. Stir in whiskey until fully incorporated. Place in a squeeze bottle and set aside.

TO ASSEMBLE & SERVE

Cut the chilled Spiced Chocolate Tart into 12 equal pieces of desired shape. Drizzle the Salted Whiskey Caramel on top, and sprinkle smoked sea salt on top of each piece. Garnish with a barbecue potato chip.

SALTED WHISKEY CARAMEL

1 (13.4-ounce) can dulce de leche

3 tablespoons whiskey

TOPPING

1–2 teaspoons smoked sea salt

12 large barbecue potato chips

CHOCOLATE-HAZELNUT TARTS

A favorite from Toy Story Land in Disney's Hollywood Studios, these are super fancy for a lunch box treat or delectable any time of day. Take your time with the dough, and the rest easily comes together. The bacon topping is optional—whatever your preference!

MAKES 8 TARTS

FROM THE WALT DISNEY WORLD RESORT

CHOCOLATE-HAZELNUT TARTS

4 cups all-purpose flour, sifted

½ cup sugar

½ cup brown sugar

2¼ teaspoons coarse salt, divided

1½ cups unsalted butter, chilled and cubed

4 tablespoons coconut oil

3 large eggs, divided

10 tablespoons water

½ cup chocolate-hazelnut spread

FOR CHOCOLATE-HAZELNUT TARTS

1. Combine flour, sugar, brown sugar, 2 teaspoons salt, butter, coconut oil, and 2 of the eggs in the bowl of an electric mixer fitted with a paddle attachment. Mix on medium speed until combined.

2. Add water and mix on low speed for 1 minute. Increase speed and blend until dough is smooth. Do not overmix. Then divide dough into 2 even balls and wrap in plastic wrap. Let it rest in refrigerator for 45 minutes.

3. Preheat oven to 375°F. Mix remaining egg and ¼ teaspoon salt in a small bowl, and set egg wash aside. Then lightly flour a large cutting board and roll first ball of dough into a ¼-inch-thick rectangle. Cut into eight 2 × 6–inch rectangles.

4. Place rectangles on a baking sheet lined with parchment paper. Brush with reserved egg wash, then spread 1 tablespoon chocolate-hazelnut spread on each rectangle.

5. Roll remaining ball of dough into ¼-inch-thick rectangle and cut into eight 2 × 6–inch rectangles. Place on top of chocolate-hazelnut-covered tarts and seal edges with a fork. Brush top of tarts with egg wash. Bake for 17 minutes, until golden brown. Cool completely.

ABOVE: A young guest at a Woody's Lunch Box table

FOR ICING

Mix powdered sugar, 1 tablespoon milk, and lemon juice in a small bowl. Slowly add remaining milk until icing is smooth and spreads easily but is not runny. Then spread icing on each cooled tart, and top with bacon pieces. (Note our photographed tart was topped with blonde chocolate crisp pearls for added flair.)

ICING

1 cup powdered sugar

2 tablespoons milk, divided

1 teaspoon lemon juice

GARNISH

4 strips bacon, cooked and crumbled

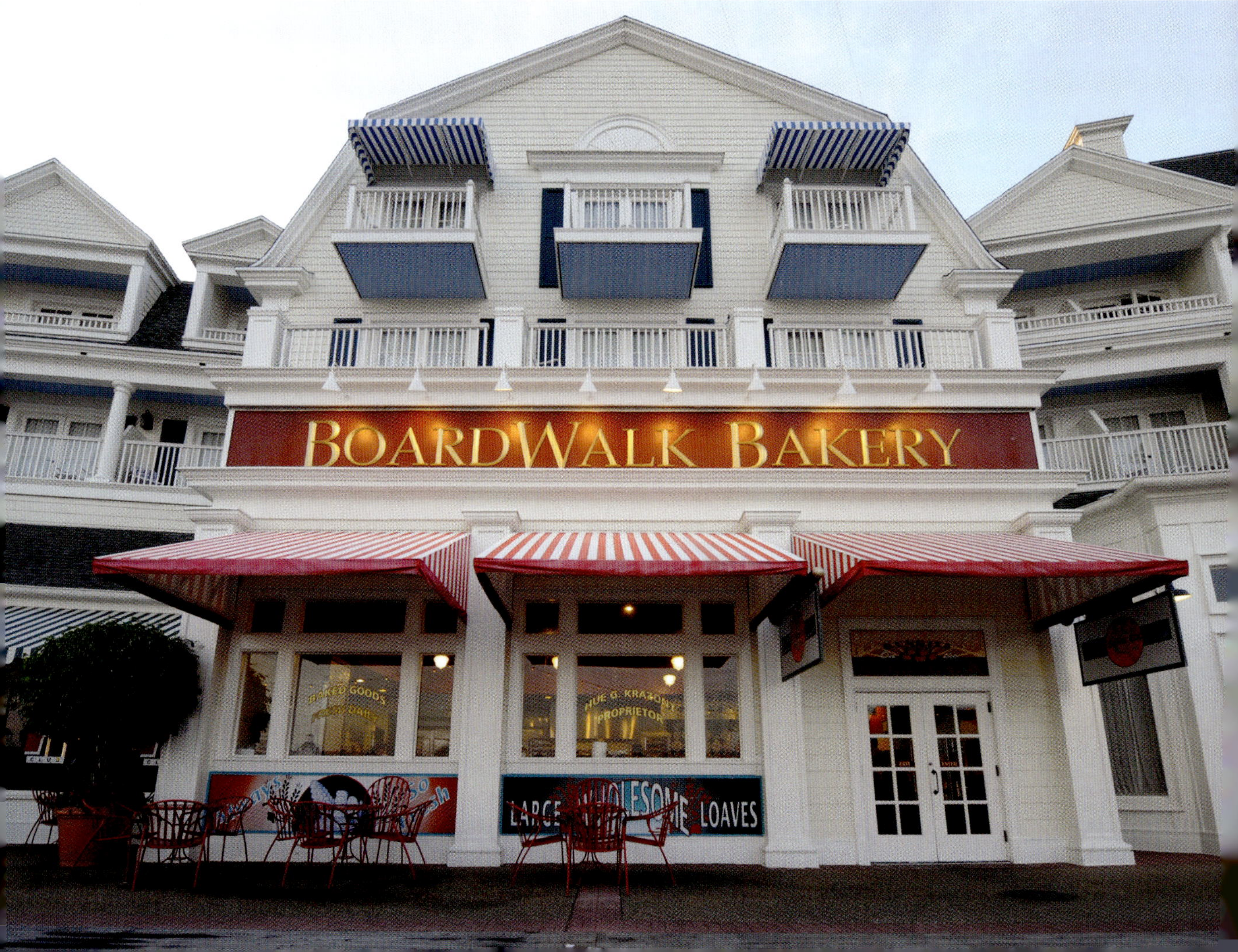

PEANUT BUTTER, BANANA & APPLEWOOD-SMOKED CANDIED BACON TREAT

The name says it all. This is basically a three-ingredient peanut butter pie in a store-bought crust with a layer of bananas and a topping of bacon candied with brown sugar. Simple! And if you're not a bacon fan, leave it off. The easy pie is dreamy.

MAKES 1 (9-INCH) PIE

FROM THE WALT DISNEY WORLD RESORT

3 thick slices applewood-smoked bacon

4 tablespoons brown sugar

1 cup peanut butter

1 cup cream cheese

2 tablespoons sugar

1 cup heavy cream

9-inch store-bought chocolate graham cracker piecrust

2 bananas, sliced

1 Preheat oven to 375°F. Line a small baking sheet with parchment paper, and place a wire rack over the baking sheet.

2 Coat bacon on both sides with brown sugar. Place on rack and bake for 20 to 30 minutes, or until crispy, depending on thickness of bacon.

3 Remove from oven. Once cooled, dice and set aside.

4 Cream together peanut butter, cream cheese, and sugar until smooth.

5 Whip cream to soft peaks in a separate bowl; gently fold into peanut butter mixture.

6 Fill pie shell halfway with mixture, then evenly top with banana slices. Top slices with remaining mixture. Sprinkle with chopped bacon. Refrigerate until ready to serve.

OPPOSITE, BOTTOM: The exterior of the former BoardWalk Bakery, 2009. The space is now home to the BoardWalk Deli.

APPLE PIE

For this Disney's Wilderness Lodge favorite, apples are layered with a rich, cake-like batter to make a "pie-meets-cake" version of a classic apple pie. We love it warm with vanilla ice cream or sliced cold straight from the fridge.

MAKES 1 (9-INCH) PIE

FROM THE WALT DISNEY WORLD RESORT

PIECRUST

4 tablespoons unsalted butter, cubed

4 tablespoons shortening

1 ¾ cups all-purpose flour

4 teaspoons sugar

⅛ teaspoon coarse salt

⅓ cup whole or 2 percent milk

SPICED APPLES

1 cup water

6 Granny Smith apples, peeled and sliced

2 teaspoons apple pie spice

APPLE PIE BATTER

½ cup unsalted butter, softened

⅔ cup sugar

2 large eggs

1 ½ cups flour

1 ½ teaspoons baking powder

⅛ teaspoon salt

4 tablespoons heavy cream

FOR PIECRUST

1   Combine butter, shortening, flour, sugar, and salt in the bowl of an electric mixer fitted with a paddle attachment. Mix at medium speed until crumbly. Then add milk and mix until incorporated.

2   Wrap dough in plastic wrap and rest in refrigerator for 30 minutes. Then roll to ¼-inch thickness, place in 9-inch pie plate, and set aside.

FOR SPICED APPLES

Bring water to simmer in a large pot. Place apples in a steamer basket and add to pot, and steam for 10 minutes. Then remove from water and cool to room temperature. Toss with apple pie spice.

FOR APPLE PIE BATTER

1   Cream butter and sugar in the bowl of a stand mixer fitted with a paddle attachment until fluffy. Add eggs and mix until just incorporated.

2   Mix flour, baking powder, and salt in a small bowl. Slowly add to mixer and beat on medium speed until combined. Add cream. Then mix until smooth, and set aside until ready to bake.

OPPOSITE, TOP: Sequenced buffalo silhouettes adorn the large lighting fixtures at Whispering Canyon Cafe.

FOR APPLE PIE

1. Preheat oven to 350°F. Place ½ cup apple pie batter on top of Piecrust, and spread until smooth. Top with Spiced Apples and remaining Apple Pie Batter.

2. Cover with foil and bake for 40 minutes. Then remove foil and bake for 20 more minutes, until golden brown. Cool to room temperature before serving. (Note our photographed pie was dusted with powdered sugar for added flair.)

GLUTEN-FREE KĪLAUEA TORTE

The Kīlauea volcano on the southeastern shore of Hawai'i's Big Island is the inspiration for this rich torte with a warm molten center (just like the volcano). With only five ingredients, it's easy to make—just don't overbake. It's delectable with a scoop of vanilla ice cream.

SERVES 6

FROM THE WALT DISNEY WORLD RESORT

½ pound bittersweet chocolate, chopped into small pieces

1 cup unsalted butter

4 large eggs

⅔ cup sugar

½ cup gluten-free baking flour, sifted

1 Preheat oven to 325°F. Spray 6 (4-ounce or larger) ramekins with cooking spray. Melt chocolate and butter using a double boiler or a heatproof bowl placed over a saucepan of simmering water, and set aside.

2 Whisk eggs and sugar in a large bowl until well blended. Then fold melted chocolate into eggs and sugar. Add sifted flour and stir until flour is mixed into chocolate.

3 Evenly divide batter among the greased ramekins. Bake for 12 to 15 minutes until the top of the cake is just beginning to set. Serve immediately.

LEFT: The elaborately detailed ceiling of Kona Cafe

CHOCOLATE-CRUSTED KEY LIME PIE

REMEMBERED FROM CÍTRICOS

Look for key limes, which are a little sweeter than other limes, to make this iconic Florida-inspired pie from Disney's Grand Floridian Resort & Spa. The dark chocolate crust pairs nicely with the creamy filling.

SERVES 8

FROM THE WALT DISNEY WORLD RESORT

6 tablespoons sugar, divided

½ cup unsalted butter, softened

5 large pasteurized eggs, divided

1⅔ cups all-purpose flour

4 tablespoons unsweetened cocoa powder, plus more for dusting

1½ teaspoons baking powder

¼ teaspoon salt

1 (14-ounce) can sweetened condensed milk

1½ teaspoons vanilla extract

½ cup key lime juice

Pinch cream of tartar

1 Beat 4 tablespoons sugar and butter in a large bowl until creamy. Beat in 1 egg until combined. Whisk together flour, cocoa powder, baking powder, and salt in a separate large bowl. Add flour mixture to butter mixture, mixing until just combined and dough holds together.

2 Remove dough from bowl and place between 2 pieces of plastic wrap. Flatten slightly into a disk and refrigerate at least 3 hours. When ready to bake, preheat oven to 350°F.

3 On a surface dusted with cocoa powder, roll dough to ⅛-inch thickness and place in a 9-inch pie pan or 9-inch tart pan. Cut a circle of parchment paper large enough to cover bottom and sides of dough. Place paper on dough; pour in enough uncooked rice or beans (or pie weights) to cover bottom of dough.

4 Bake for 10 minutes; remove parchment and weights from dough and bake for 10 minutes more. Cool to room temperature before filling. Separate yolks and whites of 4 remaining eggs, and set egg whites aside.

5 Whisk together egg yolks, sweetened condensed milk, and vanilla extract. Whisk in key lime juice until combined; mixture will thicken slightly. Pour mixture into prepared chocolate crust and bake for 15 to 20 minutes, and set aside to cool to room temperature. Then refrigerate until cold.

6 To make meringue topping, beat remaining 4 egg whites and cream of tartar with an electric mixer until soft peaks form. Gradually add 2 tablespoons sugar and continue beating until stiff peaks form, about 1 to 2 minutes.

7 Evenly spread meringue over pie. Place under a preheated broiler for 2 to 4 minutes until meringue is light golden brown.

OPPOSITE: A view of the elegant Cítricos dining room

MASCARPONE-AMARETTO TART

REMEMBERED FROM DISNEY CRUISE LINE DINING

This favorite dessert goes back almost twenty years as a treat served aboard the Disney Cruise Line ships. Almond pastry and a filling with tart cranberries, apricot jam, and amaretto make a delicate, subtly rich sweet ending.

SERVES 8-10

FROM BEYOND THE DISNEY PARKS

FOR SWEET ALMOND PASTRY

1. Cream butter and sugar in a large mixing bowl. Add almonds and egg, mixing well. Stir in sifted flour.

2. Chill dough until set, about 2 to 3 hours. Then, on a floured sheet of wax paper, roll the dough to ⅛-inch thickness. Invert dough with waxed paper into a 10½-inch tart pan with removable bottom.

3. Peel away waxed paper, gently press dough into bottom and sides of pan, and trim around the edge. Set aside.

FOR CHEESE-CRANBERRY FILLING

1. Preheat oven to 325°F. Cream butter and ⅓ cup sugar in a large mixing bowl. One at a time, add egg yolks and beat until mixture is light and fluffy.

2. Fold in mascarpone cheese, ricotta cheese, vanilla extract, orange zest, and lemon zest, and set aside.

3. In a separate large bowl, beat the egg white at high speed until soft peaks form. Gradually add 4 tablespoons sugar, 1 tablespoon at a time, and whip until stiff peaks form.

SWEET ALMOND PASTRY

1 cup unsalted butter, softened

½ cup sugar

½ cup ground almonds

1 large egg

1½ cups all-purpose flour, sifted

CHEESE-CRANBERRY FILLING

½ cup unsalted butter, softened

⅓ cup plus 4 tablespoons sugar

2 large egg yolks

1 cup mascarpone cheese

1 cup ricotta cheese

½ tablespoon vanilla extract

Zest of half an orange

Zest of half a lemon

1 large egg white

½ cup ground almonds

½ cup cake flour

2 tablespoons amaretto

½ cup cranberries

½ cup apricot jam

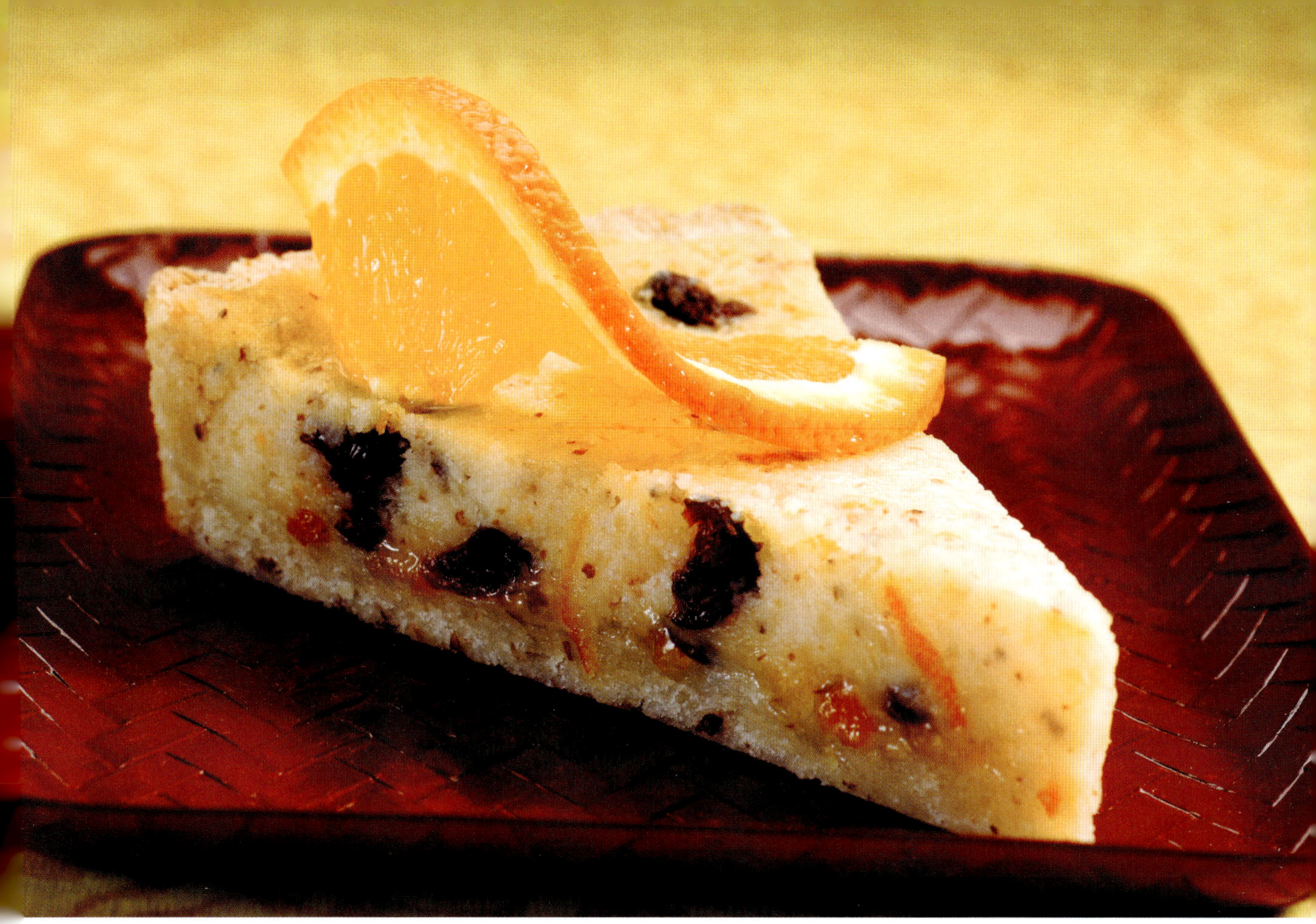

4 Fold the cheese mixture into the egg white mixture. In a small bowl, combine ground almonds and cake flour. Stir into cheese and egg whites.

5 Blend in the amaretto, then fold in cranberries. Spread the apricot jam into the bottom of the tart shell. Pour the filling into the shell on top of the jam, spreading evenly.

6 Bake for 30 to 35 minutes or until filling is set. Cool completely and remove tart from the pan. Serve at room temperature or chilled. (Note our photographed tart was garnished with an orange slice for added flair.)

RIGHT: Pluto on Deck 9 of the *Disney Wonder*

PEANUT BUTTER PIE

This pie debuted on the *Disney Magic* and the *Disney Wonder* way back in 2006, with a rich peanut butter filling and a chocolate ganache icing. It comes together quickly with a store-bought crust. And you can skip the ganache to cut back on calories—it's delicious with or without.

SERVES 8

FROM BEYOND THE DISNEY PARKS

PEANUT BUTTER PIE

1 ½ cups creamy peanut butter

8 ounces cream cheese

¾ cup sugar

2 tablespoons butter, melted

1 cup heavy cream, whipped stiff

1 baked 8-inch pie shell

GANACHE TOPPING

½ cup heavy cream

4 ounces dark chocolate

GARNISH

Whipped cream

Mint leaves

Raspberry

White chocolate curl

FOR PEANUT BUTTER PIE

With an electric mixer, blend the peanut butter, cream cheese, and sugar. Add melted butter to peanut butter mixture and fold in the whipped cream. Pour into prepared piecrust and refrigerate for 1 hour.

FOR GANACHE TOPPING

Over medium heat, bring the cream to a boil. Remove from heat and fold in chocolate. Cool until lukewarm, and glaze pie. Then refrigerate for at least 2 hours before serving. Garnish each slice with a dollop of whipped cream, mint leaves, a raspberry, and a white chocolate curl.

OPPOSITE, BOTTOM: Guests posing on a Castaway Cay beach with the *Disney Wish* docked in the background

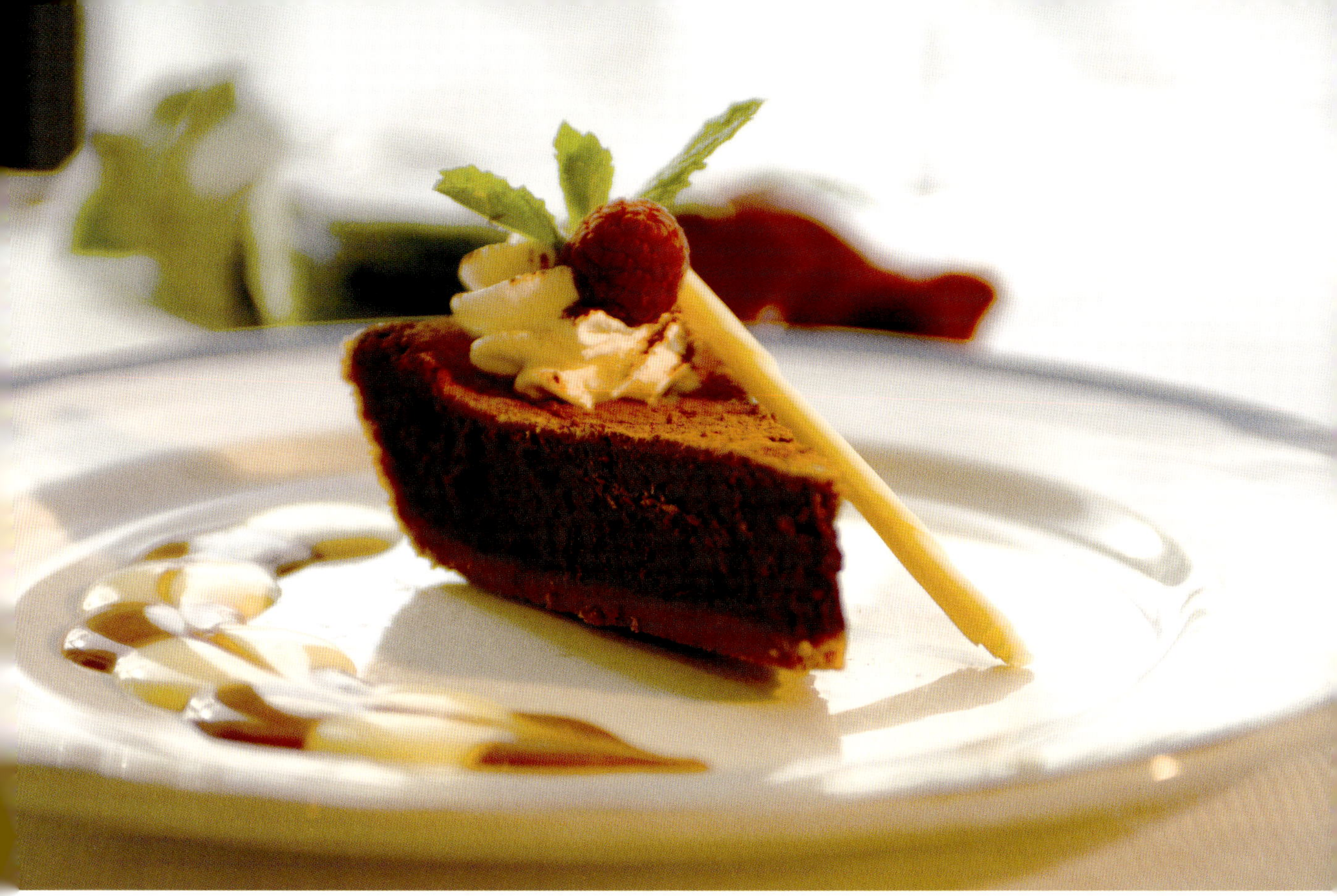

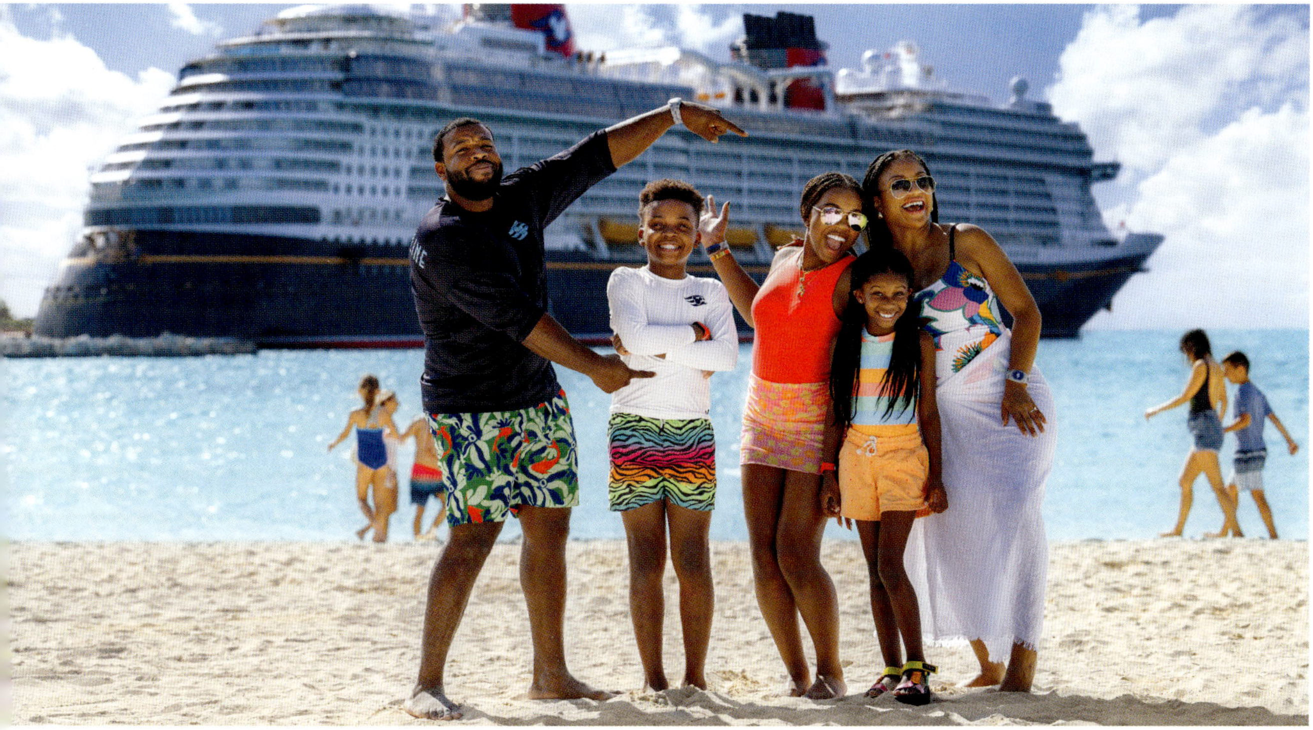

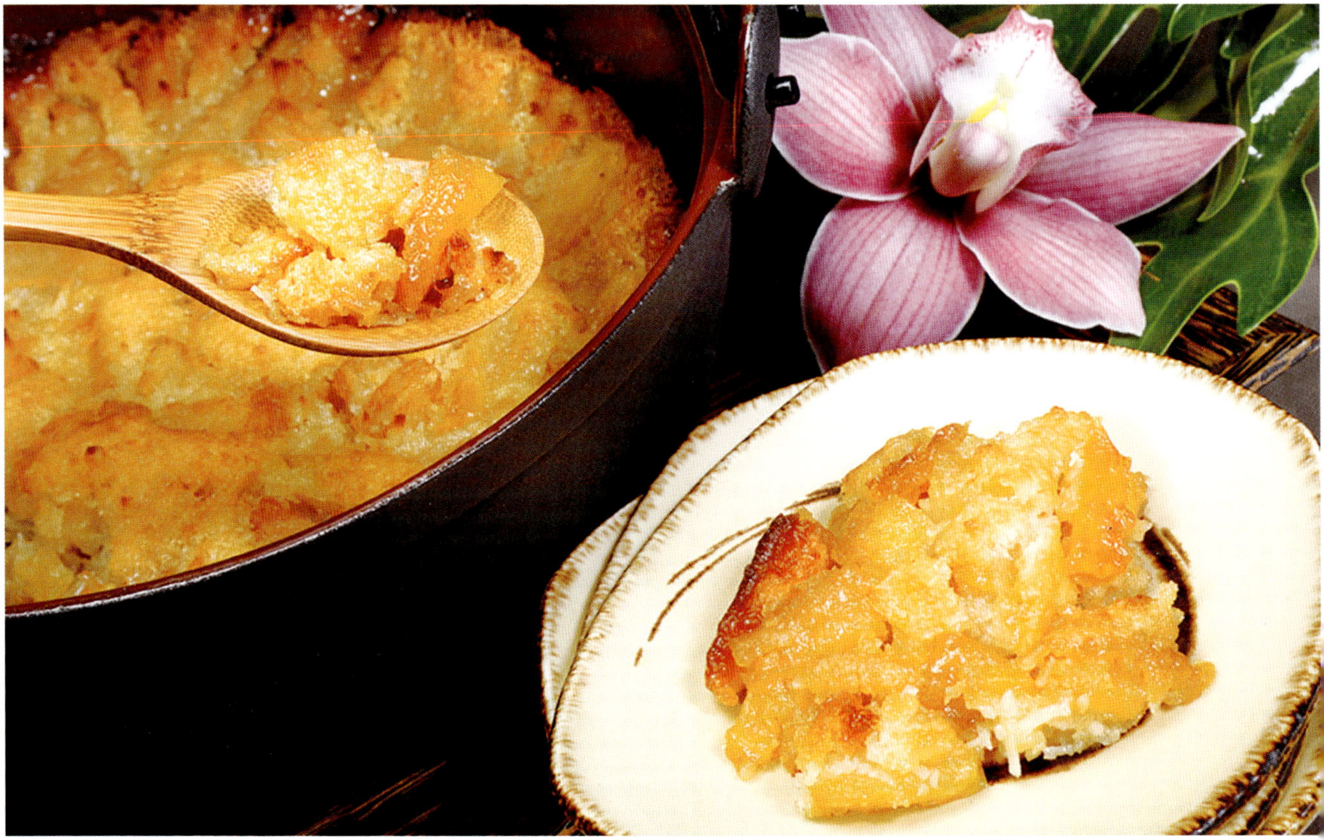

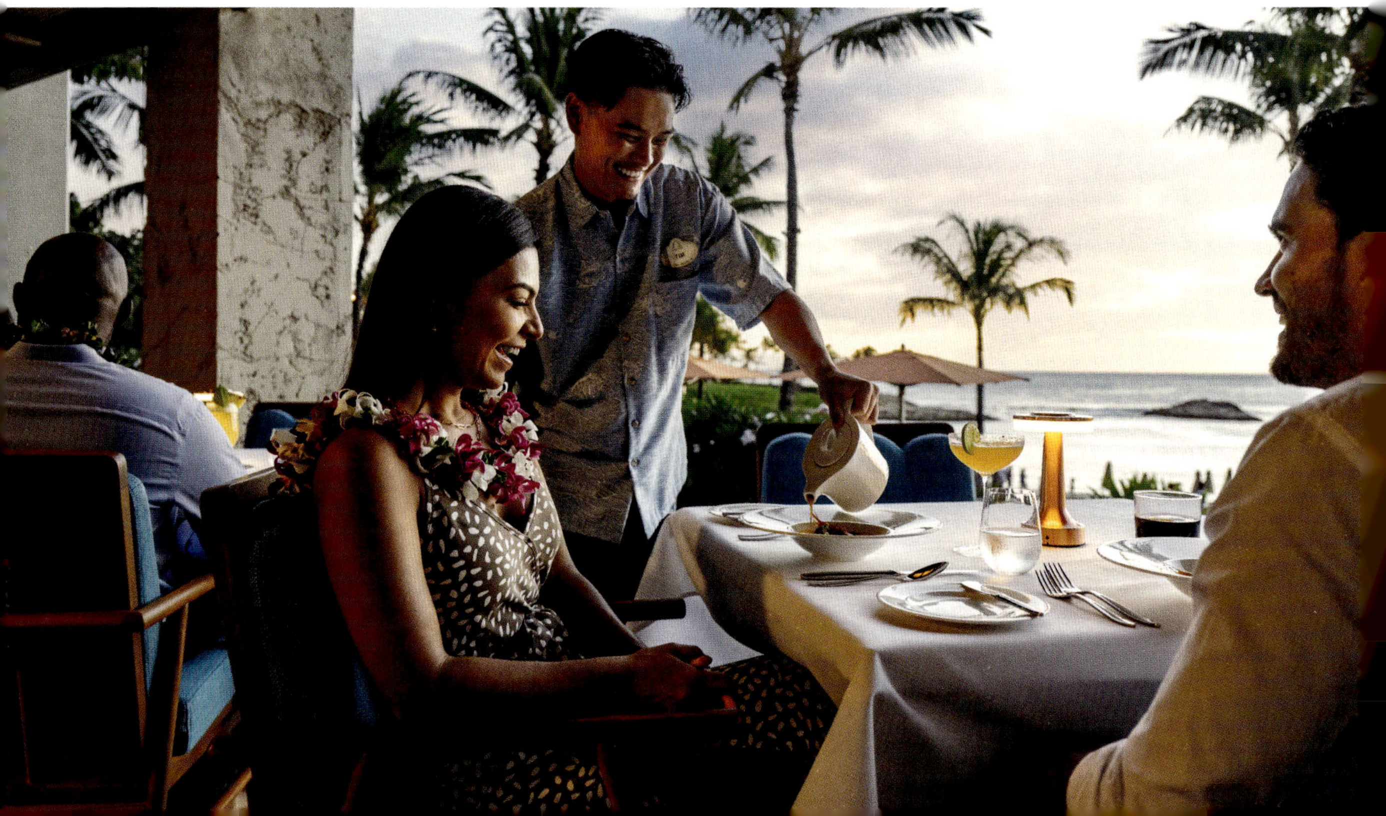

PINEAPPLE-COCONUT COBBLER

In Hawai'i, you might say this easy dessert "broke the mouth," which is local slang for "it's delicious!" Blending coconut and sweet pineapple, this treat from Aulani, A Disney Resort & Spa is even better with a scoop of vanilla or coconut ice cream.

SERVES 6

FROM BEYOND THE DISNEY PARKS

1 medium pineapple, peeled, cored, and diced

⅓ cup light brown sugar

1 cup shredded coconut

½ cup all-purpose flour

½ cup sugar

½ cup whole or 2 percent milk

4 tablespoons unsalted butter, melted

¼ teaspoon baking powder

Pinch fine salt

Vanilla or coconut ice cream, for serving

1 Preheat oven to 350°F. Butter a small (8 × 6–inch) baking pan, and set aside. Combine pineapple and brown sugar in a medium sauté pan over medium heat. Cook until sugar melts and mixture is golden.

2 Transfer mixture to a bowl, stir in coconut, and set aside. Then combine flour, sugar, milk, melted butter, baking powder, and salt in a large bowl, and stir until combined.

3 Pour batter into prepared baking pan, and top with pineapple mixture. Bake for 35 to 45 minutes, or until golden brown and cooked through. Serve warm with vanilla or coconut ice cream.

OPPOSITE, BOTTOM: Guests dining on the patio of 'AMA'AMA – Contemporary Island Cooking with Ko Olina Beach in the background

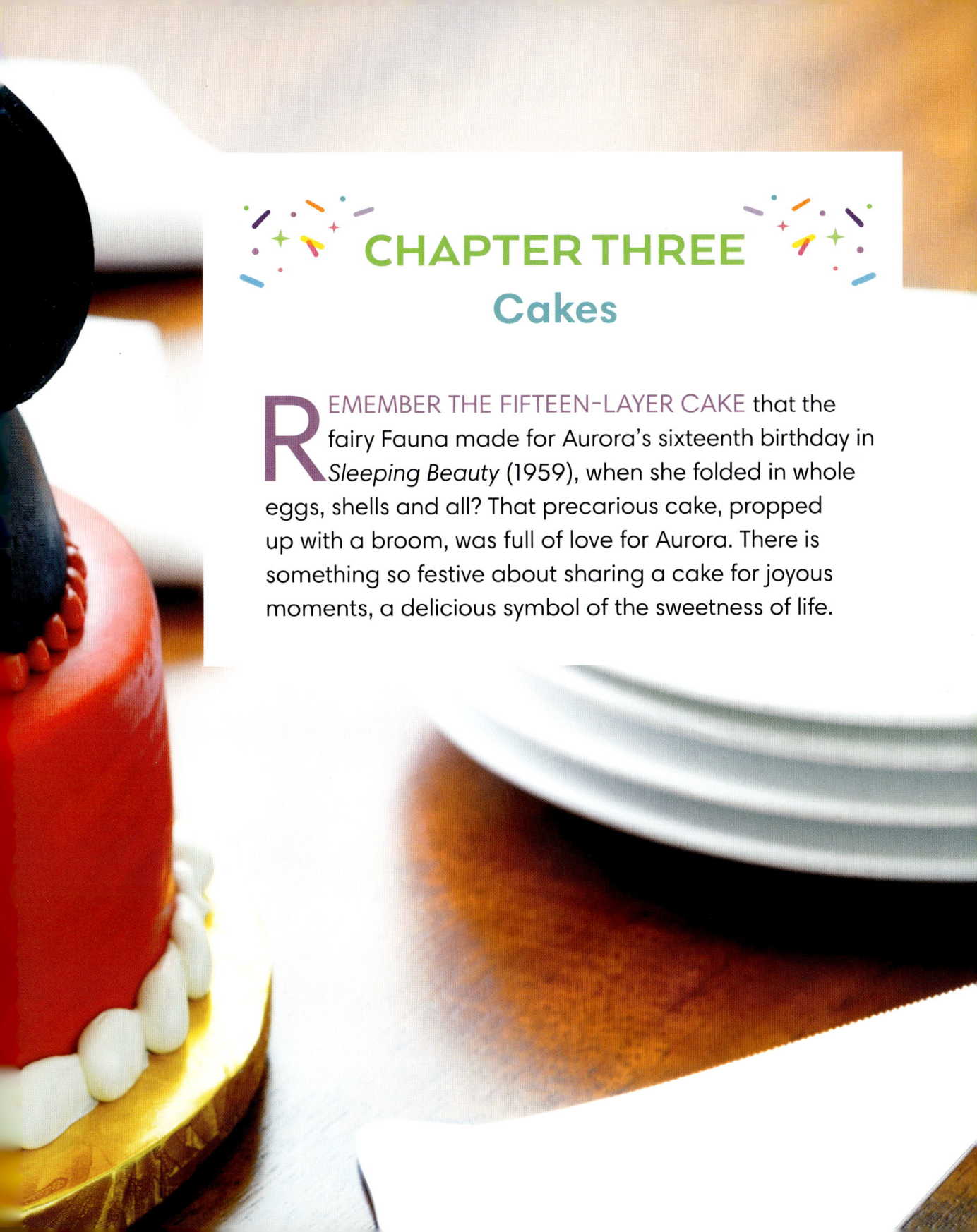

CHAPTER THREE
Cakes

REMEMBER THE FIFTEEN-LAYER CAKE that the fairy Fauna made for Aurora's sixteenth birthday in *Sleeping Beauty* (1959), when she folded in whole eggs, shells and all? That precarious cake, propped up with a broom, was full of love for Aurora. There is something so festive about sharing a cake for joyous moments, a delicious symbol of the sweetness of life.

LEMON BUMBLEBEE CUPCAKES

REMEMBERED FROM HUNGRY BEAR RESTAURANT

Start with a boxed lemon cake mix, then fill cooled cupcakes with tart lemon curd filling. The filling and frosting both need time in the refrigerator, so plan accordingly—and a little practice creates the cutest chocolate bumblebees.

MAKES 16 CUPCAKES

FROM THE DISNEYLAND RESORT

LEMON CAKE MIX CUPCAKES

1 box lemon cake mix

LEMON CURD FILLING

1 teaspoon powdered gelatin

1 tablespoon cold water

¾ cup lemon juice

¾ cup sugar, divided

3 large pasteurized eggs

3 large pasteurized egg yolks

1 tablespoon unsalted butter

FOR LEMON CAKE MIX CUPCAKES

Prepare cake mix cupcakes according to package directions, filling muffin cups three-fourths full with batter. Remove 8 cupcakes and set aside for another use. Set 16 cupcakes aside to cool completely.

FOR LEMON CURD FILLING

1 Sprinkle gelatin over cold water in a small bowl, and set aside. Then combine lemon juice and ½ cup sugar in a small saucepan over medium-low heat; bring to a simmer.

2 Whisk together remaining 4 tablespoons sugar, eggs, and egg yolks in a medium bowl. Then pour one quarter of simmering lemon-sugar mixture into egg mixture, whisking so that eggs do not cook. Pour contents of bowl back into pan with remaining lemon-sugar mixture. Continue cooking, stirring constantly for 2 minutes, until mixture thickens.

3 Remove from heat and add gelatin mixture and butter, whisking well. Then strain through a fine-mesh sieve into a bowl. Discard any solids.

4 Divide lemon curd in half and spoon into two bowls (¾ cup in each). Press a layer of plastic wrap directly onto surface of lemon curd in bowls; refrigerate 1 hour.

ABOVE: he former Hungry Bear Restaurant sign featured a honey bee nest, 2022. The venue recently reopened as Hungry Bear Barbecue Jamboree.

FOR HONEY-LEMON FROSTING

Stir honey into one bowl of Lemon Curd Filling. Then beat heavy cream on high speed with an electric mixer until stiff peaks form. Gently fold in honey–lemon curd. Refrigerate for 2 hours.

TO ASSEMBLE

1. Scoop out a small portion from the center of each Lemon Cake Mix Cupcake using a teaspoon. Place Lemon Curd Filling in a large plastic zip-top bag and cut a small hole in the end. Pipe approximately 2 teaspoons lemon curd into the center of each cupcake.

2. Place Honey-Lemon Frosting in a separate plastic zip-top bag and cut a medium-size hole in the end. Pipe frosting onto each cupcake.

TO DECORATE WITH CHOCOLATE BUMBLEBEES

1. Place 2 chocolate chips, flat sides touching, on top of a frosted cupcake so that they resemble the shape of a diamond. (One pointed end is the bee's "stinger" and the other its neck.)

2. Place another chocolate chip, flat side down, next to the bee's neck. Then use yellow writing icing to pipe three horizontal stripes onto the bee's body.

3. Tuck an almond slice under either side of the bee's body, narrow edge in frosting and angled to look like a bee's wings. Refrigerate until ready to serve.

HONEY-LEMON FROSTING

1 teaspoon honey

¾ cup Lemon Curd Filling

1 cup heavy cream

CHOCOLATE BUMBLEBEES

48 dark chocolate chips

1 small tube yellow writing icing

32 almond slices

LEMON TEA CAKE,
CELEBRATING DISNEY100

REMEMBERED FROM JOLLY HOLIDAY BAKERY CAFE

Lemon desserts were some of Walt Disney's favorites, and this sweet, dense pound cake with a ribbon of lemon down the center was created for the hundredth anniversary celebration of The Walt Disney Company. Definitely a treat worth revisiting year after year!

SERVES 8

FROM THE DISNEYLAND RESORT

FOR LEMON CURD

1. Heat double boiler or heatproof bowl over a pot of simmering water for 5 minutes. Then combine egg yolks, sugar, lemon zest, lemon juice, and salt in top of double boiler and whisk until blended.

2. Continue whisking constantly for 10 minutes, until mixture is thick enough to coat the back of a spoon. Remove from heat.

3. Whisk in cubed butter until melted. Then pour into heatproof container and cover with plastic wrap, pressing to cover top of curd. Refrigerate until ready to use.

FOR LEMON TEA CAKE

1. Preheat oven to 350°F. Grease an 8½ × 4½ × 2½–inch loaf pan with nonstick cooking spray, and set aside.

2. Cream butter and sugar in the bowl of an electric mixer fitted with a paddle attachment until fluffy. Add eggs, one at a time, and beat on medium speed until eggs are fully incorporated. Add lemon olive oil and lemon juice and beat for 1 minute.

LEMON CURD

4 large pasteurized egg yolks

⅔ cup sugar

1 tablespoon lemon zest

⅓ cup fresh lemon juice

⅛ teaspoon salt

6 tablespoons unsalted butter, softened to room temperature and cubed

LEMON TEA CAKE

1 cup unsalted butter, softened to room temperature

1 cup sugar

3 large eggs

2 tablespoons lemon olive oil

2 tablespoons fresh lemon juice

¾ cup all-purpose flour

1 teaspoon baking powder

⅛ teaspoon salt

3 Whisk flour, baking powder, and salt in a small bowl. Add 4 tablespoons flour mixture at a time to batter and beat on low speed until just mixed. Then evenly spread batter in prepared loaf pan.

4 Bake for 10 minutes, reduce heat to 325°F, and bake for an additional 25 to 30 minutes, until toothpick inserted in center comes out clean. Cool completely in pan on wire rack.

FOR WHIPPED CREAM

Whip heavy cream in the bowl of an electric mixer fitted with a whisk attachment until soft peaks form. Slowly add powdered sugar, and beat on high speed for 3 to 4 minutes, until stiff peaks form. Refrigerate until ready to serve.

FOR LEMON GLAZE

Place powdered sugar in a medium bowl. Add lemon extract, lemon juice, and food coloring (if using). Whisk until smooth, and then set aside until ready to serve.

TO ASSEMBLE & SERVE

1 Remove cake pan, and set on top of a baking sheet or cutting board. Poke 20 to 30 holes in top of cake using a chopstick. Each hole should be about 1½ inches deep.

2 Pour Lemon Curd into a piping bag fitted with a small tip. Pipe Lemon Curd into holes, making sure to wipe away any excess curd with an offset spatula.

3 Evenly spread glaze over top of tea cake, and slice loaf into 8 pieces. Place Whipped Cream into a piping bag fitted with desired tip. Pipe a rosette or desired shape on top of each cake. Sprinkle with lemon zest.

WHIPPED CREAM

½ cup heavy cream

2 tablespoons powdered sugar

LEMON GLAZE

¾ cup powdered sugar

1 teaspoon lemon extract

4 tablespoons fresh lemon juice

¼ teaspoon yellow gel food coloring, if desired

TOPPING

Zest of 1 lemon

TIRAMISU

This popular coffee-flavored Italian dessert is a mainstay at Wine Country Trattoria, where you can dine alfresco on the terrace. Inspired by Napa Valley, the restaurant offers a relaxing setting in the middle of a bustling theme park.

SERVES 6-8

FROM THE DISNEYLAND RESORT

6 large pasteurized egg yolks, room temperature

¾ cup sugar

2 tablespoons cold water

1 (¼-ounce) package powdered gelatin

⅓ cup marsala wine

1½ teaspoons vanilla extract

2½ cups mascarpone cheese, room temperature

⅓ cup buttermilk

1 cup heavy cream

20-25 packaged ladyfingers

1½ cups strongly brewed coffee

Cocoa powder, for dusting

2 chocolate curls, for garnish

1 Beat egg yolks and sugar together in a medium bowl. Set bowl over a small saucepan of simmering water and whisk until pale yellow, fluffy, and doubled in volume, about 5 minutes.

2 Place water in a small bowl; sprinkle gelatin over top, and set aside. Then heat marsala wine in a small saucepan. Stir in gelatin mixture, whisking gently to dissolve. Stir in vanilla extract, and set aside.

3 Gently whisk mascarpone into egg yolk mixture until just combined. Then whisk in buttermilk and marsala mixture. After that, whip heavy cream to medium peaks, and gently fold whipped cream into egg mixture. Refrigerate mousse until set, about 2 hours.

4 Spread a third of the mousse in the bottom of an 8-inch-square pan. Then dip ladyfingers in coffee, one at a time, and arrange half of them in a single layer on top of mousse. Spread another third of the mousse atop ladyfingers.

5 Layer with remaining coffee-dipped ladyfingers and top with remaining third of the mousse. Then refrigerate, covered, at least 4 hours. Dust with cocoa powder and top with chocolate curls just before serving.

OPPOSITE: The side Golden Vine Winery entrance

LEFT: The main entrance area of Wine Country Trattoria at the Golden Vine Winery

WARM APPLE-BUTTER CAKE

REMEMBERED FROM STEAKHOUSE 55

This nostalgic sweet was a favorite at Steakhouse 55. The cake uses a full cup of butter, thus the name. Make the caramelized apples and caramel glaze ahead of time so they'll be ready to top the warm cake for serving.

MAKES 15 (¾-CUP) RAMEKIN CAKES

FROM THE DISNEYLAND RESORT

CARAMELIZED APPLES

2 Granny Smith apples, peeled and cored

2 tablespoons unsalted butter

1 tablespoon sugar

BOURBON-CARAMEL GLAZE

¾ cup light brown sugar

½ cup unsalted butter

½ tablespoon bourbon

1 cup heavy cream

FOR CARAMELIZED APPLES

Cut apples into thin slices. Then melt butter in a large heavy skillet over medium-high heat, and add apples and sugar. Cook apples until golden and softened, and then set aside to cool.

FOR BOURBON-CARAMEL GLAZE

1. Combine brown sugar and butter in a large saucepan and bring to a boil over medium-high heat. Stir continuously until sugar dissolves.

2. Simmer over medium heat without stirring or touching pan until mixture is thick and dark amber in color, about 10 minutes.

3. Remove pan from heat. Carefully whisk in bourbon and heavy cream. Mixture will bubble vigorously and release very hot steam. Then pour caramel into a bowl to cool, and set aside.

FOR APPLE-BUTTER CAKE

1. Preheat oven to 350°F. Butter and flour 15 (¾-cup) ramekins, and set aside. Sift together flour, baking powder, baking soda, and salt in a large bowl.

2. Whisk together sugar, eggs, egg yolks, and melted butter in a separate large bowl until well combined.

ABOVE: The main entrance to the former Steakhouse 55, back in 2014

FORMERLY AT THE DISNEYLAND HOTEL · DISNEYLAND RESORT

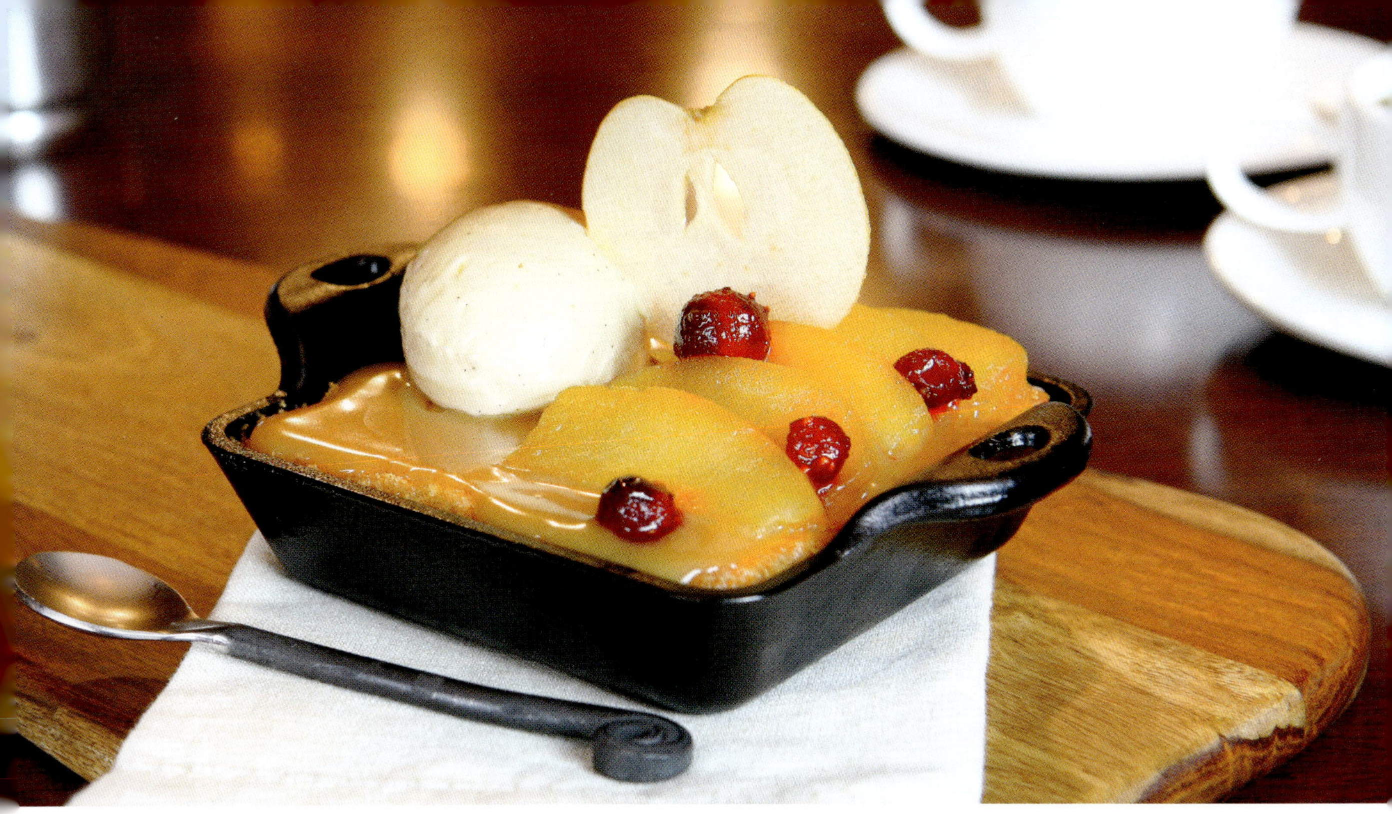

3 Combine buttermilk and almond extract in a small bowl, and set aside. Fold a third of flour mixture into egg mixture. Stir in half of buttermilk mixture. Fold in another third of flour mixture, then add remaining buttermilk mixture. Fold in remaining flour mixture.

4 Ladle ½ cup cake batter into each prepared ramekin. Bake for 20 to 22 minutes, or until a wooden pick inserted in the center of cakes comes out clean.

TO ASSEMBLE & SERVE

While Apple-Butter Cakes are warm, carefully remove from ramekins onto a serving plate. Then divide Caramelized Apples among tops of cakes, and spoon Bourbon-Caramel Glaze over top of apples and cake. Serve with vanilla ice cream and garnish with dried apple slices and cooked cranberries, if desired.

APPLE-BUTTER CAKE

1¾ cups all-purpose flour

1 tablespoon baking powder

1½ teaspoons baking soda

1½ teaspoons salt

1¾ cups sugar

8 large eggs

2 large egg yolks

1 cup unsalted butter, melted

1½ cups plus 1 teaspoon buttermilk

1½ teaspoons almond extract

Vanilla ice cream, for serving

Dried apple slices and cooked cranberries, for garnish, optional

CHOCOLATE TRUFFLE CAKES
WITH GANACHE

You can make the ganache a day ahead, as it needs plenty of time to cool. The truffle cakes are best straight from the oven, served warm with your favorite ice cream. Just make sure you use a good-quality dark chocolate for a taste to remember.

SERVES 8

FROM THE DISNEYLAND RESORT

GANACHE

4 ounces bittersweet chocolate

½ cup heavy cream

CHOCOLATE TRUFFLE CAKES

½ cup plus 6 tablespoons unsalted butter, softened; plus extra for ramekins

6½ ounces bittersweet chocolate, chopped fine

5 large eggs, room temperature, separated

½ cup sugar, divided, plus extra for ramekins

1 tablespoon all-purpose flour, sifted

Favorite ice cream, for serving

Mint leaves, for garnish

FOR GANACHE

Place chocolate in a medium heatproof bowl. Bring cream to a boil in a small saucepan over medium heat. Pour boiling cream over chopped chocolate. Slowly stir in a circular motion with a rubber spatula until all chocolate is melted, about 2 minutes. Let it sit at room temperature until ganache cools to 70°F.

FOR CHOCOLATE TRUFFLE CAKES

1 Preheat oven to 375°F. Lightly butter bottom and sides of 8 individual (¾-cup) ramekins. Coat thinly with sugar and shake out excess, and set aside.

2 Prepare a double boiler and bring water to a simmer over low heat. Place butter and chopped chocolate in the top of the double boiler, and gently stir until melted. Then whisk egg yolks and 4 tablespoons sugar in a large mixing bowl for 3 to 4 minutes or until smooth and slightly thickened. Stir in flour.

3 Ladle a small amount of melted chocolate into egg yolk mixture and whisk to combine. Add another ladle of chocolate into egg yolk mixture and continue to whisk. Once the temperature of the egg yolk mixture has been warmed, add remaining chocolate to egg yolks and vigorously whisk, and set aside.

OPPOSITE, BOTTOM: Main entrance sign of Napa Rose

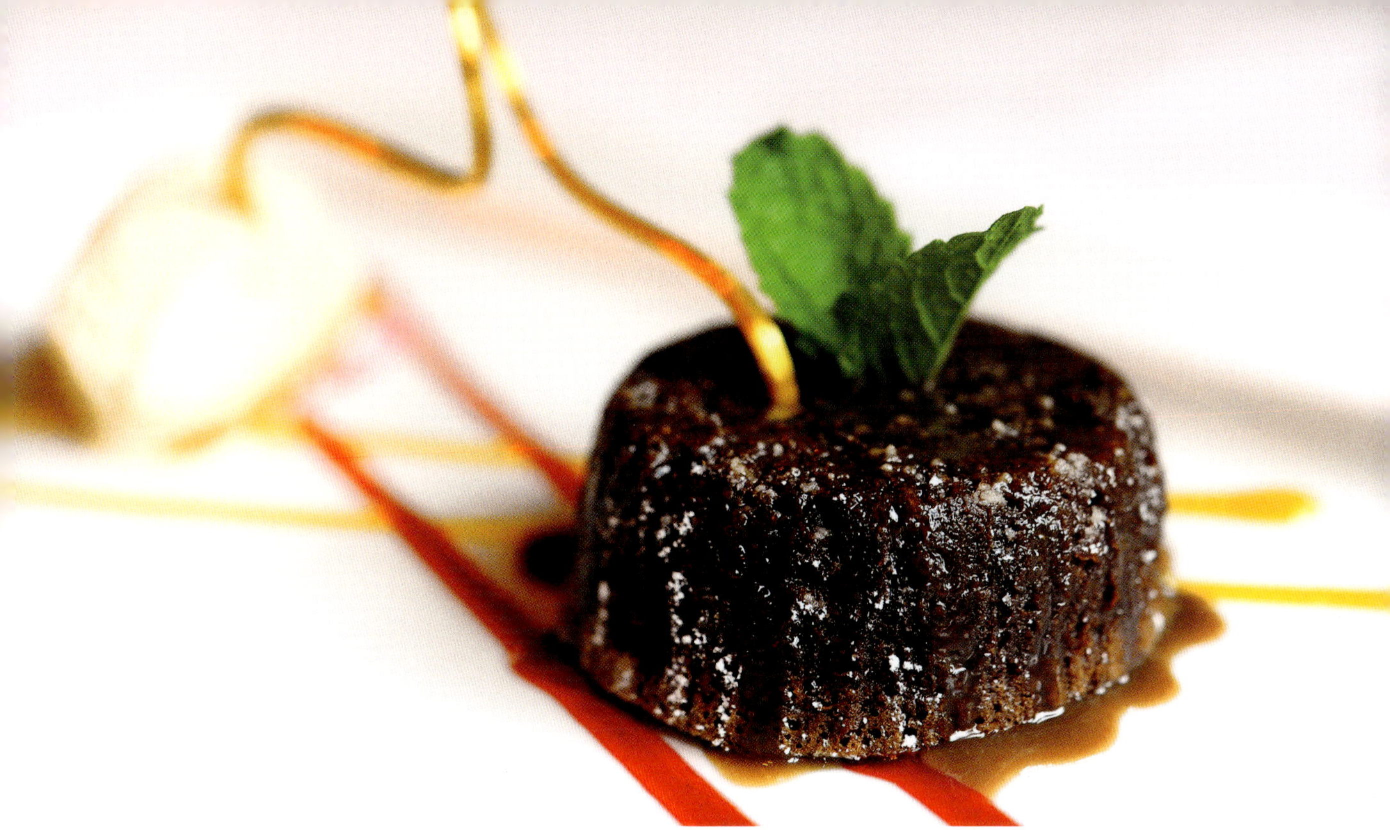

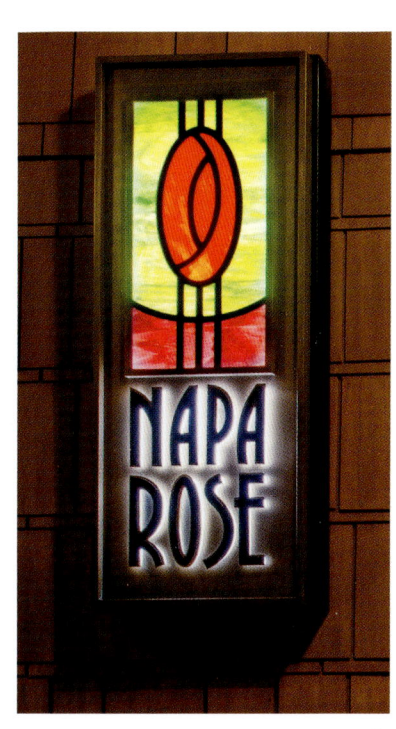

4 Combine egg whites and 1 tablespoon sugar in a stand mixer; whip on medium speed until soft peaks form.

5 Slowly add an additional 1½ tablespoons sugar while continuing to whip egg whites. Increase speed to high and slowly add remaining 1½ tablespoons sugar. Whip another 3 to 4 minutes or until stiff peaks form.

6 Gently fold egg whites into chocolate mixture, being careful not to overwork mixture. Then divide batter equally among prepared ramekins, filling three-fourths full. Place on baking sheet and bake for 9 to 10 minutes or until tops are puffy but center is still soft. Do not overbake.

7 Cut around edges of cakes using a small knife to loosen. Carefully invert cakes onto a serving plate. Top each with 1 generous tablespoon ganache. Garnish with mint leaves and serve immediately with favorite ice cream.

DISNEY'S GRAND CALIFORNIAN HOTEL & SPA · DISNEYLAND RESORT

TRIPLE CHOCOLATE CUPCAKES

REMEMBERED FROM BE OUR GUEST RESTAURANT

The menu at Be Our Guest Restaurant is French-inspired, and while the "Grey Stuff" is an option, these gourmet cupcakes with chocolate mousse filling and a ganache icing are the most popular.

MAKES 12 CUPCAKES

FROM THE WALT DISNEY WORLD RESORT

FOR CHOCOLATE-SOUR CREAM CUPCAKES

1. Preheat oven to 350°F. Then line a 12-cup muffin tin with paper liners, and set aside. Sift cocoa, flour, baking powder, and salt in a medium bowl, and set aside.

2. Combine butter and sugar in a large bowl; beat with an electric mixer until light and fluffy. Add eggs one at a time. Beat in vanilla extract.

3. With mixer on low speed, alternately add flour mixture and sour cream to the sugar mixture, beginning and ending with flour.

4. Pour batter into cups, filling each three-fourths full. Bake until a toothpick inserted in the centers comes out clean, 22 to 25 minutes.

5. Remove from oven and cool in pan 5 minutes. Transfer to a wire rack to cool completely.

FOR SIMPLE SYRUP

Combine water and sugar in a small saucepan over high heat; bring to a boil, stirring to dissolve sugar. Remove from heat and cool completely.

CHOCOLATE-SOUR CREAM CUPCAKES

¾ cup unsweetened cocoa powder

¾ cup all-purpose flour

½ teaspoon baking powder

¼ teaspoon salt

¾ cup unsalted butter, at room temperature

1 cup sugar

3 large eggs

1 teaspoon vanilla extract

½ cup sour cream

SIMPLE SYRUP

1 cup water

½ cup sugar

ABOVE: Guests enjoying a meal in the Rose Gallery of Be Our Guest Restaurant

FOR CHOCOLATE MOUSSE

1. Heat ¾ cup cream in a small saucepan until hot. Whisk together egg yolks and sugar in a medium bowl; add hot cream to egg yolk mixture in a slow stream, whisking until combined.

2. Transfer mixture to saucepan and cook over medium-low heat, stirring constantly, until it thickens slightly, about 4 to 5 minutes. Pour custard through a fine-mesh sieve into a large bowl; stir in espresso. When ready, melt chocolate in a double boiler or a bowl set over a pan of simmering water, stirring frequently until melted. Whisk chocolate into custard mixture until smooth. Refrigerate until very cold.

3. Beat remaining 1¼ cups cream in a medium bowl with an electric mixer until medium-stiff peaks form. Then whisk a quarter of the whipped cream into chocolate custard, and gently fold in remaining cream.

FOR CHOCOLATE GANACHE

Place chocolate in a medium heat-safe bowl. Then heat cream in a small saucepan until hot (do not boil). Pour cream over chocolate and stir until chocolate melts. Cool to room temperature.

TO ASSEMBLE & SERVE

Cut out centers of Chocolate–Sour Cream Cupcakes using a paring knife held at a 45° angle, cutting in a circle, to create a cone shape. Remove cupcake centers, and reserve. Then brush tops of cupcakes with Simple Syrup, or spoon it over the top, to heavily moisten. When ready, fill cupcake centers with Chocolate Mousse. Place cutout cupcake center on top of mousse, with point of cupcake center facing up. (Refrigerate any remaining mousse, tightly covered, for up to 3 or 4 days.) To finish, pipe Chocolate Ganache on top of cupcakes starting at the outer edges. (Note our photographed cupcake was garnished with a raspberry, a custom chocolate sign, and chocolate crisp pearls for added flair.)

CHOCOLATE MOUSSE

2 cups heavy cream, divided

4 large pasteurized egg yolks

3 tablespoons sugar

4 tablespoons espresso

8 ounces semisweet or bittersweet chocolate, chopped

CHOCOLATE GANACHE

12 ounces (about 1½ cups) chopped bittersweet chocolate

1 cup heavy cream

ALMOND-SWEET CORN CAKE

You might have tried this sweet treat with a subtle corn flavor during Mickey's Not-So-Scary Halloween Party, and now you can re-create it in your own kitchen with silicone corn molds. Plan ahead, as the batter needs to rest for 8 to 12 hours—and make sure to brown the butter for a nuttier, richer flavor.

MAKES 4 (7.3-INCH CORN MOLD) CAKES

FROM THE WALT DISNEY WORLD RESORT

ALMOND-SWEET CORN CAKE

10 tablespoons unsalted butter

7 large egg whites

½ cup powdered sugar

¾ cup almond flour

⅔ cup all-purpose flour

¾ teaspoon baking powder

½ teaspoon salt

2 teaspoons corn extract

1 teaspoon yellow food coloring

FOR ALMOND-SWEET CORN CAKE

1. Melt butter in a small saucepan over medium-low heat, swirling occasionally for 5 minutes. Once butter foams and begins to brown, pour butter and solids into a small bowl. Cool for 15 minutes.

2. Whip egg whites in the bowl of an electric mixer fitted with a whisk attachment for 20 seconds, and set aside.

3. Combine powdered sugar, almond flour, all-purpose flour, baking powder, and salt in a mixing bowl and whisk to combine. Add reserved egg whites, corn extract, and yellow food coloring and whisk to combine. Stir in brown butter. Cover and refrigerate batter 8 to 12 hours before baking.

4. Preheat oven to 400°F. Spread ½ cup batter into 4 (7.3-inch) silicone corn molds. Place molds on baking sheet and bake for 45 minutes, or until a toothpick inserted in the center comes out clean. Cool for 5 minutes and remove from molds. Cool completely before decorating.

FOR TOPPING

1 Melt white chocolate in a microwave-safe bowl according to package instructions.

2 Evenly divide melted white chocolate among 3 bowls. Leave one bowl white. Add desired amount of yellow and orange to remaining bowls to make yellow and orange icing to match candy corn. (Note our photographed corn cakes only show white and orange icing.)

3 Drizzle each cooled cake with the desired colors of white chocolate and decorate with candy corn.

TOPPING

1 cup white chocolate melting discs

Yellow food coloring

Orange food coloring

Candy corn

OPPOSITE: One of the dining room areas at Pecos Bill Tall Tale Inn and Cafe

GREEK YOGURT-VANILLA CAKE

FESTIVAL DEBUT: 2016 · GREECE GLOBAL MARKETPLACE

Infused with orange and lemon, this flavorful yogurt cake gets a kick from anise-flavored ouzo, Greece's most popular drink. Use full-fat yogurt to keep the cake from becoming gummy.

MAKES 1 (9 × 13-INCH) CAKE

FROM THE WALT DISNEY WORLD RESORT

OUZO SYRUP

¾ cup water

¾ cup sugar

3 tablespoons ouzo liqueur

¼ teaspoon vanilla extract

GREEK YOGURT CAKE

5 large eggs, separated

Pinch salt

¾ cup unsalted butter, room temperature

1⅛ cups sugar

2¼ cups all-purpose flour

1 tablespoon baking soda

1 cup plain Greek yogurt

1 teaspoon vanilla

Zest of 1 orange

Zest of 1 lemon

FOR OUZO SYRUP

Add all the ingredients to a small saucepan and bring to a simmer over medium heat; simmer 4 minutes, then cool.

FOR GREEK YOGURT CAKE

1. Preheat oven to 325°F. Grease a 9 × 13-inch baking pan with nonstick cooking spray. Then whip egg whites and salt in the bowl of an electric mixer fitted with a whisk attachment until stiff peaks form, and set aside.

2. Cream butter and sugar in the bowl of an electric mixer fitted with a paddle attachment for 3 minutes, until fluffy. Add one egg yolk at a time, mixing on low speed and scraping side of the bowl as needed, until eggs yolks are mixed.

3. Sift flour and baking soda, and then slowly add to mixture. Add Greek yogurt, vanilla, and orange and lemon zests. Mix on low speed until combined. Gently fold in a third of egg whites with a spatula. Fold in remaining egg whites.

4. Pour into prepared pan and evenly spread batter. Bake for 30 minutes or until a toothpick inserted in center of cake comes out clean. Immediately drizzle ⅔ cup Ouzo Syrup on top of cake. Cool completely in pan.

FOR CANDIED PISTACHIOS

1. Preheat oven to 350°F. Place all ingredients in a small bowl. Stir with a spatula until pistachios are coated.

2. Place on sheet pan and bake for 4 minutes; stir and bake for an additional 4 minutes. Remove from oven, stir to break up any large pieces, and set aside.

FOR GREEK YOGURT WHIPPED CREAM

Whip heavy cream and powdered sugar in the bowl of an electric mixer until medium peaks form. Then add Greek yogurt and whip to medium peaks. Refrigerate until ready to serve.

TO ASSEMBLE & SERVE

Place a cooling rack on top of a baking sheet. Turn cooled Greek Yogurt Cake onto the rack. Pour remaining Ouzo Syrup on top of cake. Top each slice with the Greek Yogurt Whipped Cream and then Candied Pistachios.

CANDIED PISTACHIOS

1 cup chopped pistachios

1 tablespoon egg white

4 tablespoons sugar

GREEK YOGURT WHIPPED CREAM

2 cups heavy cream

1 cup powdered sugar

1½ cups Greek yogurt

PISTACHIO-CARDAMOM CAKES
WITH CHOCOLATE-COCONUT CREAM

FESTIVAL DEBUT: 2017 · INDIA GLOBAL MARKETPLACE

Pistachio and cardamom are a classic combination in Indian sweets. A dollop of silky Chocolate-Coconut Cream adds extra richness. At the festival, the cake was paired with sweet Tokaji wine from Hungary.

MAKES 12 MINI BUNDT CAKES

FROM THE WALT DISNEY WORLD RESORT

CHOCOLATE-COCONUT CREAM

3 cups coconut milk, divided

½ cup sugar, divided

4 tablespoons cornstarch

3 ounces semisweet chocolate, chopped

PISTACHIO-CARDAMOM CAKES

1½ cups all-purpose flour

¼ teaspoon baking soda

1¼ teaspoons ground cardamom

½ cup unsalted butter, at room temperature

1½ cups sugar

½ cup sour cream

3 large eggs

1 teaspoon almond extract

1½ cups ground unsalted pistachios

FOR CHOCOLATE-COCONUT CREAM

1 Whisk ½ cup coconut milk, 4 tablespoons sugar, and cornstarch in a small bowl, and set aside. Combine remaining coconut milk and sugar in a medium saucepan. Bring to a boil over medium-high heat.

2 Reduce heat to medium and slowly whisk in reserved coconut milk mixture from bowl. Cook, stirring constantly, until boiling. Remove from heat.

3 Stir in chocolate and strain into a medium bowl. Cover cream with plastic wrap touching the top to avoid skin forming. Refrigerate until ready to use.

FOR PISTACHIO-CARDAMOM CAKES

1 Preheat oven to 325°F. Spray 12 (1½-inch diameter, 2½-inch deep) mini Bundt pans with nonstick cooking spray, and set aside. Sift flour, baking soda, and cardamom into a medium bowl and set aside.

2 Cream together butter and sugar in the bowl of an electric mixer until fluffy. Mix in sour cream until blended.

OPPOSITE, TOP: Guests on a sunny day in front of Spaceship Earth at EPCOT

3 Add a third of the flour mixture and one egg until just mixed. Repeat with remaining flour mixture and eggs. Add almond extract and ground pistachios and mix until blended.

4 Pour into the prepared pans and bake for 15 to 20 minutes, until a toothpick inserted in the center comes out clean. Cool each pan on wire rack for 15 minutes and remove from pan. (Note if you have less than 12 mini Bundt pans, then repeat process for remaining cakes once a pan opens up.)

TO SERVE

Serve each cake with 2 tablespoons of Chocolate-Coconut Cream.

OLIVE OIL CAKE WITH LEMON CURD

FESTIVAL DEBUT: 2017 · SPAIN GLOBAL MARKETPLACE

Olive oil makes a moist, dense cake, and the lemon curd brightens the flavors. At the festival it was paired with a sip of savory Oloroso sherry.

MAKES 1 (8-INCH) SQUARE CAKE

FROM THE WALT DISNEY WORLD RESORT

LEMON CURD

3 large pasteurized eggs

3 large pasteurized egg yolks

½ cup sugar

Zest of 1 lemon

¾ cup fresh lemon juice

4 tablespoons unsalted butter, cubed

OLIVE OIL CAKE

1 cup all-purpose flour

¼ teaspoon baking powder

½ teaspoon salt

½ cup whole milk

⅓ cup extra-virgin olive oil

¾ cup sugar

2 large eggs

FOR LEMON CURD

1   Whisk together eggs, egg yolks, sugar, lemon zest, and lemon juice in a double boiler or heatproof bowl. Set bowl over boiling water.

2   Cook for 10 minutes, whisking constantly, until curd thickens and top bubbles disappear. Remove from heat.

3   Stir in butter, one cube at a time, and strain into a bowl. Cover top of Lemon Curd with plastic wrap and refrigerate until ready to serve.

FOR OLIVE OIL CAKE

4   Preheat oven to 325°F. Grease an 8 × 8-inch cake pan with nonstick cooking spray, and set aside. Then sift flour, baking powder, and salt into a medium bowl and set aside.

5   Whisk milk and olive oil together into a small bowl, and set aside. Mix sugar and eggs together with an electric mixer on high speed until pale. Add half of the flour mixture and beat until mixed. Then add half of the olive oil mixture. Repeat with remaining flour and olive oil mixtures.

6   Pour batter into the cake pan. Bake for 25 to 30 minutes, until a toothpick inserted in the center comes out clean.

TO SERVE

Cut cake to desired size pieces and serve each slice with 1 to 2 tablespoons of Lemon Curd.

OPPOSITE: As part of the new World Celebration Gardens, the statue of Walt Disney, named *Walt the Dreamer*, invites guests to sit down and soak in the sights, sounds, and smells of EPCOT.

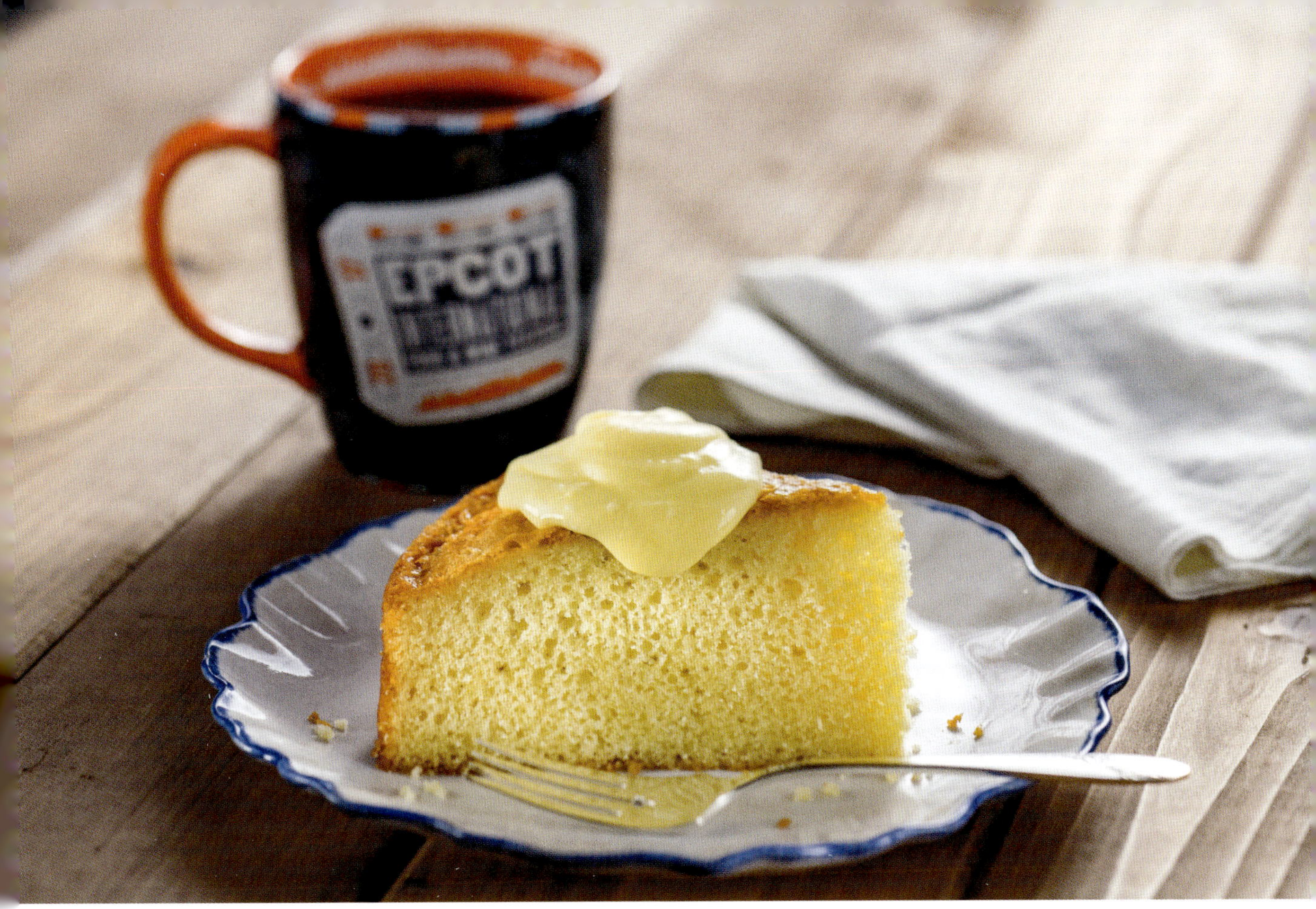
EPCOT

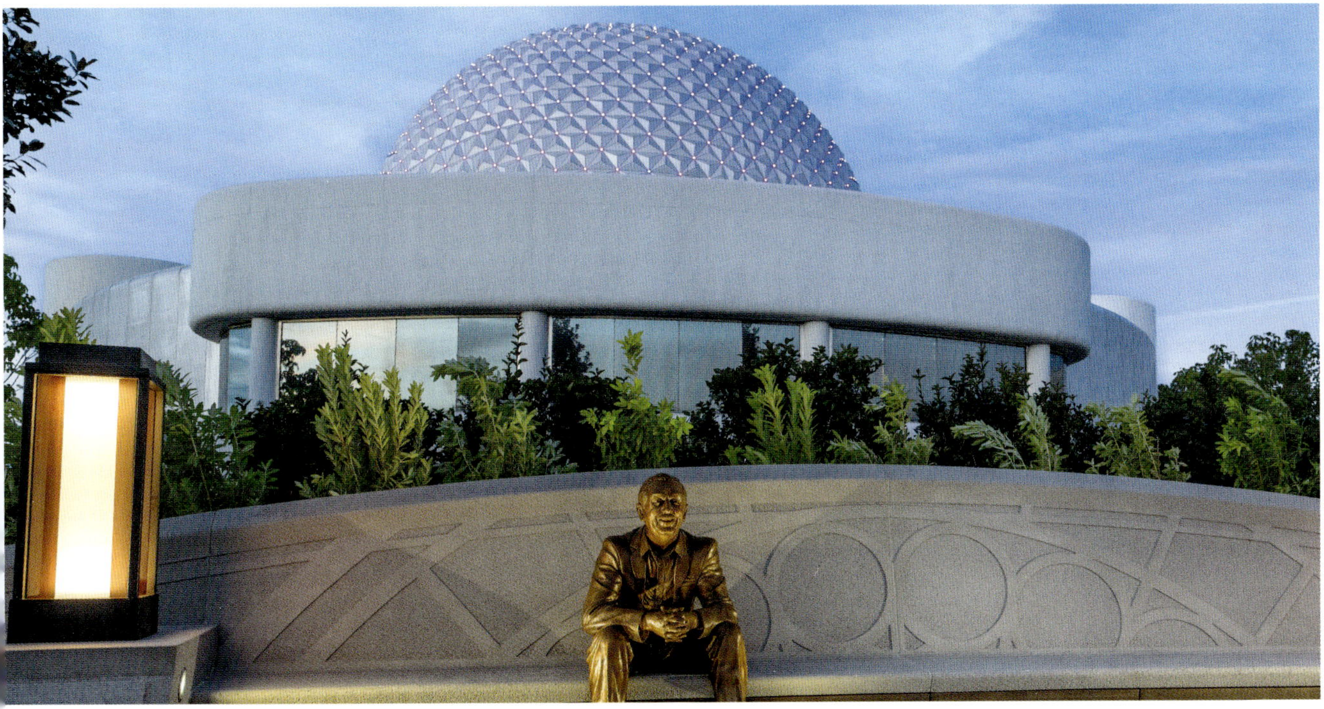

ROCKY ROAD CAKE

FESTIVAL DEBUT: 2022 · FLAVORS FROM FIRE GLOBAL MARKETPLACE

This recipe might look time-consuming, but it's actually easy to make, and the individual cakes topped with marshmallows, almonds, and ganache really set this apart from an everyday chocolate cake.

SERVES 8

FROM THE WALT DISNEY WORLD RESORT

FOR SPICY SUGARED ALMONDS

1 Line a baking sheet with parchment paper, and set aside. Combine 1 teaspoon sugar with the cinnamon and cayenne in a small bowl, and set aside.

2 Stir remaining ⅓ cup sugar and water in a medium saucepan over medium-high heat until boiling. Carefully add almonds and stir frequently for 8 to 10 minutes, until water evaporates. Continue stirring for 2 to 3 minutes, until sugar begins to caramelize. Sprinkle reserved cinnamon-cayenne-sugar mixture over almonds and stir to mix.

3 Carefully pour almonds onto prepared baking sheet, separating with spatula. Cool completely, then coarsely chop. Store in airtight container for up to 3 days.

FOR CHOCOLATE GANACHE SAUCE

1 Spray eight 6-ounce ramekins with nonstick cooking spray, and set aside. Place chopped chocolate in a medium glass bowl.

2 Bring heavy cream to simmer in a small saucepan over medium heat. Pour over chocolate. Let chocolate sit for 5 minutes, then stir until smooth.

3 Place 1½ tablespoons of ganache in each ramekin and refrigerate for 20 minutes. Keep remaining ganache at room temperature until ready to serve.

SPICY SUGARED ALMONDS

⅓ cup plus 1 teaspoon sugar

⅛ teaspoon cinnamon

⅛ teaspoon ground cayenne

3 tablespoons water

¾ cup unsalted almonds

CHOCOLATE GANACHE SAUCE

6 ounces dark chocolate, chopped

⅔ cup heavy cream

CHOCOLATE-BUTTERMILK CAKES

1 cup all-purpose flour

1 cup sugar

4 tablespoons unsweetened cocoa powder

1 teaspoon baking soda

½ teaspoon baking powder

¼ teaspoon salt

1 egg

½ cup vegetable oil

½ cup buttermilk

½ cup hot water

FOR CHOCOLATE-BUTTERMILK CAKES

1 Preheat oven to 350°F. In a large mixing bowl, whisk together flour, sugar, cocoa powder, baking soda, baking powder, and salt. Add egg, oil, and buttermilk. Whisk to combine. Carefully add hot water and whisk until batter is smooth.

2 Remove ramekins filled with ganache from refrigerator and fill each with ⅓ cup cake batter. Bake for 20 to 25 minutes, until a toothpick inserted in the center comes out clean. Cool 5 to 10 minutes before serving.

TO ASSEMBLE & SERVE

Carefully remove the Chocolate-Buttermilk Cakes from ramekins. Top each with 2 tablespoons mini marshmallows and 1 tablespoon Spicy Sugared Almonds. Warm the reserved Chocolate Ganache Sauce in microwave for 30 seconds on 50 percent power. Then drizzle it over each cake, and sprinkle with sea salt.

TOPPINGS

1 cup mini marshmallows

Spicy Sugared Almonds

Chocolate Ganache Sauce

Sea salt

AVOCADO CUSTARD CAKES

Jiko – The Cooking Place at Disney's Animal Kingdom Lodge celebrates the cuisine of Africa and India, and this pale green cake combines lime, believed to have originated in India, and avocado, better known as "butter fruit" in parts of India where it grows. Whipped egg whites make it extra fluffy.

MAKES 24 MINI CAKES

FROM THE WALT DISNEY WORLD RESORT

4 large eggs, separated

2 large egg yolks

3 limes, divided

4½ tablespoons unsalted butter

1½ cups sugar

2 Hass avocados, mashed

1 cup whole milk

1 cup crème fraîche

1½ cups all-purpose flour

1 cup heavy cream

2 tablespoons powdered sugar

1 Preheat oven to 300°F. Lightly grease 2 standard (12-well) muffin tins with nonstick spray, and set aside.

2 Separate 6 egg yolks and 4 egg whites into separate bowls, and set aside.

3 Zest all 3 limes, and set aside a third of the zest for garnish. Juice 2 limes and combine juice with two-thirds of the zest, and set aside.

4 Cream butter and sugar in an electric mixer until light and fluffy. Add mashed avocados and lime juice–zest mixture. Mix until combined.

5 Add egg yolks, mixing until combined. Mix in milk and crème fraîche. Add flour and mix until just incorporated, being careful not to overmix. Pour batter into a large bowl. Clean mixing bowl.

6 Whisk egg whites in a stand mixer until soft peaks form. Gently fold beaten egg whites into avocado batter.

7 Place batter into the greased muffin tins, filling wells three-fourths full. Bake for 35 to 40 minutes. (Cakes should yield slightly when pressed on top.)

8 Remove from oven and cool completely before unmolding. Just before serving, whip cream and powdered sugar together until the cream reaches stiff peaks.

9 Place a dollop of whipped cream on top of each avocado custard cake. Garnish with remaining lime zest.

OPPOSITE: Chefs in the open kitchen area of Jiko – The Cooking Place

CAFÉ CON LECHE CHOUX

Toledo's menu, inspired by the cuisine of Spain, includes this sweet ending with chocolate mousse and coffee custard. This recipe takes some time, and skill with making the pâte à choux, but the delicate dessert is worth the effort.

SERVES 12

FROM THE WALT DISNEY WORLD RESORT

FOR COFFEE CUSTARD

1. Bloom gelatin sheet in ice water. Heat espresso and milk in a medium saucepan over medium-low heat for 5 minutes, until warm. Remove from heat.

2. Whisk together egg yolk and sugar in a small bowl. Slowly whisk in half of the warm milk-coffee mixture to temper the eggs. Strain egg mixture into saucepan with remaining milk-coffee mixture, and stir custard until combined.

3. Add bloomed gelatin sheet, melted milk chocolate, and coarse salt to custard. Stir until smooth. Whip heavy cream to soft peaks. Fold into custard. Refrigerate for at least 8 hours.

FOR DARK CHOCOLATE MOUSSE

1. Bloom gelatin sheet in ice water. Heat ½ cup of the heavy cream in a medium saucepan until warm. Add bittersweet chocolate chips and stir until smooth. Remove from heat.

2. Heat bloomed gelatin and orange liqueur in microwave for 15 seconds, until 113°F. Stir in egg yolks, then pour into chocolate-cream mixture.

3. Whip remaining ¾ cup heavy cream to soft peaks. Fold into chocolate mousse. Pour into 1½-inch molds and freeze for at least 4 hours.

COFFEE CUSTARD

1 (silver) gelatin sheet

4 tablespoons brewed espresso

¼ cup whole milk

1 large pasteurized egg yolk

2 teaspoons sugar

1 cup milk chocolate, melted

1 pinch coarse salt

½ cup heavy cream

CHOCOLATE MOUSSE

1 (silver) gelatin sheet

1¼ cups heavy cream, divided

1 cup bittersweet chocolate chips

½ teaspoon orange liqueur

4 large pasteurized egg yolks

DISNEY'S CORONADO SPRINGS RESORT · DISNEY'S ANIMAL KINGDOM RESORT AREA

FOR CHOCOLATE CRAQUELIN

Place all ingredients in the bowl of a food processor. Blend until combined. Wrap dough in plastic wrap and chill for 45 minutes. Roll dough to ⅛-inch thickness and cut into 1¼-inch circles, and set aside until ready to serve.

FOR CHOCOLATE PÂTE À CHOUX

1. Preheat oven to 300°F. Line a baking sheet with parchment paper. Combine water, milk, butter, sugar, and salt in a medium saucepan. Bring to a boil over medium heat.

2. Quickly stir in flour and cocoa powder using a spatula. Cook over medium heat, stirring constantly for 1 minute, until mixture pulls away from sides of the pan.

3. Transfer to an electric mixer fitted with a paddle attachment and mix on low speed for 2 minutes, until slightly cooled. Add eggs, one at a time, and beat until soft peaks form.

4. Transfer to a piping bag fitted with a large round tip. Pipe into 1¼-inch circles onto prepared pan. Bake for 30 to 35 minutes, until puffy and lightly browned on the sides.

CHOCOLATE CRAQUELIN

½ cup sugar

½ cup all-purpose flour

2 tablespoons unsweetened cocoa powder

½ cup unsalted butter

½ teaspoon coarse salt

CHOCOLATE PÂTE À CHOUX

½ cup water

½ cup whole milk

7 tablespoons unsalted butter

1½ teaspoons sugar

1 teaspoon coarse salt

⅔ cup all-purpose flour, sifted

2 tablespoons unsweetened cocoa powder

5 large eggs

OPPOSITE: Guests toast in the main dining room of Toledo – Tapas, Steak & Seafood.

RECIPE CONTINUES ON NEXT PAGE

CAFÉ CON LECHE CHOUX

FOR VANILLA CHANTILLY

1. Bloom gelatin sheet in ice water. Combine ¾ cup heavy cream with the powdered sugar and vanilla bean. Whisk by hand to soft peaks.

2. Place remaining 4 tablespoons of heavy cream and bloomed gelatin sheet in a small saucepan. Heat over medium heat, stirring constantly, until gelatin is melted.

3. Add to whipped cream mixture and beat until smooth. Refrigerate until ready to serve.

FOR DARK CHOCOLATE GLAÇAGE

1. Bloom gelatin sheets in ice water. Combine water, sugar, and glucose syrup in a medium saucepan and bring to a boil. Add bloomed gelatin and condensed milk.

2. Place dark chocolate chips in a medium bowl. Pour the warm gelatin-sugar mixture over chocolate and mix with a hand blender. Keep at 95°F until ready to serve.

TO ASSEMBLE & SERVE

1. Whip the Coffee Custard and Vanilla Chantilly each by hand to soft peaks. Then place the whipped Coffee Custard in a piping bag fitted with a round tip.

2. Fill Chocolate Pâte à Choux with the Coffee Custard, and then set aside. Spoon Vanilla Chantilly onto a plate. Top with the filled Chocolate Pâte à Choux and a Chocolate Craquelin.

3. Remove Chocolate Mousse from freezer and glaze with Dark Chocolate Glaçage. Add to top of each Chocolate Craquelin. Garnish each with fleur de sel and a chocolate decoration.

VANILLA CHANTILLY

½ (silver) gelatin sheet

1 cup heavy cream, divided

½ cup powdered sugar

½ vanilla bean, scraped

DARK CHOCOLATE GLAÇAGE

4 (silver) gelatin sheets

4 tablespoons water

4 tablespoons sugar

4 tablespoons glucose syrup

2½ tablespoons condensed milk

½ cup dark chocolate chips

TOPPING

Fleur de sel

10 chocolate decorations

ABOVE: Toledo – Tapas, Steak & Seafood is the rooftop restaurant in the Gran Destino Tower.

WARM CHOCOLATE CAKE
WITH MOLTEN RASPBERRY-CARAMEL CENTER

This elegant dessert is a favorite at Topolino's Terrace, with tart raspberry, rich caramel, and milk chocolate filling in the center of a dark chocolate cake. Time this recipe so that you're ready to serve it warm with a scoop of vanilla gelato.

SERVES 12

FROM THE WALT DISNEY WORLD RESORT

RASPBERRY-CARAMEL CENTER

2 cups fresh raspberries

1 cup chopped milk chocolate

1 cup sugar

4 tablespoons water

4 tablespoons heavy cream

2 tablespoons unsalted butter

⅛ teaspoon salt

FOR RASPBERRY-CARAMEL CENTER

1 Place raspberries in food processor and purée until smooth. Set aside. Melt chopped chocolate in microwave-safe bowl on 50 percent power, stirring every 30 seconds until melted, and set aside.

2 Combine sugar and water in a small saucepan. Bring to boil over medium heat and cook until golden brown.

3 Remove from heat and whisk in heavy cream and puréed raspberries. Pour over melted chocolate and stir with spatula. Add butter and salt; stir until incorporated, and set aside.

RECIPE CONTINUES ON NEXT PAGE

WARM CHOCOLATE CAKE
WITH MOLTEN RASPBERRY-CARAMEL CENTER

(CONTINUED)

FOR CHOCOLATE CAKE BATTER

1. Sift powdered sugar, all-purpose flour, and salt into small bowl, and set aside. Melt butter and chopped dark chocolate in microwave-safe bowl on 50 percent power, stirring every 30 seconds until melted.

2. Whisk eggs and egg yolks in medium bowl and add to chocolate mixture. Add in sifted powdered sugar mixture and whisk until smooth.

FOR WARM CHOCOLATE CAKE WITH MOLTEN RASPBERRY-CARAMEL CENTER

1. Preheat oven to 350°F. Grease ½ cup muffin tins or aluminum baking cups with unsalted butter. Add 4 tablespoons cake batter into each tin. Top with 1 tablespoon Raspberry-Caramel Center and another 4 tablespoons Chocolate Cake Batter.

2. Bake for 9 to 10 minutes, until edges are baked but center is still soft. Let it rest for 5 minutes before removing from pan. Serve warm.

CHOCOLATE CAKE BATTER

1½ cups powdered sugar

1 cup all-purpose flour

¼ teaspoon salt

1 cup unsalted butter

4 cups chopped dark chocolate

6 large eggs

6 large egg yolks

LEFT: Donald Duck poses for a photo with a guest of Topolino's Terrace – Flavors of the Riviera.

DISNEY'S RIVIERA RESORT · EPCOT RESORT AREA

CHOCOLATE CREAM COOKIE CUPCAKES

REMEMBERED FROM BOARDWALK BAKERY

When Disney's BoardWalk Inn & Villas first opened in summer 1996, it featured the BoardWalk Bakery, where the cases were filled with freshly made savories and sweets. These days, the space is known as the BoardWalk Deli and offers overstuffed sandwiches and other delicious deli notables. But we still smile at these over-the-top cupcakes: a trifecta of cake, cookies, and freshly whipped cream.

MAKES 12 CUPCAKES

FROM THE WALT DISNEY WORLD RESORT

VANILLA CUPCAKES

1 ½ cups cake flour

1 ½ teaspoons baking powder

¼ teaspoon salt

½ cup unsalted butter, softened

⅔ cup sugar

3 large eggs

1 teaspoon vanilla extract

4 tablespoons milk

FOR VANILLA CUPCAKES

1 Preheat oven to 350°F and line two jumbo 6-well muffin tins with baking cups, or grease with nonstick spray. Then sift together flour, baking powder, and salt into a mixing bowl, and set aside.

2 In a separate bowl, cream butter and sugar with an electric mixer until light and fluffy. Add eggs with mixer on low speed; add vanilla extract. Then add dry ingredients and stir until just moistened.

3 Add milk and mix 1 minute on low speed. Then scoop approximately ½ cup batter into each muffin cup. Bake for 17 to 20 minutes, or until a toothpick inserted in center comes out clean. Cool on wire rack for 20 minutes before removing from pan.

RECIPE CONTINUES ON NEXT PAGE

CHOCOLATE CREAM COOKIE CUPCAKES

(CONTINUED)

FOR CHOCOLATE CREAM COOKIE MOUSSE

1 Whip ¾ cup heavy cream with mixer on medium speed to medium-firm peaks, and set aside. Finely crumble 6 chocolate sandwich cookies, and set aside.

2 Melt white chocolate chips in double boiler or heatproof bowl on top of a pot of simmering water. Remove from heat and set aside.

3 Pour remaining 4 tablespoons cream into a small saucepan; stir in gelatin, and set aside until gelatin softens and swells, about 3 minutes. Stir over low heat until gelatin dissolves. Don't let mixture boil.

4 Remove from heat and gently add egg yolks, then melted white chocolate, stirring quickly to avoid lumps. Fold together whipped cream and crumbled chocolate sandwich cookies; fold into white chocolate mixture.

TO ASSEMBLE & SERVE

1 Whip cream and sugar together until medium peaks form, and then refrigerate until ready to use. Cut out centers of Vanilla Cupcakes using a paring knife held at a 45° angle, cutting in a circle to create a cone shape. Remove cupcake centers and set aside.

2 Fill each cupcake center with about 2 tablespoons Chocolate Cream Cookie Mousse. Place cutout cupcake center on top of mousse, with point facing up.

3 Pipe whipped cream on tops of cupcakes, starting at outer edges and then slowly moving in and up to the top.

4 Gently press candy gems around base of whipped cream, and place 1 chocolate sandwich cookie on top of each cupcake.

CHOCOLATE CREAM COOKIE MOUSSE

1 cup heavy cream, divided

6 chocolate sandwich cookies

⅔ cup white chocolate chips

1 (¼-ounce) package powdered gelatin

2 large pasteurized egg yolks

TOPPINGS

2 cups heavy cream

½ cup sugar

Candy gems for decorating, optional

12 chocolate sandwich cookies

CHOCOLATE-PEANUT BUTTER PRETZEL CAKE

Layers of brownie, silky ganache, and airy peanut butter mousse get a topping of salty pretzels and a scoop of ice cream (dulce de leche is the perfect pairing). Give yourself plenty of time to chill the dessert.

SERVES 10-12

FROM THE WALT DISNEY WORLD RESORT

FOR CHEWY CHOCOLATE BROWNIE

1. Preheat oven to 325°F. Grease a 9 × 6-inch loaf pan, and set aside. (As an alternate to greasing, line the pan with two sheets of parchment paper so they hang over all sides of the pan; this can make it easier to remove the brownies later.)

2. Place butter and sugar in the bowl of a stand mixer fitted with a paddle attachment and mix on medium speed until light and fluffy.

3. Add melted chocolate, vanilla extract, and salt; mix well, scraping down sides of bowl. Add cocoa powder and flour; mix on low speed until combined, scraping down sides of bowl.

4. Add milk and egg; mix on low speed until combined, scraping down sides of bowl. Pour batter into prepared pan, and spread evenly.

5. Bake until a toothpick inserted in center has moist crumbs, about 25 to 28 minutes. Remove the loaf pan from oven, and let it cool completely.

CHEWY CHOCOLATE BROWNIE

½ cup unsalted butter, softened

¾ cup sugar

⅓ cup semisweet chocolate chips, melted

½ teaspoon vanilla extract

½ teaspoon salt

4 tablespoons unsweetened cocoa powder

½ cup cake flour

2 tablespoons milk

1 large egg

ABOVE: The dramatic vaulted ceiling of Yachtsman Steakhouse

FOR CHOCOLATE–PEANUT BUTTER GANACHE

1 Combine chocolate chips and peanut butter chips in a microwave-safe bowl; melt 20 seconds at a time until the chips are almost melted (some small lumps are okay).

2 Combine cream, corn syrup, milk, and butter in a small saucepan and heat just to scalding. Pour hot liquid over melted chocolate mixture. Stir well, and set aside.

CHOCOLATE–PEANUT BUTTER GANACHE

4 tablespoons semisweet chocolate chips

4 tablespoons peanut butter chips

4 tablespoons heavy cream

2 teaspoons corn syrup

2 teaspoons milk

1 tablespoon unsalted butter

RECIPE CONTINUES ON NEXT PAGE

CHOCOLATE-PEANUT BUTTER PRETZEL CAKE

(CONTINUED)

FOR PEANUT BUTTER MOUSSE

1. Place cream in a mixing bowl and whip on medium speed until soft peaks form, and set aside. In a separate bowl, beat cream cheese, peanut butter, milk, and vanilla on medium speed in a stand mixer using a paddle attachment until combined and smooth, scraping down sides of bowl.

2. Beat in the powdered sugar and mix on low speed until smooth, scraping down sides. Then use a rubber spatula to gently fold whipped cream into peanut butter mixture a third at a time until well mixed.

TO ASSEMBLE & SERVE

1. Remove Chewy Chocolate Brownie from loaf pan. Line loaf pan with plastic wrap overhanging sides for easy removal, then return brownie to pan. (If you lined the pan with parchment paper prior to baking as an alternate to greasing the pan, you may skip this step.)

2. Drizzle half of the Chocolate–Peanut Butter Ganache evenly over the brownie. Chill until set, about 15 minutes.

3. Pour Peanut Butter Mousse over the ganache and spread evenly until flat. Chill until set, at least 1 hour. Warm remaining ganache in microwave for 20 seconds at a time until mixture is fluid but not hot.

4. Pour remaining ganache over mousse and spread evenly. Chill completely, 4 hours or overnight.

5. Carefully lift chilled cake out of loaf pan with plastic wrap. Then transfer cake to a cutting board, and cut cake into slices, running knife under hot water and wiping with a dry cloth before each cut. Garnish each slice with crushed pretzels and serve with ice cream.

PEANUT BUTTER MOUSSE

⅓ cup heavy cream

4 ounces cream cheese, softened

⅔ cup creamy peanut butter

2 tablespoons milk

½ teaspoon vanilla extract

½ cup powdered sugar

TOPPINGS

½ cup coarsely crushed pretzels

Ice cream, preferably dulce de leche flavor

OPPOSITE, TOP: A couple share a table in the main dining room of California Grill, 2020.

PLANT-BASED PEANUT & BANANA TORTE

This elegant dessert has lots of steps, but you can make the miso caramel, peanut crumble, and blackberry-banana sauce while the peanut butter filling chills. And leftovers are delicious with a cup of coffee for breakfast.

SERVES 12

FROM THE WALT DISNEY WORLD RESORT

FOR SHORTBREAD CRUST

1. Preheat oven to 300°F. Melt coconut oil in microwave at 50 percent power for 30 to 45 seconds. Combine melted coconut oil, almond flour, gluten-free flour, maple syrup, and vanilla extract in a large bowl. Stir to combine.

2. Firmly press into an 8 × 8-inch baking dish. Bake for 13 to 15 minutes, until golden brown. Cool at room temperature for at least 30 minutes.

SHORTBREAD CRUST

⅔ cup coconut oil

2 cups almond flour

⅔ cup gluten-free flour

4 tablespoons maple syrup

1 tablespoon vanilla extract

RECIPE CONTINUES ON NEXT PAGE

PLANT-BASED PEANUT & BANANA TORTE

(CONTINUED)

FOR PEANUT BUTTER TORTE

1 Melt peanut butter and coconut oil in a large microwave-safe bowl, stirring every 30 seconds, until smooth.

2 Add maple syrup and vanilla extract. Stir until combined. Pour on top of cooled Shortbread Crust. Freeze for 4 hours to set.

FOR WHITE CHOCOLATE GLAZE

1 Melt chopped white chocolate in a large microwave-safe bowl, stirring every 30 seconds, until melted.

2 Combine coconut milk and coconut oil in a small saucepan. Heat over medium-low heat until hot. Pour into melted white chocolate and stir until smooth.

3 Pour on top of peanut butter–topped shortbread, making sure to evenly cover the top. Freeze until ready to serve.

FOR BLACKBERRY-BANANA SAUCE

1 Place blackberries in food processor or blender and purée until smooth. If desired, strain blackberries with a mesh strainer to remove seeds. Place in a small saucepan.

2 Purée bananas and add to blackberries. Stir in ⅓ cup sugar. Bring to a boil over medium-high heat, stirring occasionally.

3 Once purée is boiling, combine pectin and remaining 2 tablespoons sugar in a small bowl. Sprinkle over top of Blackberry-Banana Sauce and stir constantly for 30 seconds. Remove from heat and stir in salt. Cool at room temperature for 30 minutes before serving.

PEANUT BUTTER TORTE

3 cups creamy peanut butter

¾ cup coconut oil

¾ cup maple syrup

2 teaspoons vanilla extract

Shortbread Crust, cooled

WHITE CHOCOLATE GLAZE

16 ounces plant-based white chocolate, chopped

½ cup canned coconut milk

4 tablespoons coconut oil

BLACKBERRY-BANANA SAUCE

1 ½ cups fresh blackberries

2 ripe bananas

⅓ cup plus 2 tablespoons sugar, divided

¾ teaspoon pectin

⅛ teaspoon salt

OPPOSITE: California Grill is situated on the top floor of the original tower at Disney's Contemporary Resort.

FOR MISO CARAMEL

Combine sugar, corn syrup, and water in a small saucepan. Cook over medium-high heat until boiling. Then cook undisturbed for 10 to 12 minutes until dark amber in color. When ready, remove from heat and slowly stir in coconut milk. Stir until smooth. Add miso and set aside until ready to serve.

FOR PEANUT CRUMBLE

1 Preheat oven to 275°F. Mix chopped peanuts, almond flour, coconut oil, agave syrup, and baking soda in a medium bowl until crumbs form.

2 Spread on ungreased baking sheet and bake for 10 minutes, stirring after 5 minutes, until golden brown, and set aside until ready to serve.

FOR CARAMELIZED BANANAS

1 Slice each banana into approximately ½-inch-thick circles for a total of 24 slices. Then place sugar in a small bowl, and dip top of each banana slice in sugar.

2 Use a cooking torch to melt sugar on each slice until melted and browned. Banana slices can also be broiled on top rack of oven for 1 to 2 minutes. Cool completely before serving, but do not refrigerate.

TO ASSEMBLE & SERVE

1 Remove Peanut Butter Torte (as topped with White Chocolate Glaze) from freezer. Cut into 12 rectangles, each one approximately 4 inches long and 1¼ inches wide. Then smear 1 to 2 tablespoons Blackberry-Banana Sauce in the center of each plate. Top with a piece of the Peanut Butter Torte.

2 Spoon 1 tablespoon Miso Caramel around the plate, and sprinkle desired amount of Peanut Crumble around plate. Then place 2 Caramelized Bananas and 2 fresh blackberries on each plate, and sprinkle flaked sea salt on top of torte.

MISO CARAMEL

1 cup sugar

4 tablespoons corn syrup

⅓ cup water

½ cup canned coconut milk

1½ teaspoons miso paste

PEANUT CRUMBLE

½ cup chopped peanuts

1¼ cups almond flour

½ cup softened coconut oil

⅓ cup agave syrup

1½ teaspoons baking soda

CARAMELIZED BANANAS

3 bananas

4 tablespoons sugar

TOPPING

Flaked sea salt, to taste

24 fresh blackberries

PEANUT BUTTER & JELLY CUPCAKES

REMEMBERED FROM TRAIL'S END RESTAURANT

The classic childhood combo starts with peanut butter batter and peanut butter icing; then it's filled with a dollop of your favorite jelly—we're partial to grape jelly with this much peanut butter, but you could get fancy with fig or apricot jam.

MAKES 10-12 CUPCAKES

FROM THE WALT DISNEY WORLD RESORT

PEANUT BUTTER CUPCAKES

- 1 ½ cups all-purpose flour
- 1 ½ teaspoons baking powder
- ¼ teaspoon coarse salt
- ½ cup unsalted butter, at room temperature
- ½ cup creamy peanut butter
- ½ cup sugar
- ½ cup brown sugar
- 2 large eggs
- ¼ teaspoon vanilla extract
- ½ cup whole milk

FOR PEANUT BUTTER CUPCAKES

1. Preheat oven to 350°F. Line muffin pan with paper liners, and set aside. Whisk flour, baking powder, and salt together in a medium mixing bowl, and set aside.

2. Cream butter and peanut butter in the bowl of an electric mixer fitted with a paddle attachment until smooth. Add both sugars and cream until fluffy. Then add eggs and vanilla, and beat on medium speed until fully combined. Reduce to low speed.

3. Add half of the flour mixture and beat until just combined. Add milk and remaining flour mixture and beat on low speed for 1 minute, until combined. Then scoop batter into prepared pan, filling each cup about two-thirds full. Bake for 15 to 18 minutes, until top of cupcakes spring back when touched.

4. Cool in pan for 5 minutes, then move to cooling rack. Cool completely before filling and frosting.

ABOVE: A decor detail from Trail's End Restaurant

FOR JELLY FILLING

Cut a 1-inch-wide hole in the center of each cupcake, to about two-thirds down, being careful not to cut through to the bottom. Discard extra cake pieces. Then fill centers of cupcakes with 2 tablespoons of jam or jelly. Wipe away any excess filling with an offset spatula.

FOR PEANUT BUTTER BUTTERCREAM

1. Cream butter in the bowl of an electric mixer fitted with a whisk attachment until smooth. Then add sugar and mix on low speed until combined. Increase speed to medium and beat until fluffy.

2. Add vanilla and peanut butter and beat on medium speed until combined. Then place in a piping bag fitted with a star tip. Pipe buttercream on top of filled cupcakes.

3. Top each cupcake with one peanut butter sandwich cookie, and refrigerate until ready to serve.

JELLY FILLING

1½ cups favorite jelly or jam

PEANUT BUTTER BUTTERCREAM

¾ cup unsalted butter, softened

2 cups powdered sugar

¾ teaspoon vanilla extract

¾ cup creamy peanut butter

TOPPING

12 peanut butter sandwich cookies

PINEAPPLE CUPCAKES, INSPIRED BY DOLE WHIP®

REMEMBERED FROM CONTEMPO CAFE

Use your favorite yellow cupcake recipe or box mix for the pineapple mousse–filled cupcake, then top with yellow and white buttercream to create the look of the classic DOLE Whip® swirl. If you have leftover pineapple mousse, it tastes great with graham crackers or as a fruit dip. It's even delicious on its own!

MAKES 12 CUPCAKES

FROM THE WALT DISNEY WORLD RESORT

FOR PINEAPPLE MOUSSE

1. Whip heavy cream in the bowl of an electric mixer fitted with a whisk attachment until soft peaks form, and set aside.

2. Heat milk in a small saucepan over medium heat until very hot but not boiling. Whisk in gelatin, and stir until dissolved. Remove from heat and cool for 10 minutes.

3. Fold gelatin mixture into whipped cream until fully incorporated. Refrigerate for at least 4 hours, up to 2 days.

FOR PINEAPPLE BUTTERCREAM

1. Combine pineapple juice and gelatin in a small bowl, stirring until gelatin is dissolved, and set aside. Cream shortening and softened butter in the bowl of an electric mixer fitted with a paddle attachment until fluffy.

2. Add gelatin mixture and beat on medium speed until fully incorporated. Then add powdered sugar, one cup at a time, and beat on low speed until fully mixed. Increase to medium speed and beat, scraping side of bowl as needed, until frosting is stiff.

PINEAPPLE MOUSSE

½ cup heavy cream

⅓ cup whole or 2 percent milk

3 tablespoons pineapple-flavored powdered gelatin

PINEAPPLE BUTTERCREAM

1 tablespoon pineapple juice

3 tablespoons pineapple-flavored powdered gelatin

½ cup vegetable shortening

½ cup unsalted butter, softened

4 cups powdered sugar

2 tablespoons whole or 2 percent milk

3 Add milk, one teaspoon at a time, until buttercream is light and fluffy. Then divide the Pineapple Buttercream in half and store in two airtight containers until ready to use.

TO ASSEMBLE & SERVE

1 Using a 1-inch cookie cutter or apple corer, cut hole about two-thirds down the center of each premade cupcake. Fill with reserved Pineapple Mousse. Using an offset spatula, remove any excess mousse from the top of the cupcake.

2 Add a few drops of yellow and orange food coloring to one of the reserved Pineapple Buttercream containers until desired shade of yellow is achieved.

3 Place white buttercream in a piping bag fitted with a star tip. Spoon yellow buttercream in a second piping bag fitted with a star tip of the same size.

4 Pipe buttercream on cupcakes, alternating between yellow and white to create a soft-serve swirl look. Top with maraschino cherry.

PINEAPPLE CUPCAKES

12 vanilla cupcakes, made from a favorite recipe or box mix

Yellow food coloring

Orange food coloring

12 maraschino cherries

OPPOSITE: The entrance area of Contempo Cafe on the Grand Canyon Concourse level, 2013

BANANAS FOSTER ANGEL FOOD CAKE
WITH VANILLA ICE CREAM

Store-bought angel food cake goes upscale with a buttery banana sauce with a generous splash of rum and a fresh mint simple syrup that gives it an extra kick.

SERVES 4-6

FROM THE WALT DISNEY WORLD RESORT

FOR BANANAS FOSTER SAUCE

1. Cut bananas in 1-inch pieces. Top with 2 tablespoons water, and set aside. Then melt butter in a heavy skillet over medium heat. Add sugar and cinnamon and cook, stirring until sugar is almost dissolved, about 2 minutes.

2. With caution, add banana liqueur (mixture will bubble). Then carefully add the rum, which will make the alcohol flame on its own and then die down. Add bananas and water to the skillet, turning bananas with a spoon as the liquid caramelizes. Remove from heat and keep warm.

FOR MINT SIMPLE SYRUP

1. Purée the mint in a blender. Then bring water to a boil in a small heavy-bottomed pot. Add mint and steep for 10 minutes. Pour liquid through a fine-mesh strainer. Keep the water and discard the mint.

2. Bring the mint water back to a boil, and add the sugar, boiling about 3 minutes until clear and reduced to a thin syrup.

TO ASSEMBLE & SERVE

Place 2 slices of angel food cake in a generous serving bowl. Then add a scoop of vanilla ice cream to the side. Pour Bananas Foster Sauce over the angel food cake. Drizzle mint syrup over ice cream; garnish ice cream with a sprig of mint.

BANANAS FOSTER SAUCE

4 ripe bananas, peeled and sliced in half lengthwise

2 tablespoons water

4 tablespoons unsalted butter

1 cup brown sugar

½ tablespoon cinnamon

2 tablespoons banana liqueur

4 tablespoons dark rum

MINT SIMPLE SYRUP

3 tablespoons fresh mint, chopped

¾ cup water

¾ cup sugar

TO ASSEMBLE & SERVE

Angel food cake

Vanilla ice cream

6 fresh mint sprigs, for garnish

MOIST APPLE CAKE

REMEMBERED FROM DISNEY CRUISE LINE DINING

Use juicy, crisp Granny Smith apples to make this easy cake. There's no need to ice; just dust with powdered sugar or top yours with a dollop of whipped cream.

SERVES 8-12

FROM BEYOND THE DISNEY PARKS

1. Preheat oven to 350°F. Spray bottom and sides of a 9-inch springform pan with nonstick spray. Note that a springform pan is a two-piece pan that has sides that can be removed, which makes it easier to take the cake out of the pan later.

2. Sift flour, baking soda, nutmeg, cinnamon, and salt into a large bowl, and set aside. Then combine brown sugar and oil in the bowl of an electric mixer fitted with a whisk attachment. Beat on medium speed to combine.

3. Add eggs, and beat at medium speed for 5 minutes. With a spoon or rubber spatula, stir in diced apples. Then fold flour mixture into batter, and pour the mixture into prepared pan.

4. Bake for 45 to 50 minutes, or until the cake springs back when touched. Top with powdered sugar, if desired.

1¾ cups all-purpose flour

1 teaspoon baking soda

⅛ teaspoon ground nutmeg

⅛ teaspoon ground cinnamon

Pinch salt

1⅓ cups brown sugar

1 cup extra-virgin olive oil

2 large eggs

3 Granny Smith apples, peeled, cored, and diced

Powdered sugar, optional

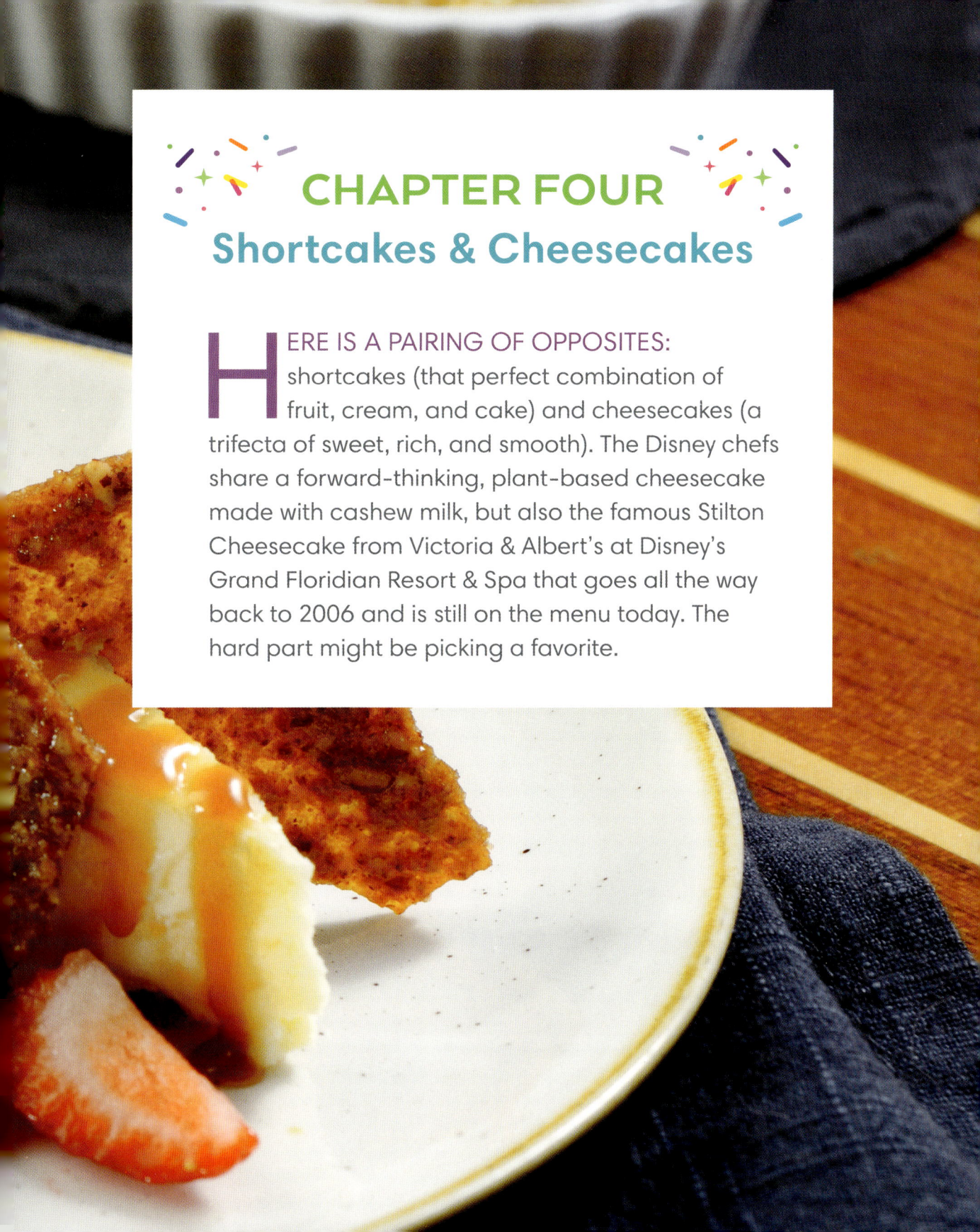

CHAPTER FOUR
Shortcakes & Cheesecakes

HERE IS A PAIRING OF OPPOSITES: shortcakes (that perfect combination of fruit, cream, and cake) and cheesecakes (a trifecta of sweet, rich, and smooth). The Disney chefs share a forward-thinking, plant-based cheesecake made with cashew milk, but also the famous Stilton Cheesecake from Victoria & Albert's at Disney's Grand Floridian Resort & Spa that goes all the way back to 2006 and is still on the menu today. The hard part might be picking a favorite.

CRÈME FRAÎCHE CHEESECAKE

REMEMBERED FROM CARNATION CAFE

For this longtime favorite on Main Street, U.S.A., start with an easy graham cracker crust and a classic cheesecake filling. But the crème fraîche topping takes it to another level. The finished cheesecake needs to chill at least four hours, so plan accordingly.

MAKES 1 (9-INCH) CHEESECAKE

FROM THE DISNEYLAND RESORT

GRAHAM CRACKER CRUST

1½ cups graham cracker crumbs (from about 9–12 graham crackers)

6 tablespoons unsalted butter, melted

STRAWBERRY COMPOTE

1 pint strawberries, hulled and rinsed

⅓ cup sugar

Juice of ½ lime (about 1 tablespoon juice)

CRÈME FRAÎCHE TOPPING

½ cup plus 1 tablespoon crème fraîche

1 tablespoon sugar

FOR GRAHAM CRACKER CRUST

1. Butter the inside of a 9-inch springform pan. Note that a springform pan is a two-piece pan that has sides that can be removed, which makes it easier to take the cake out of the pan later.

2. Mix together graham cracker crumbs and melted butter in a medium bowl. Press graham cracker mixture into bottom and about ¼ inch up the sides of the pan, and set aside.

FOR STRAWBERRY COMPOTE

1. Bring strawberries and sugar to a boil in a medium saucepan over medium heat. Turn heat to low and simmer, stirring frequently to break up strawberries. (Alternatively, you also can mash the strawberries with a potato masher or fork.)

2. Simmer 3 to 5 minutes, or until sauce is slightly thickened. Then remove from heat and carefully transfer to a bowl. Stir in lime juice, and refrigerate to chill.

FOR CRÈME FRAÎCHE TOPPING

Use handheld electric mixer to beat crème fraîche in a medium bowl until smooth. Beat in sugar, and then cover and refrigerate.

FOR NEW YORK CHEESECAKE

1 Add cream cheese to bowl of a stand mixer fitted with a paddle attachment. Mix on low speed until smooth and creamy, about 3 minutes.

2 Add sour cream and mix until creamy, scraping down bowl with a rubber spatula. Then add powdered sugar and mix on very low speed until well combined with no lumps, scraping down the bowl with a rubber spatula.

3 Add orange juice and lemon juice and mix on low speed until combined. Then add vanilla, then eggs, one at a time, mixing on low speed until fully mixed, scraping down bowl with a rubber spatula. Continue mixing until smooth and creamy.

NEW YORK CHEESECAKE

2 (8-ounce) blocks cream cheese, room temperature

1 cup sour cream

1 ½ cups powdered sugar, sifted

1 ½ teaspoons fresh orange juice

1 ½ teaspoons fresh lemon juice

1 ½ teaspoons vanilla extract

5 large eggs

RECIPE CONTINUES ON NEXT PAGE

CRÈME FRAÎCHE CHEESECAKE

(CONTINUED)

4   Preheat oven to 325°F. Take a large piece of foil and place the springform pan in the middle; gently fold up sides of foil around pan. (Do this gently so that you don't create any holes in the foil. This will prevent water from the water bath getting into your cheesecake.)

5   Pour cheesecake batter into prepared pan, making sure top is smooth. Then place foil-wrapped pan in a large high-sided roasting pan. Prepare 2 quarts of boiling water. Place the roasting pan with cheesecake in oven on the lower rack. Carefully pour the hot water into the roasting pan (it should reach halfway up the cheesecake). This will create a water bath for the cheesecake.

6   Bake until cheesecake is nearly set but still slightly jiggly in the center, about 1–1¼ hours. When ready, take roasting pan with cheesecake out of oven and pour crème fraîche topping over hot cheesecake.

7   Place cheesecake (still in water bath) back into oven and turn off heat, and leave cheesecake in oven for 10 minutes. Then remove from oven and cool to room temperature.

8   Cover cheesecake tightly and refrigerate until fully chilled, at least 4 hours or overnight. Unmold from the springform pan, and then slice. Serve each slice topped with strawberry compote.

FOR ALTERNATE BRÛLÉE TOPPING

Omit crème fraîche topping. Once cheesecake is fully chilled, evenly sprinkle with 4 tablespoons sugar, then gently shake pan from side to side to ensure even coverage. Wipe off any stray granules of sugar. Use a chef's torch to caramelize the sugar, being careful to keep the flame moving so you don't over-caramelize any one spot.

ABOVE: Donald Duck poses with guests on Main Street, U.S.A. in front of Sleeping Beauty Castle.

STRAWBERRY-RHUBARB SHORTCAKE

REMEMBERED FROM CARNATION CAFE

This old-fashioned shortcake that combines sweet strawberries and tart rhubarb was created for the Diamond Celebration marking the sixtieth anniversary of the Disneyland park. The recipe takes time to re-create, but it's an elegant ending.

SERVES 12

FROM THE DISNEYLAND RESORT

RHUBARB

3 stalks fresh rhubarb

1 cup water

1 cup sugar

1 (6-ounce) package fresh raspberries

SHORTCAKE

1 box favorite white cake mix

FROZEN WHITE CHOCOLATE BAVARIAN MOUSSE

1 (¼-ounce) package gelatin

1½ tablespoons cold water

2½ cups heavy cream, divided

4 tablespoons sugar

4 large pasteurized egg yolks

½ cup white chocolate chips

FOR RHUBARB

1 Clean and peel the rhubarb stalks, making sure to save the rhubarb peels. Cut peeled rhubarb stalks into 2-inch pieces, and set aside.

2 Combine the water and sugar in a medium saucepan. Add rhubarb peels and raspberries. Cook over medium-high heat until mixture boils.

3 Strain syrup into a second medium saucepan. Cook over medium-high heat until syrup boils. Turn off heat.

4 Add sliced rhubarb to syrup. Allow rhubarb to marinate in syrup for 2 hours, until tender. Remove from syrup and set aside.

FOR SHORTCAKE

Prepare cake, according to package directions, in a 9 × 13-inch pan. Let cake cool in pan for at least 2 hours.

FOR FROZEN WHITE CHOCOLATE BAVARIAN MOUSSE

1 Combine gelatin and water in a small bowl, and set aside. Heat 1 cup of heavy cream and all the sugar in a medium saucepan over medium heat, for 5 to 7 minutes, until simmering.

RECIPE CONTINUES ON NEXT PAGE

STRAWBERRY-RHUBARB SHORTCAKE

(CONTINUED)

2 Whisk egg yolks in a medium bowl. Slowly pour in half of the hot cream mixture, stirring constantly.

3 Pour the egg yolk and cream mixture into the saucepan of warm cream. Cook over medium heat for 4 to 6 minutes, until it begins to boil.

4 Remove from heat and stir in gelatin and white chocolate chips until mixture is smooth. Let mixture cool for 30 to 45 minutes, until it is just above room temperature.

5 Place remaining 1½ cups of heavy cream in the bowl of an electric mixer. Whip on high speed 5 to 7 minutes, until soft peaks form.

6 Fold into cooled white chocolate–cream mixture. Pour mousse into silicone muffin pan with 12 wells. Refrigerate any mousse that does not fit in the molds. Place muffin pan in the freezer for 2 hours.

FOR STRAWBERRY SAUCE

1 Place thawed strawberries and any reserved juice into a food processor or blender. Purée until smooth. Strain puréed berries through a fine-mesh strainer into a medium saucepan.

2 Stir in ⅓ cup sugar and the lemon juice. Cook over medium-high heat for 5 to 7 minutes, until mixture almost boils. Remove syrup from heat and cool for 45 minutes.

3 In a large microwave-safe bowl, combine the Clear Jel® mixture with the remaining 1 tablespoon sugar. Cook in microwave for 1 to 2 minutes, until sugar is dissolved. Slowly whisk strawberry syrup and orange zest into the Clear Jel® cornstarch mixture.

STRAWBERRY SAUCE

1 (20-ounce) package frozen unsweetened strawberries, thawed, with juices reserved

⅓ cup plus 1 tablespoon sugar, divided

Juice of 1 lemon

1 tablespoon orange zest

1 cup Clear Jel® modified cornstarch mixture

TO ASSEMBLE & SERVE

1 Using a round 3-inch cookie cutter, cut cooled Shortcake into 12 circles. Place each circle of cake in the center of a bowl. Lay 4 strawberry halves and a few slices of the reserved rhubarb stalks around each circle of cake.

2 Pour ⅓ cup of the Strawberry Sauce around each cake, making sure to spoon sauce over the sliced strawberries and rhubarb.

3 Gently place the Frozen White Chocolate Bavarian Mousse over the top of each cake. Top with shimmer dust. Allow mousse to sit at room temperature for 10 to 15 minutes, until soft, before serving.

GARNISH

16 fresh strawberries, cut in half

Shimmer dust

VANILLA BEAN-YOGURT CHEESECAKE

This orange-scented cheesecake was a favorite sweet ending from Steakhouse 55, a restaurant that paid homage to the glory days of Hollywood. (The "55" was for 1955, the year Disneyland opened.)

MAKES 1 (8-INCH) CHEESECAKE

FROM THE DISNEYLAND RESORT

FOR CRUST

1 Tightly wrap an 8-inch springform pan with 2 layers of aluminum foil, and set aside. Note that a springform pan is a two-piece pan that has sides that can be removed, which makes it easier to take the cake out of the pan later.

2 Combine graham cracker crumbs and butter in a medium bowl. Press mixture into bottom of prepared pan with hands. Refrigerate until ready to use.

FOR CHEESECAKE

1 Preheat oven to 300°F. Combine sugar, flour, and orange zest in a small bowl; mix with a fork until well combined, and set aside.

2 Beat cream cheese in a large bowl with an electric mixer until smooth and creamy. Add vanilla bean seeds, beating to combine. Add sugar mixture, beating to combine. Scrape down bowl.

3 Add eggs and egg yolks one at a time, beating well after each addition. Scrape down bowl. Add yogurt, beating well to combine.

4 Pour filling over crust in springform pan. Cover loosely with a piece of aluminum foil. Place pan into a larger roasting pan. Pour boiling water into pan halfway up sides of cheesecake. Carefully transfer larger pan to oven.

GRAHAM CRACKER CRUST

1½ cups crushed graham cracker

5 tablespoons unsalted butter, melted

CHEESECAKE

1½ cups sugar

3 tablespoons flour

Zest of ½ orange

4 cups cream cheese at room temperature

½ vanilla bean, split lengthwise and scraped, seeds reserved

5 large eggs

2 large egg yolks

½ cup plain whole milk yogurt

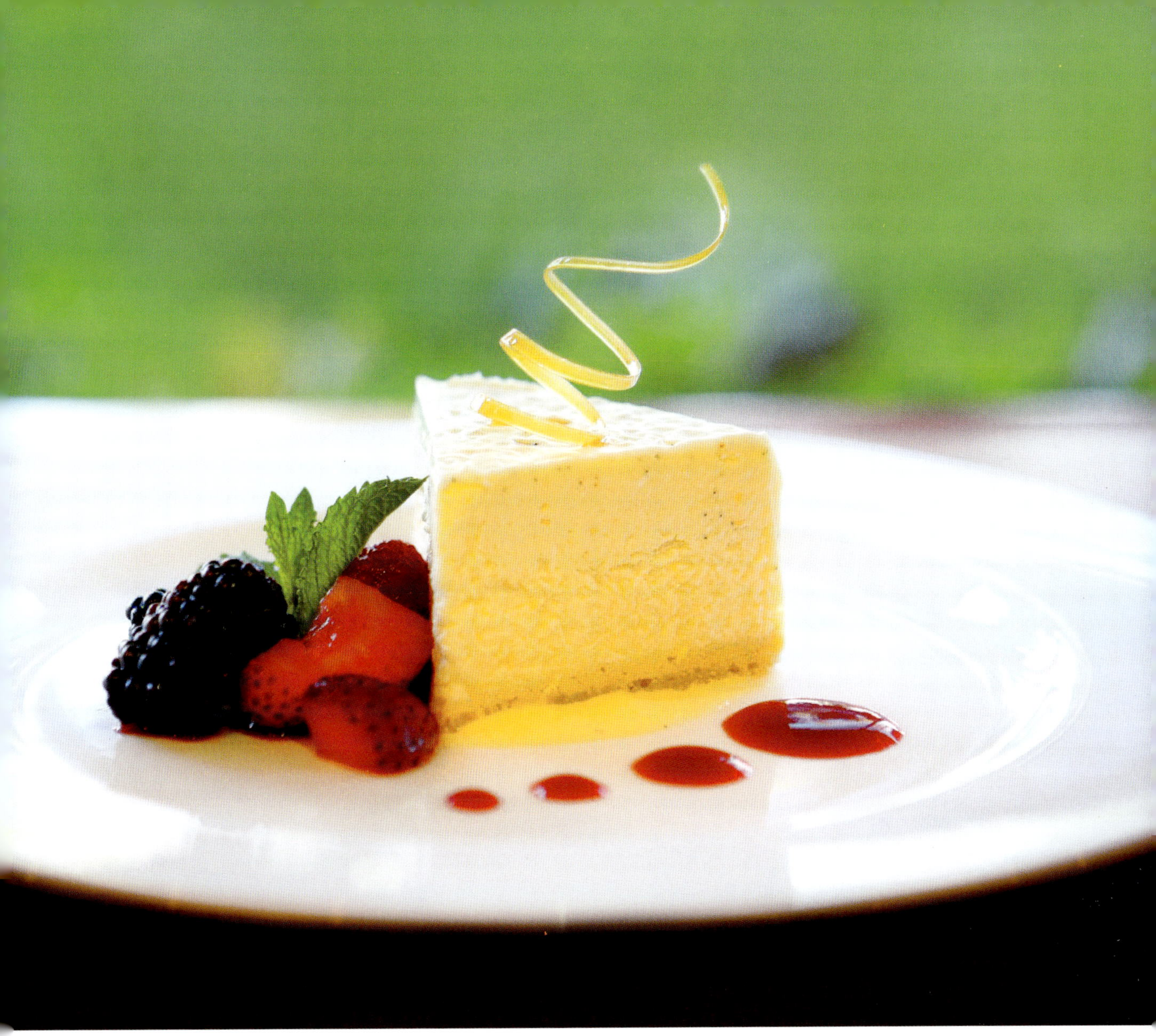

5 Bake for 1 hour, or until sides of cheesecake are firm but center still wobbles slightly when pan moves, and set aside for 5 minutes before serving. (Note our photographed cheesecake slice was topped with a spun sugar spiral and garnished with strawberry syrup, blackberries, raspberries, strawberries, and mint leaves for added flair.)

FORMERLY AT THE DISNEYLAND HOTEL · DISNEYLAND RESORT

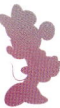

BLUEBERRY-LIME CHEESECAKE ROLL

FESTIVAL DEBUT: 2014 · DESSERTS & CHAMPAGNE GLOBAL MARKETPLACE

Blueberry purée flavors the chiffon cakes, with a tart lime cheesecake filling. At the EPCOT festival the cake was paired with crisp apple ice wine for a fun sweet ending.

MAKES 2 (9-INCH) CHEESECAKE ROLLS

FROM THE WALT DISNEY WORLD RESORT

FOR BLUEBERRY CHIFFON CAKE

1. Preheat oven to 350°F. Line a 12 × 18 × 1-inch half-sheet pan with parchment paper. Sift flour, baking powder, ⅓ cup sugar, and salt in a large mixing bowl. Then add 2 eggs, oil, milk, and blueberry purée, mixing well, and set aside.

2. In separate medium mixing bowl, whip 4 egg whites for 5 minutes until almost double in size. Slowly add ½ cup sugar and cream of tartar. Whip meringue for 7 to 10 minutes on high speed, or until stiff peaks form.

3. Slowly fold a third of meringue mixture into cake batter, mixing well, then fold in remaining meringue. Spread batter evenly onto sheet pan. Place a sheet of parchment paper over the top of batter and gently smooth so there are no air bubbles. (The parchment paper will help maintain the purple color.)

4. Bake for 15 to 17 minutes, or until top of cake springs back when touched. Cool completely, then carefully remove top parchment paper. Turn onto clean sheet of parchment paper, carefully removing bottom parchment paper.

BLUEBERRY CHIFFON CAKE

½ cup cake flour

¼ teaspoon baking powder

½ cup plus ⅓ cup sugar, divided

Pinch salt

2 large eggs

4 tablespoons vegetable oil

½ cup milk

½ cup blueberry purée

4 large egg whites

⅛ teaspoon cream of tartar

FOR LIME CHEESECAKE FILLING

1 Preheat oven to 300°F. Spray an 8½-inch round cake pan with cooking spray. Mix cream cheese and sugar in the large bowl of an electric mixer with a paddle attachment until smooth. Add eggs, one at a time, mixing on low until blended.

2 Prepare a water bath for baking by filling a pan that is large enough to hold the cake pan with enough boiling water to reach halfway up the sides of the cake pan.

3 Pour batter into cake pan and bake in water bath for about 45 minutes, or until center is firm but jiggles (it will firm more as it cools). Cool completely in refrigerator.

4 Once cooled, spoon cheesecake into large mixing bowl and mix with paddle attachment for 3 minutes or until smooth. Mix in lime zest and lime juice.

FOR BLUEBERRY GLAZE

Spoon purée into a small saucepan, and stir in sugar. Heat over medium-high heat until boiling. Remove from heat and add gelatin, stirring until dissolved. Allow to cool and thicken.

TO ASSEMBLE & SERVE

Spread Lime Cheesecake Filling evenly on the Blueberry Chiffon Cake. Cut cake in half to make two 9-inch-long rolls. Carefully roll each cake, seam side down, and trim ends. Brush desired amount of Blueberry Glaze on top and side of each roll. Refrigerate until ready to serve.

LIME CHEESECAKE FILLING

2 (8-ounce) packages cream cheese, softened

½ cup sugar

2 large eggs

2 limes, zested and juiced

BLUEBERRY GLAZE

½ cup blueberry purée

1 ½ teaspoons sugar, or to taste

3 (¼-ounce) packages powdered gelatin

ABOVE: Pluto nosing around EPCOT

CHEESECAKE
WITH PASSION FRUIT CURD

FESTIVAL DEBUT: 2017 · HAWAI'I GLOBAL MARKETPLACE

The tart sweetness of passion fruit curd, lavishly spread over the cooled cheesecake, takes this straightforward sweet to new heights.

MAKES 1 (9-INCH) CHEESECAKE

FROM THE WALT DISNEY WORLD RESORT

SOUR CREAM-VANILLA CHEESECAKE

1 ½ cups graham cracker crumbs

⅓ cup unsalted butter, melted

¼ teaspoon cinnamon

4 (8-ounce) packages cream cheese, at room temperature

1 ¼ cups sugar

½ cup sour cream

2 teaspoons vanilla extract

5 large eggs

FOR SOUR CREAM-VANILLA CHEESECAKE

1 Preheat oven to 325°F. Take a large piece of foil and place a 9-inch springform pan in the middle; gently fold up sides of foil around pan. (Do this carefully so that you don't create any holes in the foil. This will prevent water from the eventual water bath getting into your cheesecake.)

2 Mix graham cracker crumbs, melted butter, and cinnamon in a small bowl until graham cracker crumbs are moist. Pat into the foil-wrapped pan. Place in freezer for 20 minutes to set crust.

3 Cream the cream cheese and sugar with an electric mixer until fluffy. Add sour cream and vanilla and mix until just blended. Add in eggs, one at a time, until just mixed.

4 Remove crust from freezer and pour cheesecake batter into pan. Then place pan in a large high-sided roasting pan. Prepare 2 quarts of boiling water. Place the roasting pan with cheesecake in oven on the lower rack. Carefully pour the hot water into the roasting pan (it should reach halfway up the cheesecake). This will create a water bath for the cheesecake. Bake for 60 minutes, until center is set and top begins to brown.

5 Cool in pan at room temperature for 2 hours. Refrigerate for 1 hour before removing from springform pan.

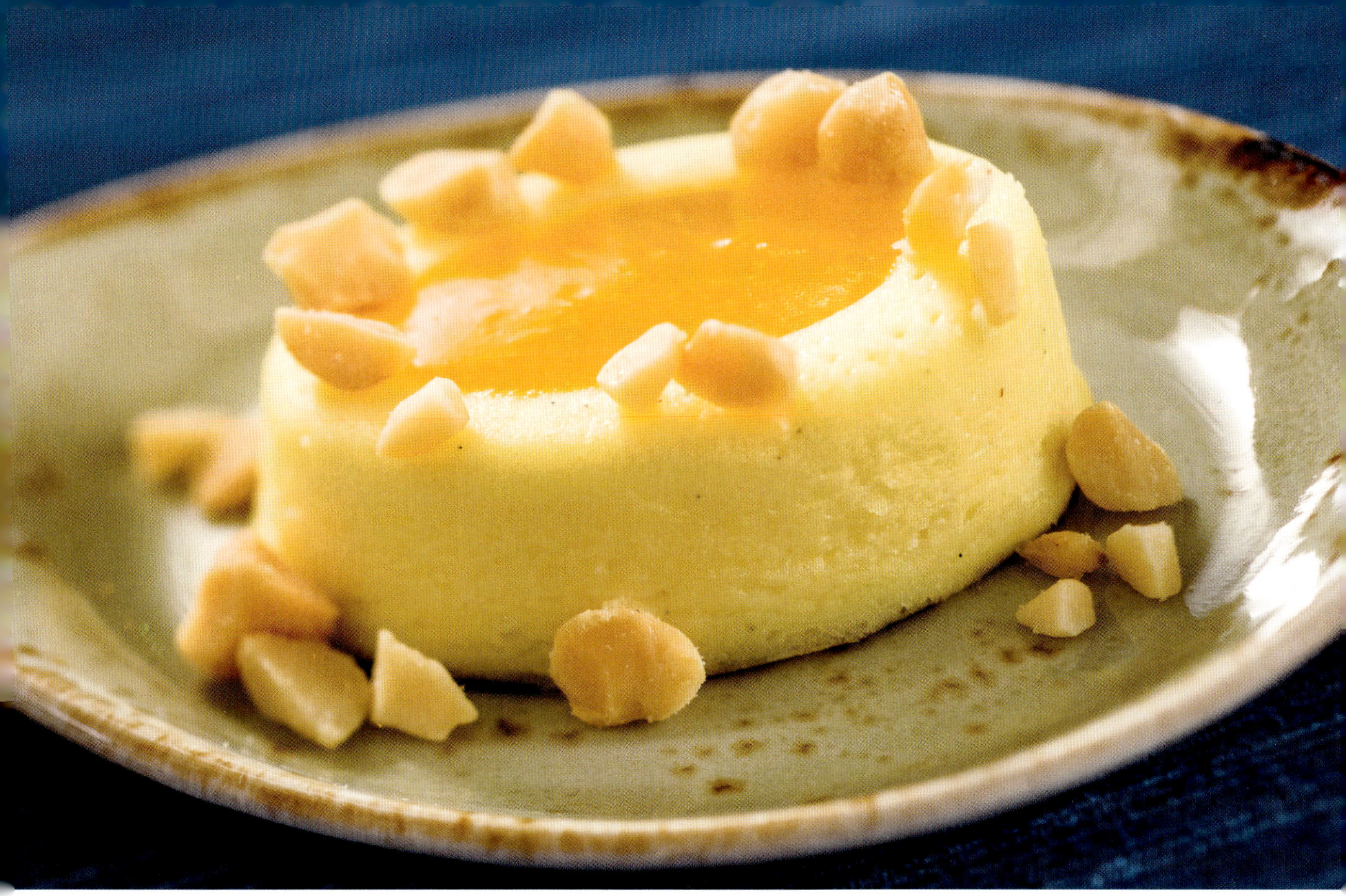

FOR PASSION FRUIT CURD

1. Whisk together eggs, egg yolks, sugar, and passion fruit purée in a double boiler or heatproof bowl. Set pan or bowl over boiling water.

2. Cook for 10 minutes, whisking constantly, until curd thickens and top bubbles disappear. Remove from heat.

3. Stir in butter, one cube at a time. Strain into a bowl. Cover top of passion fruit curd with plastic wrap and refrigerate until ready to serve.

TO ASSEMBLE & SERVE

Spread Passion Fruit Curd over Sour Cream–Vanilla Cheesecake and garnish with dry roasted macadamia nuts before slicing and serving.

PASSION FRUIT CURD

3 large pasteurized eggs

3 large pasteurized egg yolks

½ cup sugar

¾ cup passion fruit purée

4 tablespoons unsalted butter, cubed

GARNISH

Dry roasted macadamia nuts

MAPLE-BOURBON CHEESECAKE

FESTIVAL DEBUT: 2018 · CHEESE STUDIO GLOBAL MARKETPLACE

Silky goat cheese with maple-bourbon flavoring is the star of this cool, creamy, not-too-sweet treat. The candied pecans add a perfect crunch, and leftovers make a great salad topping or snack.

MAKES 1 (9-INCH) CHEESECAKE

FROM THE WALT DISNEY WORLD RESORT

GRAHAM CRACKER CRUST

1½ cups graham cracker crumbs

⅓ cup unsalted butter, melted

¼ teaspoon cinnamon

MAPLE-BOURBON CHEESECAKE

2 (8-ounce) packages cream cheese, room temperature

10 ounces maple-bourbon goat cheese, room temperature

1¼ cups sugar

½ cup sour cream

1 tablespoon maple extract

5 large eggs

Graham Cracker Crust, cooled

FOR GRAHAM CRACKER CRUST

1. Preheat oven to 325°F. Fill large roasting pan with ½-inch water and place in the oven while preparing crust and filling.

2. Spray 9-inch springform pan with cooking spray. Note that a springform pan is a two-piece pan that has sides that can be removed, which makes it easier to take the cake out of the pan later.

3. Cut a circle of parchment paper the same size as the bottom of springform pan and place on bottom of pan. Then place prepared springform pan on a double layer of aluminum foil large enough to cover underside and extend to top of rim. Press foil to sides of springform pan.

4. Mix graham cracker crumbs, butter, and cinnamon in medium bowl. Then press crust mixture firmly to bottom of springform pan. Place springform pan in freezer to set crust while making filling.

FOR MAPLE-BOURBON CHEESECAKE

1. Cream together cream cheese, maple-bourbon goat cheese, and sugar in a large mixing bowl until just blended.

2 Add sour cream and maple extract; continue to mix until blended. Then add eggs, one at a time, and blend until batter is smooth. Do not over blend. Remove Graham Cracker Crust from freezer and pour filling over crust.

3 Carefully place aluminum foil–lined pan in roasting pan with water. Bake for 60 to 70 minutes until center of cheesecake jiggles slightly.

4 Carefully remove roasting pan from oven and allow cheesecake to cool completely in pan for 2 hours at room temperature. Refrigerate for at least 1 hour or as long as overnight.

RECIPE CONTINUES ON NEXT PAGE

MAPLE-BOURBON CHEESECAKE

(CONTINUED)

FOR CANDIED PECANS

Preheat oven to 330°F. Place pecans, sugar, and egg white in a medium bowl. Mix until pecans are fully coated. Place pecans on parchment paper–lined sheet pan. Bake for 8 to 10 minutes, until pecans are lightly browned. After baking, stir pecans and allow to cool. Once cheesecake is assembled, there will be leftover Candied Pecans, which can be stored in an airtight container for up to 2 months and used in salads or for snacking.

FOR MAPLE-BOURBON CREAM TOPPING

Whip maple-bourbon goat cheese with an electric mixer on medium speed until smooth. Gradually add cream while still on medium speed. Add maple extract and bourbon until mixture forms light peaks.

TO ASSEMBLE & SERVE

1   Remove Maple-Bourbon Cheesecake from the refrigerator. Carefully run a small knife around the edge of the pan to loosen the sides.

2   Unbuckle the springform pan while the cheesecake is still very cold. Run a long, thin spatula between the parchment paper and the bottom of the springform pan. Transfer to a serving dish and remove parchment paper.

3   Top cheesecake with the Maple-Bourbon Cream Topping, and sprinkle top with desired number of Candied Pecans.

4   Cutting the cheesecake can be tricky. Try dipping a long, thin knife in hot water, wipe dry, then slice. Repeat this method with each slice. Slicing and transferring are easiest when the cheesecake is very cold. Allow slices to stand at room temperature for 5 to 10 minutes before serving.

CANDIED PECANS

2 cups chopped pecans

2 tablespoons sugar

1 large egg white

MAPLE-BOURBON CREAM TOPPING

5 ounces maple-bourbon goat cheese, room temperature

4 tablespoons heavy cream

1 teaspoon maple extract

1 tablespoon bourbon

OPPOSITE: A view of the main tower of Disney's Contemporary Resort from the pool area

GLUTEN-FRIENDLY LEMON MERINGUE CHEESECAKE (NO SUGAR ADDED)

For its filling, this fancy gluten-free cheesecake uses Italian mascarpone—made similarly to American cream cheese but with a base of whole cream instead of milk, so it's richer and sweeter with a velvety texture. The lemon-orange shortbread crust adds extra citrus zing.

SERVES 6

FROM THE WALT DISNEY WORLD RESORT

LEMON MASCARPONE CHEESECAKE

7 tablespoons sugar substitute, divided

4 tablespoons fresh lemon juice

4 large pasteurized egg yolks (reserve whites)

4 tablespoons unsalted butter

2½ teaspoons powdered gelatin

2 tablespoons cold water

½ cup mascarpone cheese

½ cup sour cream

¾ cup heavy cream

FOR LEMON MASCARPONE CHEESECAKE

1 Combine 4 tablespoons sugar substitute, lemon juice, and egg yolks in a heatproof bowl, and place over a small saucepan filled with a few inches of water, being sure bottom of bowl doesn't touch water.

2 Cook over medium-high heat, stirring constantly, until the mixture is thick, about 5 to 7 minutes. Remove from heat and whisk in butter. Cover lemon curd and refrigerate until cool.

3 Spray a 9 × 5-inch loaf pan with nonstick spray, then line with plastic wrap, letting edges hang over sides of pan, smoothing out as many wrinkles as possible.

4 Combine gelatin and water in a small bowl, stir, and set aside. Then combine mascarpone, sour cream, and 3 tablespoons sugar substitute in the bowl of an electric mixer fitted with a paddle attachment; mix until smooth. Scrape down sides of bowl.

RECIPE CONTINUES ON NEXT PAGE

GLUTEN-FRIENDLY LEMON MERINGUE CHEESECAKE
(NO SUGAR ADDED)

5 Add cooled lemon curd and mix well. Whip heavy cream in a separate bowl using an electric mixer until it holds soft peaks.

6 Microwave gelatin-water mixture 15 to 30 seconds on high until dissolved. Stir in a tablespoon of whipped cream, then stir the mixture into mascarpone mixture. Fold remaining whipped cream into mascarpone mixture.

7 Pour into prepared pan and cover tightly with plastic wrap, pressing wrap directly onto top. Freeze at least 6 hours.

FOR CITRUS SHORTBREAD CRUST

1 Combine butter and sugar substitute in an electric mixer fitted with a paddle attachment; beat until smooth. Add egg yolk, mixing until combined. Scrape down sides of bowl and mix 30 seconds longer.

2 Add baking powder, salt, flour, and lemon and orange zest, mixing just until dough comes together. Pat dough into a ½-inch-thick rectangle and refrigerate 1 hour.

3 Preheat oven to 350°F. Remove citrus shortbread dough from freezer and cut into 6 (1½ × 5-inch) rectangles.

4 Place on a baking sheet lined with parchment paper and bake for 10 minutes, until light golden brown, and set aside to cool.

CITRUS SHORTBREAD CRUST

½ cup unsalted butter, softened

2 tablespoons sugar substitute

1 large pasteurized egg yolk (reserve white)

2 teaspoons baking powder

¼ teaspoon salt

1¼ cups gluten-free flour

Zest of half a lemon

Zest of half an orange

FOR MERINGUE CLOUDS

1. Preheat oven to 200°F. Line a baking sheet with parchment paper, and set aside. Then combine egg whites, sugar substitute, and cream of tartar in an electric mixer fitted with a whisk attachment, and beat until stiff but not dry.

2. Using a teaspoon, drop mounds of meringue onto prepared baking sheet. Bake until set and firm, about 1 hour. When ready, run the flame of a small kitchen torch over meringues slowly to just brown edges.

TO ASSEMBLE & SERVE

1. Remove cheesecake from freezer. Briefly dip loaf pan into a larger pan of hot water, then pull the ends of the plastic wrap up to remove cheesecake from pan. Remove plastic wrap and discard.

2. Cut cheesecake into 6 (1½ × 5-inch) rectangles using a sharp knife dipped in hot water. Place 1 slice of cheesecake onto each citrus shortbread cookie. Arrange cheesecakes on a serving platter, and place 3 Meringue Clouds on top of each cheesecake.

MERINGUE CLOUDS

5 large pasteurized egg whites (use reserved whites)

4 tablespoons sugar substitute

1 teaspoon cream of tartar

STILTON CHEESECAKE

REMEMBERED FROM VICTORIA & ALBERT'S

This elegant small bite goes way back to 2006, when we featured it in our first Delicious Disney cookbook. More savory than sweet, with a shortbread crust, it's perfect with a cheese course and fresh fruit.

MAKES 1 (9½-INCH) CHEESECAKE, OR 48 MINI CHEESECAKES

FROM THE WALT DISNEY WORLD RESORT

FOR SHORTBREAD CRUST

Preheat oven to 350°F. Blend together flour and sugar. Then add butter and blend until mixture resembles coarse meal (it will not form a dough). When ready, press into the bottom of 48 buttered mini-muffin cups (1¾ × 1 inch) or transfer into a buttered 9½-inch springform pan. Spread evenly and press into bottom. (Note that a springform pan is a two-piece pan with sides that can be removed, which makes it easier to take the cake out of the pan later.) Bake for 7 to 9 minutes on the middle rack of the oven until pale golden. Cool in pan on a wire rack.

FOR FILLING

1 Beat together crumbled Stilton, cream cheese, and sugar in a large bowl with mixer on low speed. Then add in eggs (one at a time), beating well after each addition.

2 Add flour, and beat in sour cream and vanilla until just blended. Then pour filling over cooled crust in mini-muffin cups or a springform pan.

3 If using a springform pan, line with aluminum foil and carefully place in roasting pan with water. Bake in middle of oven for 30 minutes, until puffed and pale golden around the edge. When ready, transfer to rack and run a knife around edge of pan to loosen. Cool completely, about 2 hours. Chill, covered, at least 4 hours.

SHORTBREAD CRUST

1¼ cups all-purpose flour

4 tablespoons sugar

½ cup unsalted butter, softened and cubed

FILLING

¾ cup Stilton cheese, rind discarded and cheese crumbled

1¼ cups (or 10 ounces) cream cheese, softened

⅓ cup plus 1 tablespoon sugar

2 large eggs

2 tablespoons all-purpose flour

⅓ cup plus 1 tablespoon sour cream

1 teaspoon vanilla

ABOVE: Lush decor details at Victoria & Albert's

PLANT-BASED COFFEE & CASHEW CHEESECAKE

REMEMBERED FROM CALIFORNIA GRILL

This cheesecake starts with a Marcona almond crust, and cashews with a generous splash of coffee create the creamy filling. The cheesecake takes eight to twelve hours to freeze, so plan ahead. The warm chocolate glaze adds another dimension.

MAKES 1 (9-INCH) CHEESECAKE

FROM THE WALT DISNEY WORLD RESORT

COFFEE-SOAKED CASHEWS

2¼ cups raw cashews

3 cups coffee, at room temperature

COFFEE-CASHEW CHEESECAKE

1½ cups Marcona almonds, finely ground

Coffee-Soaked Cashews

4 tablespoons agave nectar

2 tablespoons vanilla extract

½ cup coffee, at room temperature

6 tablespoons organic coconut oil

WARM CHOCOLATE GLAZE

4 tablespoons vegetable shortening

4 tablespoons unsweetened cocoa powder

⅔ cup agave nectar

FOR COFFEE-SOAKED CASHEWS

Place cashews in a medium bowl. Pour cooled coffee over cashews. Cover, and let it rest for 8 to 12 hours. Drain excess coffee from cashews, and set aside.

FOR COFFEE-CASHEW CHEESECAKE

1   Spray a 9-inch springform pan with nonstick cooking spray. Note that a springform pan is a two-piece pan that has sides that can be removed, which makes it easier to take the cake out of the pan later.

2   Pat ground Marcona almonds in bottom of pan, and set aside. Then lace Coffee-Soaked Cashews, agave nectar, vanilla extract, coffee, and coconut oil in a food processor and blend until smooth. Spread cashew mix on top of almonds. Freeze 8 to 12 hours.

FOR WARM CHOCOLATE GLAZE

Melt shortening in a small saucepan over medium heat. Remove from heat. Whisk in cocoa powder. Add agave nectar and whisk until smooth. Keep warm until ready to serve.

TO ASSEMBLE & SERVE

Remove outer ring from springform pan. Pour Warm Chocolate Glaze over frozen Coffee-Cashew Cheesecake. Sprinkle chopped almonds on top. Cut with a warm knife and garnish with fresh fruit.

TOPPING

½ cup chopped Marcona almonds

Fresh fruit of your choice

STRAWBERRY SHORTCAKE
WITH LEMON CORN BREAD

REMEMBERED FROM YACHTSMAN STEAKHOUSE

Though this recipe goes all the way back to 2008, its take on shortcake—lemon corn bread soaked in lemon syrup, then seared in butter to serve warm—is as fresh as ever. Look for the best berries to soak in the orange-brandy liqueur. Our topping preference is freshly whipped cream to let the flavors shine.

SERVES 12

FROM THE WALT DISNEY WORLD RESORT

ORANGE-BRANDY LIQUEUR STRAWBERRIES

7 ½ cups hulled and sliced fresh strawberries, divided

⅓ cup orange-brandy liqueur

3 tablespoons sugar

LEMON CORN BREAD

½ cup canola oil

1 ¼ cups whole or 2 percent milk

2 large eggs

½ cup all-purpose flour

1 ¼ cups sugar

2 tablespoons baking powder

½ cup cornmeal

4 tablespoons lemon juice

3 tablespoons fresh lemon zest

FOR ORANGE-BRANDY LIQUEUR STRAWBERRIES

Combine 1 ½ cups strawberries, liqueur, and sugar in a blender, blending until smooth. Then combine remaining strawberries with puréed mixture in a large mixing bowl, and set aside to marinate.

FOR LEMON CORN BREAD

1 Preheat oven to 300°F. Grease and flour a 13 × 9 × 2-inch baking pan. Beat oil, milk, and eggs in a large bowl using an electric mixer.

2 Sift together flour, sugar, and baking powder in a separate bowl. Gradually mix the flour mixture into the egg mixture, stirring until smooth. Stir in cornmeal, then lemon juice and zest.

3 Transfer the batter to the prepared baking pan. Bake until a toothpick inserted in the center comes out with a few moist crumbs attached, about 40 minutes.

FOR LEMON SYRUP

1 Mix sugar and water in a small saucepan; bring to a boil over high heat. Then reduce heat to medium and continue to cook for 1 minute.

2 Remove from heat and add lemon juice and zest. If not using immediately, refrigerate in an airtight container.

TO ASSEMBLE & SERVE

1 Cut cooled corn bread into 12 squares, trimming off top crust. Drizzle each square of corn bread with 1 tablespoon Lemon Syrup. Allow syrup to soak in for 2 to 3 minutes.

2 In a buttered frying pan, carefully sear both sides of the corn bread until golden brown. Top corn bread square with Orange-Brandy Liqueur Strawberries, then top with whipped cream, crème fraîche, or vanilla ice cream.

LEMON SYRUP

½ cup sugar

½ cup water

4 tablespoons lemon juice

Zest of half a lemon

TOPPING

Fresh whipped cream, crème fraîche, or vanilla ice cream

CHAPTER FIVE
Bread, Transformed

TIANA'S PILLOWY BEIGNETS IN *The Princess and the Frog* (2009) make it possible for her to open the restaurant of her dreams. A version of those dreamy French-style donuts has been on the menu at the Disneyland theme park since the 1960s—and remains one of the most popular indulgences at Disney eateries. But maybe you haven't tried the Banana Split Monte Cristo from Carthay Circle Restaurant at Disney California Adventure Park, or the Malasadas from Aulani, A Disney Resort & Spa. These recipes take "bread" to a whole new level.

BANANA SPLIT MONTE CRISTO

Our version never looks as pretty as the dessert at Carthay Circle, but it's okay to be a little messy. The chiffon cake is the most challenging part to prepare, but once it's baked and filled, the rest comes together quickly—you have to eat it while it's warm!

SERVES 10

FROM THE DISNEYLAND RESORT

FOR CHIFFON CAKE SANDWICHES

1. Preheat oven to 375°F. Lightly spray a 15 × 10 × 1–inch jelly roll pan with nonstick spray. Fit with parchment paper and lightly spray again with nonstick spray.

2. Using whip attachment of mixer, beat eggs on low speed in deep-sided bowl until broken down. Slowly add sugar to eggs and continue mixing for 1 to 2 minutes.

3. Scrape sides of bowl and continue beating until mixture is light and fluffy. Then add vanilla and cold water; continue whipping until all ingredients are thoroughly incorporated.

4. Mix flour, cream of tartar, and baking soda in medium bowl. Add dry ingredients to wet mixture on low speed until no flour lumps remain.

5. Pour batter into prepared jelly roll pan and bake until it appears golden brown and springs to touch, about 10 to 12 minutes. Cool completely on wire rack.

6. Run small knife around edges of pan once cake is cooled. Place another 15 × 10 × 1–inch jelly roll pan on counter and cover pan with large sheet of waxed paper. Invert cake onto second pan and remove waxed paper from bottom of cake.

CHIFFON CAKE SANDWICHES

3 large eggs

1 cup sugar

2 teaspoons vanilla extract

⅓ cup cold water

1 cup flour

1 teaspoon cream of tartar

½ teaspoon baking soda

1½ cups raspberry preserves

2–3 bananas, cut into ¼-inch slices

OPPOSITE: Carthay Circle Restaurant is proudly situated at the end of Buena Vista Street.

7 Cut cake in half and spread raspberry preserves on half, leaving about ½-inch border around edges. Top evenly with sliced bananas.

8 Place other half of cake on top and press together lightly to ensure top sticks to filling. Slice into 10 square pieces and refrigerate until ready to batter.

FOR BANANAS FOSTER SAUCE

While cake is baking, melt butter over medium heat in a small saucepan. Add brown sugar and bring to a boil. Add cream and stir well. Return to a boil, then reduce heat and stir until mixture thickens. Keep warm until ready to serve.

FOR BREADCRUMB BATTER

1 Mix panko crumbs and corn flake crumbs in shallow bowl, and set aside. Then whisk together eggs, milk, brown sugar, orange zest, vanilla extract, and banana liqueur in a separate bowl.

2 Dip Chiffon Cake Sandwiches into batter for about 30 seconds, then remove and coat in breadcrumb mixture.

3 With caution, heat canola oil to 350°F in a large pot. Carefully drop coated sandwiches two at a time into pot and fry until golden brown, about 1 to 2 minutes, turning after about 30 seconds. Drain on paper towel–lined plate.

TO ASSEMBLE & SERVE

Place a desired amount of banana slices in 10 shallow serving bowls. Drizzle each with warm Bananas Foster Sauce. Then set the fried Chiffon Cake Sandwiches on top of the banana bases. Top each with your favorite ice cream and ice cream syrups, including more of the warm Bananas Foster Sauce. Garnish with a sugar cookie, and serve immediately.

BANANAS FOSTER SAUCE

½ cup unsalted butter

¾ cup brown sugar

1½ cups heavy cream

BREADCRUMB BATTER

1 cup panko breadcrumbs

1 cup corn flake cereal crumbs

4 large eggs

1½ cups milk

½ cup brown sugar

Zest of half an orange

1 teaspoon vanilla extract

4 tablespoons banana liqueur

4 cups canola oil

GARNISH

2–3 bananas, cut as desired

Bananas Foster Sauce

Favorite ice cream

Favorite ice cream syrups

Sugar cookies, dusted with powdered sugar

COOKIES & CREAM BREAD PUDDING

REMEMBERED FROM PACIFIC WHARF CAFE

Put day-old Italian bread to good use in this easy recipe with sandwich cookies for sweet chocolate flavor. The supersweet whipped topping is a decadent finish.

SERVES 12

FROM THE DISNEYLAND RESORT

FOR COOKIES & CREAM BREAD PUDDING

1. Preheat oven to 350°F. Spray 9 × 13-inch baking pan with nonstick cooking spray, and set aside. Cut bread into 1-inch cubes, place in a large mixing bowl, and set aside.

2. Combine eggs, sugar, half-and-half, and vanilla extract in a medium mixing bowl. Whisk until fluffy. Pour over cubed bread, stirring gently to mix.

3. Set aside for 15 minutes and allow egg mixture to soak into bread. When ready, gently stir in chocolate sandwich cookies.

4. Pour bread pudding mixture into prepared baking pan, and spread it out evenly. Bake for 45 to 50 minutes, until top has set and a thermometer placed in the center reads 165°F. Cool for 15 minutes.

TO ASSEMBLE & SERVE

1. Whip heavy cream in the bowl of an electric mixer fitted with a whisk attachment until medium peaks form.

2. Cut Cookies & Cream Bread Pudding using a Mickey Mouse-shaped cookie cutter, and place on a plate. Drizzle with 1 to 2 teaspoons sweetened condensed milk.

3. Top each serving with 2 tablespoons whipped cream and 1 tablespoon crushed chocolate sandwich cookies.

COOKIES & CREAM BREAD PUDDING

1 (1-pound) loaf day-old Italian bread

5 large eggs

1 ½ cups sugar

4 cups half-and-half

1 tablespoon vanilla extract

24 chocolate sandwich cookies, quartered

TOPPINGS

½ cup heavy cream

1 (14-ounce) can sweetened condensed milk

12 chocolate sandwich cookies, crushed

OPPOSITE, BOTTOM: When Pacific Wharf Cafe closed in 2023, the space reopened as Aunt Cass Café, a part of the San Fransokyo Square transformation.

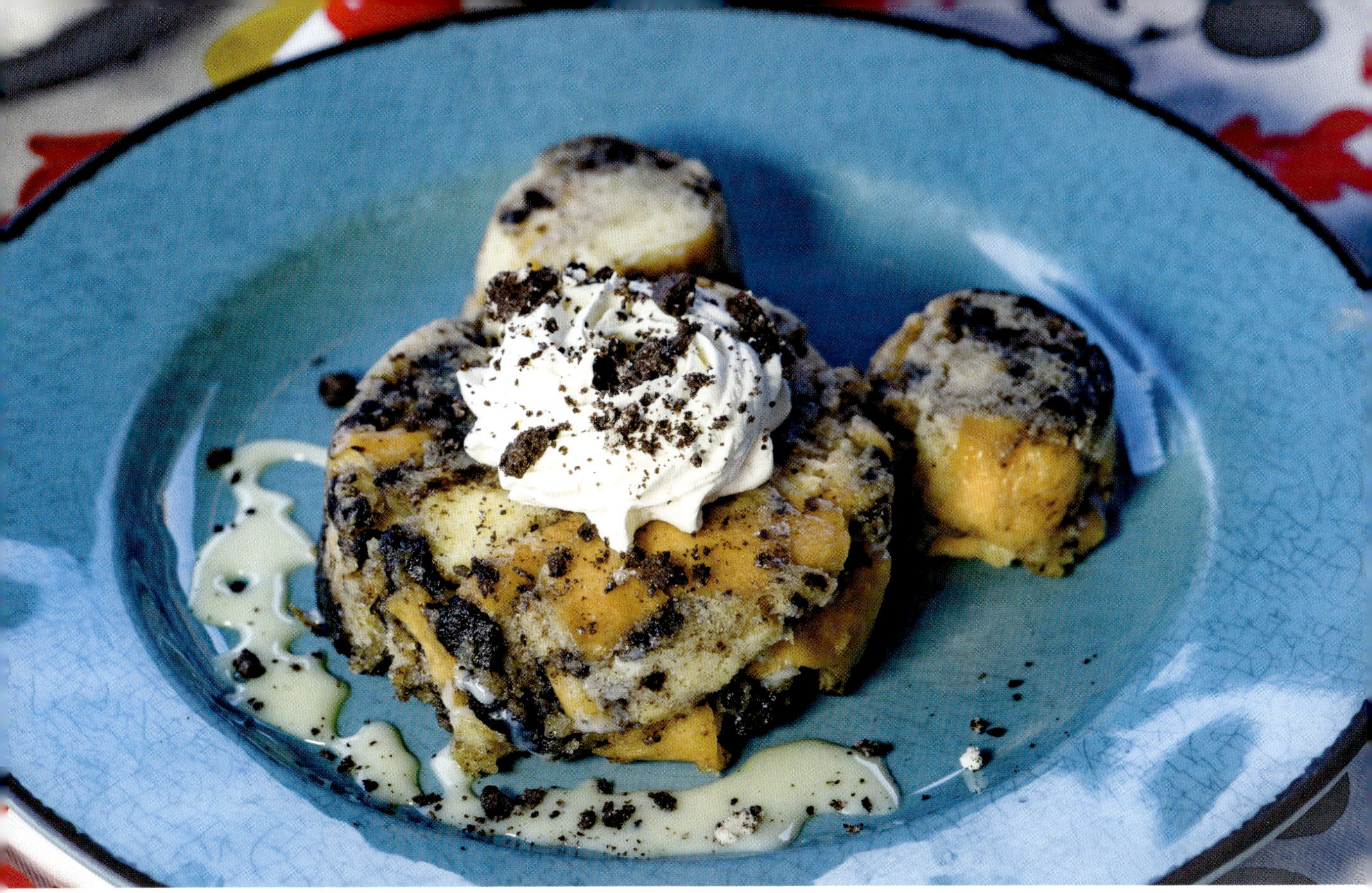

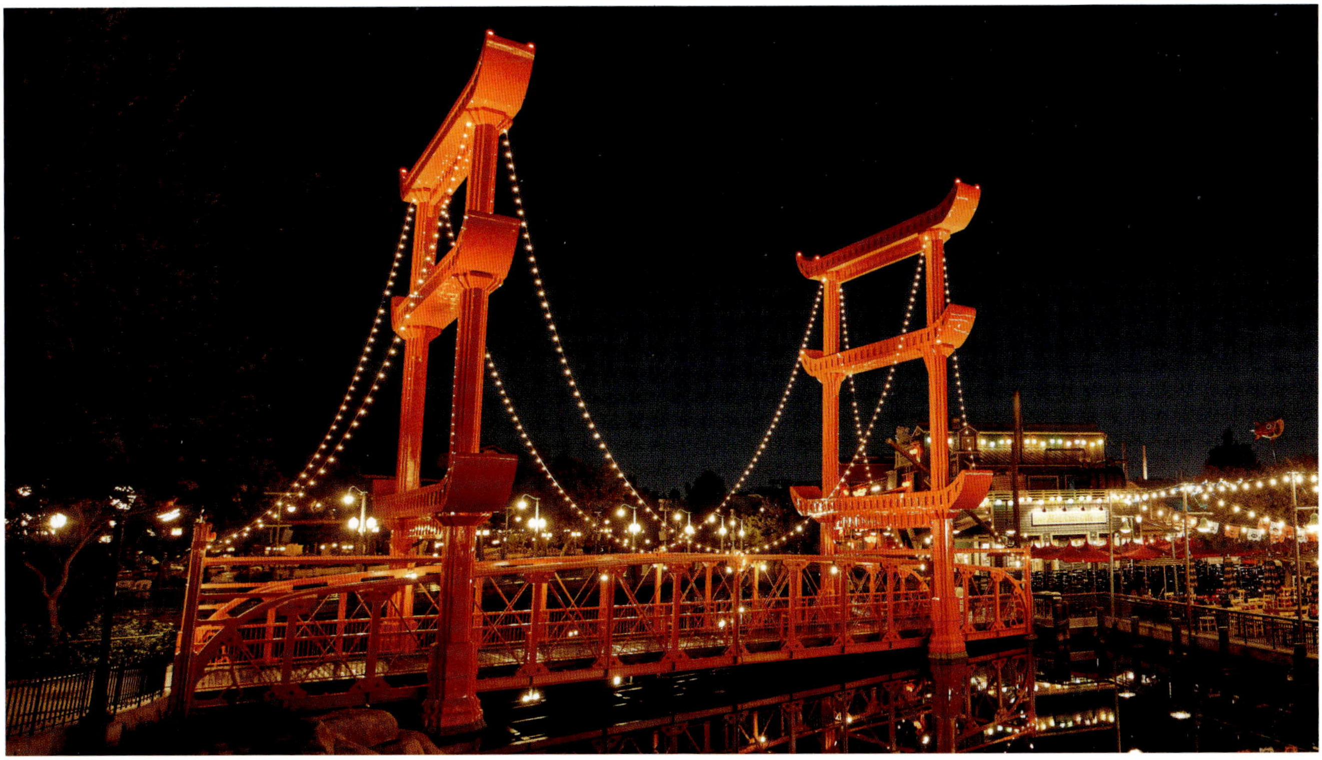

ORANGE-CRANBERRY BREAD PUDDING
WITH WARM ORANGE-VANILLA SAUCE

FESTIVAL DEBUT: 2013 · HOPS AND BARLEY GLOBAL MARKETPLACE

Use plain frozen Texas toast as the base. Cranberries, white chocolate, and orange zest add the flavor, with a warm vanilla sauce and a dash of an orange-flavored liqueur.

SERVES 8-10

FROM THE WALT DISNEY WORLD RESORT

ORANGE-CRANBERRY BREAD PUDDING

8 pieces Texas toast or favorite thick-sliced bread

½ cup dried cranberries

2 cups whole or 2 percent milk, divided

6 ounces white baking chocolate, melted

3 large eggs

½ cup sugar

2 teaspoons vanilla extract

½ teaspoon table salt

½ teaspoon cinnamon

Zest of 2 medium oranges

FOR ORANGE-CRANBERRY BREAD PUDDING

1 Preheat oven to 350°F. Lightly grease an 8 × 8–inch baking dish. Cut bread into 1 × 1–inch cubes. Spread evenly in baking dish. Sprinkle cranberries evenly over bread, and set aside.

2 Heat 1 cup milk and melted white chocolate in a small saucepan over medium-low heat, stirring until milk and chocolate are combined.

3 Whisk eggs, remaining 1 cup milk, sugar, vanilla, salt, cinnamon, and orange zest in a small bowl; add to melted chocolate mixture, stirring to combine.

4 Pour mixture over bread. Let it sit 10 minutes, allowing bread to absorb the liquid. Bake for 30 to 35 minutes in a water bath until a knife inserted comes out clean.

FOR WARM ORANGE-VANILLA SAUCE

1 Whisk egg yolks, vanilla, sugar, and cornstarch in medium bowl until fully combined and slightly foamy, and set aside.

ABOVE: The Orange Bird, who made his Magic Kingdom debut in 1971, has become a popular Walt Disney World Resort mascot.

2 Heat milk and cream in a medium saucepan over medium heat for 3 to 5 minutes, until bubbly around edges. Gradually add hot milk mixture to egg mixture, stirring constantly with a whisk.

3 Transfer mixture to saucepan and cook over medium-low heat for 2 to 3 minutes until thick and bubbly, stirring constantly. Remove from heat and stir in the orange-brandy liqueur, and set aside until ready to serve.

TO SERVE

Cut Orange-Cranberry Bread Pudding into squares, and drizzle with Warm Orange-Vanilla Sauce.

WARM ORANGE-VANILLA SAUCE

2 large pasteurized egg yolks

1 tablespoon vanilla

⅓ cup sugar

2 teaspoons cornstarch

1 cup milk

½ cup heavy cream

2 tablespoons orange-brandy liqueur

PLANT-BASED BANANA BREAD
WITH WARM MIXED-BERRY COMPOTE

FESTIVAL DEBUT: 2021 · SHIMMERING SIPS GLOBAL MARKETPLACE

If you're used to cooking vegan, the ingredients in this banana cake will be familiar (but you can also create the cake with dairy products replacing the vegan cream and butter). The streusel adds a nice crunch.

MAKES 1 (9-INCH) LOAF

FROM THE WALT DISNEY WORLD RESORT

PLANT-BASED STREUSEL

2 tablespoons plant-based butter substitute

2 tablespoons brown sugar

⅔ cup gluten-free flour

½ teaspoon cinnamon

BANANA BREAD LOAF

2 cups gluten-free flour

4 teaspoons baking soda

1 tablespoon baking powder

½ teaspoon salt

¼ teaspoon ground ginger

¼ teaspoon ground nutmeg

1 ½ cups sugar

¾ cup canola oil

1 ¼ cups plant-based cooking cream

1 teaspoon vanilla extract

1 tablespoon apple cider vinegar

2 cups mashed ripe bananas

Plant-Based Streusel

FOR PLANT-BASED STREUSEL

Melt plant-based butter substitute in microwave-safe bowl. Add brown sugar, gluten-free flour, and cinnamon. Stir with a fork until crumbs form, and set aside.

FOR BANANA BREAD LOAF

1. Preheat oven to 325°F. Grease a 9-inch round cake pan with cooking spray and line bottom of pan with parchment, and set aside.

2. Combine flour, baking soda, baking powder, salt, ginger, and nutmeg in the bowl of an electric mixer fitted with a paddle attachment. Mix on low speed for 30 seconds.

3. Add sugar, canola oil, plant-based cooking cream, vanilla extract, and apple cider vinegar. Beat on low speed, occasionally scraping sides, for 2 minutes, until well mixed.

4. Add mashed banana and beat on medium speed until combined. Pour into prepared pan. Top with reserved Plant-Based Streusel.

5. Bake for 45 minutes, until a toothpick inserted in the center comes out clean. Cool completely before serving.

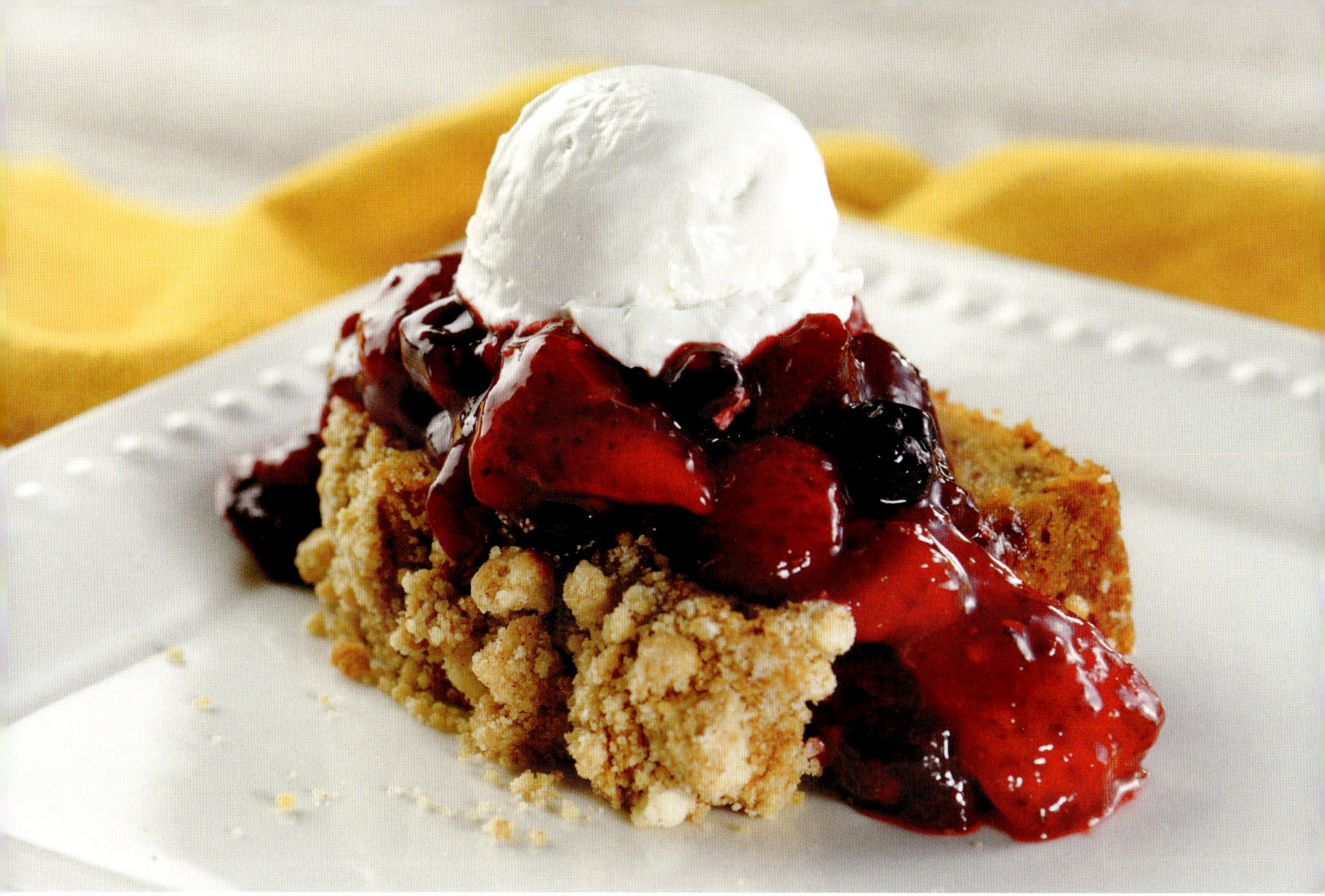

WARM MIXED-BERRY COMPOTE

1 cup frozen strawberries

4 tablespoons frozen blackberries

4 tablespoons frozen raspberries

4 tablespoons frozen blueberries

3 tablespoons sugar

1 teaspoon lime juice

TOPPING

Dairy-free ice cream

FOR WARM MIXED-BERRY COMPOTE

1. Combine strawberries, blackberries, raspberries, blueberries, sugar, and lime juice in a small saucepan. Bring to a simmer over medium-low heat.
2. Cook, stirring occasionally to break up fruit, for 10 minutes, until sauce begins to thicken. Keep warm until ready to serve.

TO SERVE

Cut Banana Bread Loaf to desired size. Serve with Warm Mixed-Berry Compote. If desired, add a scoop of dairy-free ice cream.

EPCOT INTERNATIONAL FOOD & WINE FESTIVAL, SEASONALLY

PRETZEL BREAD PUDDING
WITH WARM VANILLA SAUCE

REMEMBERED FROM SOMMERFEST

If you love sweet-savory desserts, this is a balanced combination of salty pretzel bread and sweet vanilla sauce and caramel. The pretzel bread needs to be refrigerated at least four hours before baking, so give yourself plenty of time, then serve it straight from the oven with warm vanilla sauce. And leftovers are great for breakfast.

MAKES 15 SERVINGS

FROM THE WALT DISNEY WORLD RESORT

WARM VANILLA SAUCE

1 large pasteurized egg

4 tablespoons sugar

¾ cup heavy cream

1 cup milk, divided

2½ teaspoons cornstarch

¾ teaspoon vanilla extract

FOR WARM VANILLA SAUCE

1 Beat egg and sugar in a small bowl, and set aside. Bring cream and ¾ cup milk to a simmer in a small saucepan over medium heat. Slowly add a third of the simmering cream mixture to the eggs, whisking constantly to temper eggs.

2 Carefully pour back into saucepan. Whisk cornstarch and remaining 4 tablespoons milk together in a small bowl, and add to saucepan.

3 Cook over medium heat, stirring constantly until sauce thickens. Remove from heat and add vanilla extract.

4 Place a mesh strainer over a bowl. Pour sauce through strainer and cool to room temperature. Cover and refrigerate for up to 7 days.

ABOVE: The outdoor and open air tables of Sommerfest, 2013

FOR PRETZEL BREAD PUDDING

1 Tear or chop pretzel bread into large pieces. Place in a food processor and pulse until coarse crumbs form. Whisk milk, heavy cream, sugar, eggs, vanilla paste, baking powder, and cinnamon in a large bowl. Add pretzel bread pieces.

2 Cover and refrigerate 4 to 12 hours. When ready, preheat oven to 375°F. Spray 15 (1-cup) ramekins or wells of muffin tins with nonstick cooking spray.

3 Add ⅓ cup pretzel bread pudding mix into each ramekin or muffin tin well. Bake for 25 to 30 minutes, until centers of pretzel bread puddings are firm. Cool for 5 minutes before removing from molds.

TO ASSEMBLE & SERVE

Remove vanilla sauce from refrigerator. Heat in a small saucepan over medium-low heat until warm. Place warm pretzel bread pudding on small plates. Top each with 2 to 3 tablespoons vanilla sauce. Drizzle caramel on top, if desired.

PRETZEL BREAD PUDDING

1 pound pretzel bread

1 cup milk

1⅔ cups heavy cream

1⅓ cups sugar

4 large eggs

1¾ teaspoons vanilla paste

½ teaspoon baking powder

⅛ teaspoon cinnamon

TOPPINGS

Warm Vanilla Sauce

Caramel sauce, optional

BANANA BREAD PUDDING
WITH VANILLA SAUCE

REMEMBERED FROM TUSKER HOUSE RESTAURANT

Start with your favorite cinnamon rolls for this easy sweet. Make the vanilla sauce while it's baking; then eat it warm from the oven drizzled with the rich sauce.

SERVES 10

FROM THE WALT DISNEY WORLD RESORT

FOR BREAD PUDDING

1. Preheat oven to 325°F. Spray a 9 × 13–inch baking dish with cooking spray. Dice cinnamon roll dough into 1-inch pieces and place in baking dish.

2. Whisk together milk, eggs, sugar, cinnamon, vanilla extract, and nutmeg in a large bowl until very well combined.

3. Mash 6 bananas in a small bowl and whisk into egg mixture. Thinly slice remaining 2 bananas and add to cinnamon rolls in baking dish.

4. Sprinkle with chocolate chips and raisins. Pour egg mixture over mixture in baking dish and set aside 20 to 30 minutes.

5. Bake for 55 minutes, or until top is golden and center is set. Brush the top of bread pudding with melted butter and sprinkle with sanding sugar before serving.

FOR VANILLA SAUCE

1. Combine butter and flour in a medium saucepan over medium heat and cook 5 minutes, stirring frequently. Whisk together milk, cream, sugar, egg, and salt in a large bowl.

2. Add milk mixture to butter-flour mixture, gently whisking continuously until mixture thickens (it will thicken further as it cools). Stir in vanilla extract. Serve sauce over warm bread pudding.

BREAD PUDDING

16-ounce package cinnamon roll dough

3¼ cups whole milk

10 large eggs

1½ cups sugar

1 tablespoon cinnamon

1 tablespoon vanilla extract

¼ teaspoon nutmeg

8 ripe bananas, divided

½ cup chocolate chips

½ cup raisins

3 tablespoons unsalted butter, melted

4 tablespoons coarse sanding sugar

VANILLA SAUCE

1 tablespoon plus 1 teaspoon unsalted butter

1 tablespoon plus 1 teaspoon flour

1¼ cups whole milk

1 cup heavy cream

¾ cup sugar

1 large pasteurized egg, beaten

Pinch coarse salt

1½ teaspoons vanilla extract

ORANGE-CRANBERRY MUFFINS

REMEMBERED FROM BOARDWALK BAKERY

Tart dried cranberries and sweet orange flavor these easy-to-make muffins that are perfect for breakfast or brunch—or any time of day with a cup of coffee or a glass of cold milk.

MAKES 15 MUFFINS

FROM THE WALT DISNEY WORLD RESORT

FOR STREUSEL TOPPING

Combine flour, sugar, butter, and vanilla extract in a small bowl. Mash with a fork until crumbly, and set aside.

FOR MUFFINS

1. Preheat the oven to 350°F. Line 15 muffin cups with paper or foil liners, and set aside. Combine flour, cornstarch, and baking powder in a medium bowl, whisking to combine.

2. Combine sugar, butter, vanilla extract, and lemon extract in a medium bowl; beat with an electric mixer for 5 minutes, or until light and creamy.

3. Add eggs one at a time to the sugar-butter mixture, beating well after each addition; add 3 tablespoons of flour mixture with the last egg. (Mixture may seem curdled.)

4. Beat for 3 to 4 minutes, or until creamy. Then fold in remaining flour mixture, orange zest, and dried cranberries, mixing until just incorporated.

5. Fill prepared muffin cups three-fourths full with batter; sprinkle Streusel Topping over tops of muffins. Bake for 20 to 25 minutes, or until a wooden pick inserted in the center comes out clean.

STREUSEL TOPPING

4 tablespoons cake flour

4 tablespoons sugar

2 tablespoons unsalted butter, softened

½ teaspoon vanilla extract

MUFFINS

1 cup plus 2 tablespoons sifted cake flour

1 cup cornstarch

½ teaspoon baking powder

1¼ cups sugar

1 cup unsalted butter, at room temperature

½ teaspoon vanilla extract

¼ teaspoon lemon extract

4 large eggs

Zest of 1 orange

1 cup dried cranberries

OPPOSITE, BOTTOM: A 2012 view of Disney's BoardWalk Inn & Villas, with BoardWalk Bakery on the left

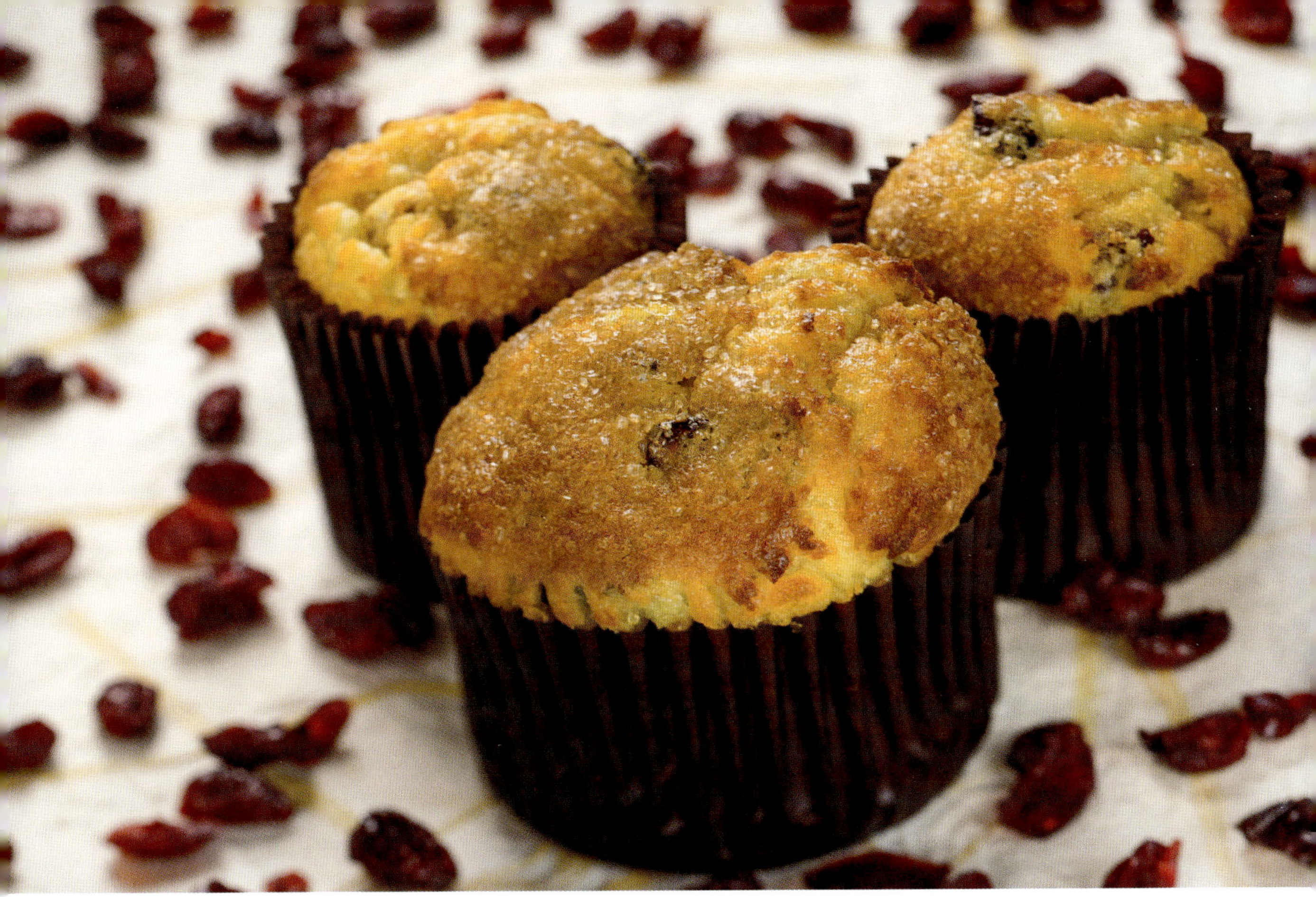

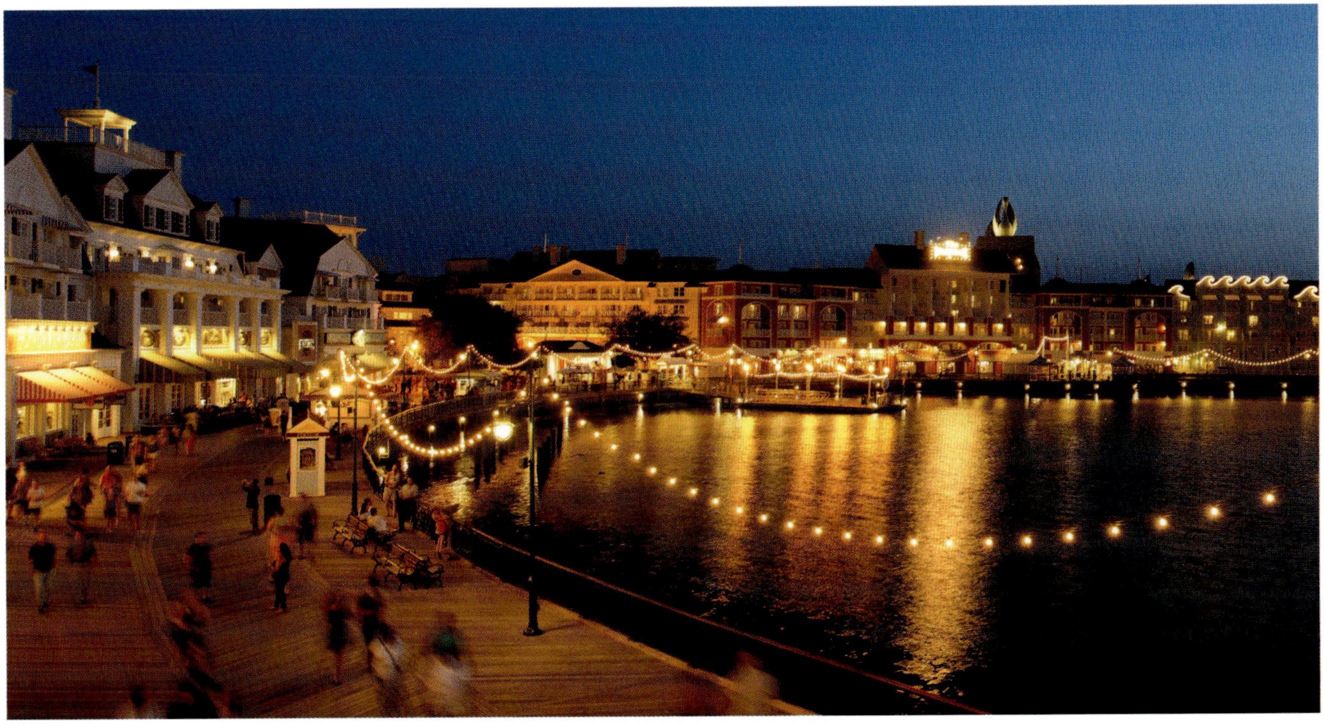

HOUSE-MADE DONUTS

Tart, sweet marionberries, a type of blackberry, thrive in the Pacific Northwest, and these filled donuts were on the menu before Artist Point became Story Book Dining at Artist Point with Snow White. If you can't find marionberries, blackberries work as well.

MAKES 24 DONUTS

FROM THE WALT DISNEY WORLD RESORT

FOR MARIONBERRY JAM

1 Combine berries, sugar, cinnamon stick, star anise, and orange juice in a 2-quart saucepan. Cook over medium heat, stirring occasionally for 15 minutes or until berries are soft and jam begins to reduce.

2 Stir in pectin and remove from heat. Remove cinnamon stick and star anise. Place in a blender and purée for 30 seconds or until smooth. Pour through a fine-mesh strainer and refrigerate until ready to use.

FOR WARM DONUTS

1 Whisk together eggs and sugar in a medium mixing bowl. Split vanilla bean in half, lengthwise, and scrape out seeds. Add seeds to egg-sugar mixture.

2 Whisk in crème fraîche, milk, all-purpose flour, and baking powder. Cover and refrigerate for 2 to 12 hours. When ready to serve, with caution, heat oil in a deep fryer to 350°F.

3 Using a small cookie scoop, carefully drop dough into the fryer, frying in batches so as not to overcrowd. Turn frequently for 3 to 5 minutes, or until donuts are golden brown. Remove from fryer and drain on paper towels.

FOR CINNAMON SUGAR

Mix sugar and cinnamon together in a small bowl.

MARIONBERRY JAM

4 cups marionberries or blackberries

⅓ cup sugar

½ cinnamon stick

1 star anise

3 tablespoons freshly squeezed orange juice

1 tablespoon pectin

WARM DONUTS

4 large eggs

4 tablespoons sugar

½ vanilla bean

1 cup crème fraîche

4 tablespoons whole or 2 percent milk

1½ cups all-purpose flour

¾ teaspoon baking powder

CINNAMON SUGAR

¾ cup sugar

½ teaspoon ground cinnamon

FOR CHOCOLATE-HAZELNUT GANACHE

1 Heat heavy cream in a small saucepan over medium-low heat until warm, and set aside. Melt chocolate in a double boiler or heatproof bowl on top of a pot of simmering water.

2 Add warm cream to melted chocolate and stir until combined. Turn off heat and stir in chocolate-hazelnut spread. Cool for 15 minutes before serving.

TO ASSEMBLE & SERVE

Place 1½ cups of Marionberry Jam in a large piping bag fitted with a ¼-inch round tip. Roll Warm Donuts in Cinnamon Sugar. Fill each with Marionberry Jam, and serve with Chocolate-Hazelnut Ganache for dipping.

CHOCOLATE-HAZELNUT GANACHE

½ cup heavy cream

2 cups chopped dark chocolate

1 cup chocolate-hazelnut spread

PLANT-BASED LAVENDER DONUTS

Made with chickpea liquid, flaxseed, coconut milk, and coconut oil, these donuts with their unusual flavors create a sublime dessert. Culinary lavender is available online and in specialty stores, and contains less oil than the aromatic lavender used in perfumes.

MAKES 24-36 DONUTS

FROM THE WALT DISNEY WORLD RESORT

LAVENDER SUGAR

1 cup sugar

1 tablespoon dried culinary lavender

DONUTS

¾ cup lukewarm water

1 tablespoon active dry yeast

¾ cup liquid brine from canned chickpeas

5 teaspoons ground flaxseed

1¼ cups coconut milk

½ cup coconut oil

6⅔ cups all-purpose flour

½ cup sugar, plus more for topping

1 teaspoon coarse salt

Vegetable oil, for frying

FOR LAVENDER SUGAR

Toss sugar and dried culinary lavender in medium bowl. Cover, and let it rest for several hours or overnight. Sift out lavender with a fine-mesh strainer, and set aside.

FOR DONUTS

1 Combine water and yeast in the bowl of an electric mixer fitted with a dough hook. Then let it rest for 5 minutes until yeast is frothy.

2 Whisk chickpea brine and ground flaxseed in medium bowl. Add to water and yeast. Then add coconut milk, coconut oil, flour, sugar, and salt.

3 Mix on low speed until soft dough ball forms. Increase to medium-high speed and knead for 5 minutes. Then transfer dough to large bowl coated with nonstick cooking spray.

4 Cover with plastic wrap and let dough rise at room temperature for 90 minutes, or until doubled in size. When ready, place parchment paper on two baking pans and spray with nonstick cooking spray, and set aside.

5   Place dough on large board covered with flour, roll to ¼-inch thickness, and cut with desired size donut cutter. Place cut donuts on prepared baking pans. Cover with plastic wrap and let rise for 15 minutes, or until doubled in size.

6   With caution, heat oil to 350°F. Carefully add donuts and cook for 1 to 2 minutes, or until browned on one side, then flip and brown other side. Remove from oil and drain on paper towels to cool. While still warm, toss with Lavender Sugar. If desired, serve with a pistachio crumble, blueberries, and dairy-free frozen yogurt (as pictured).

GLUTEN-FRIENDLY BEIGNETS

While the classic fried dough treats have flour, we think this gluten-friendly version is just as delicious, soft, and fluffy. Enjoy them hot with a generous dusting of powdered sugar.

MAKES 20 BEIGNETS

FROM THE WALT DISNEY WORLD RESORT

½ cup plus 2 tablespoons warm water (100°F)

1½ teaspoons dry active yeast

½ cup plus 2 tablespoons apple juice

4 tablespoons unsweetened applesauce

3 tablespoons sugar

2½ teaspoons powdered gluten-free egg substitute

¼ teaspoon salt

½ teaspoon canola oil

Pinch ground cinnamon

1 pound gluten-free pizza crust mix

Powdered sugar, for finishing

1. Combine warm water and yeast in a small bowl, and set aside 5 minutes. Combine apple juice, applesauce, sugar, egg substitute, salt, oil, and cinnamon in the bowl of an electric mixer fitted with a paddle attachment. Mix until well combined.

2. Add pizza crust mix, 4 tablespoons at a time, until soft dough forms (you will not use all of mix). Turn dough out onto a work surface dusted with remaining pizza crust mix. Knead until dough is no longer sticky but still soft.

3. Roll dough to ¼-inch thickness, cut into 2 × 3–inch pieces, and set aside at room temperature for 20 minutes. Pour enough oil into a deep-sided pot until it reaches 2 inches up sides. With caution, heat oil over medium heat to 350°F.

4. Lightly press beignets to slightly flatten. Carefully add a few beignets to oil; fry until golden brown on both sides, turning once.

5. Remove from hot oil with a slotted spoon and place on a baking sheet lined with paper towels. Dust with a generous amount of powdered sugar, and serve hot.

OPPOSITE, BOTTOM: Guests enjoy the jazzy atmosphere of Scat Cat's Club – Lounge.

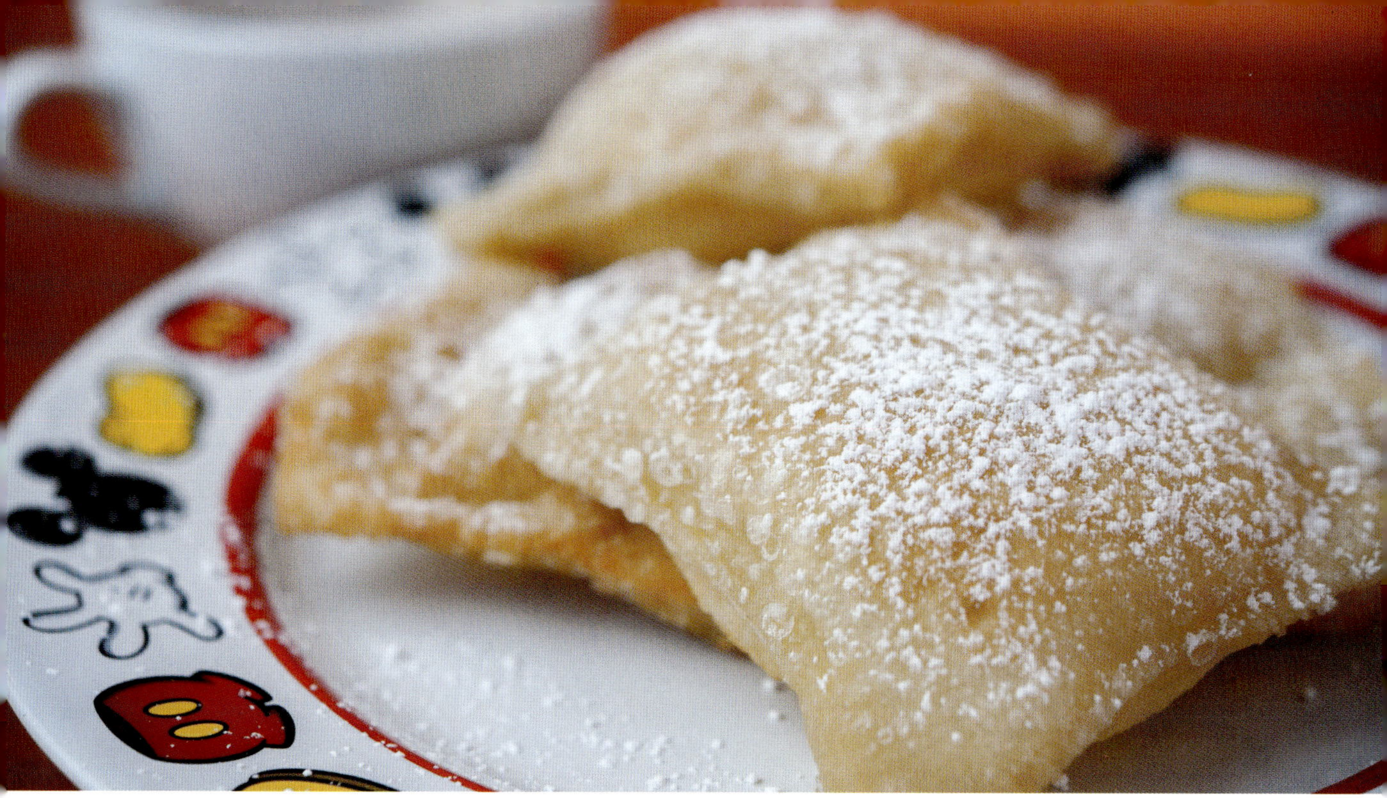

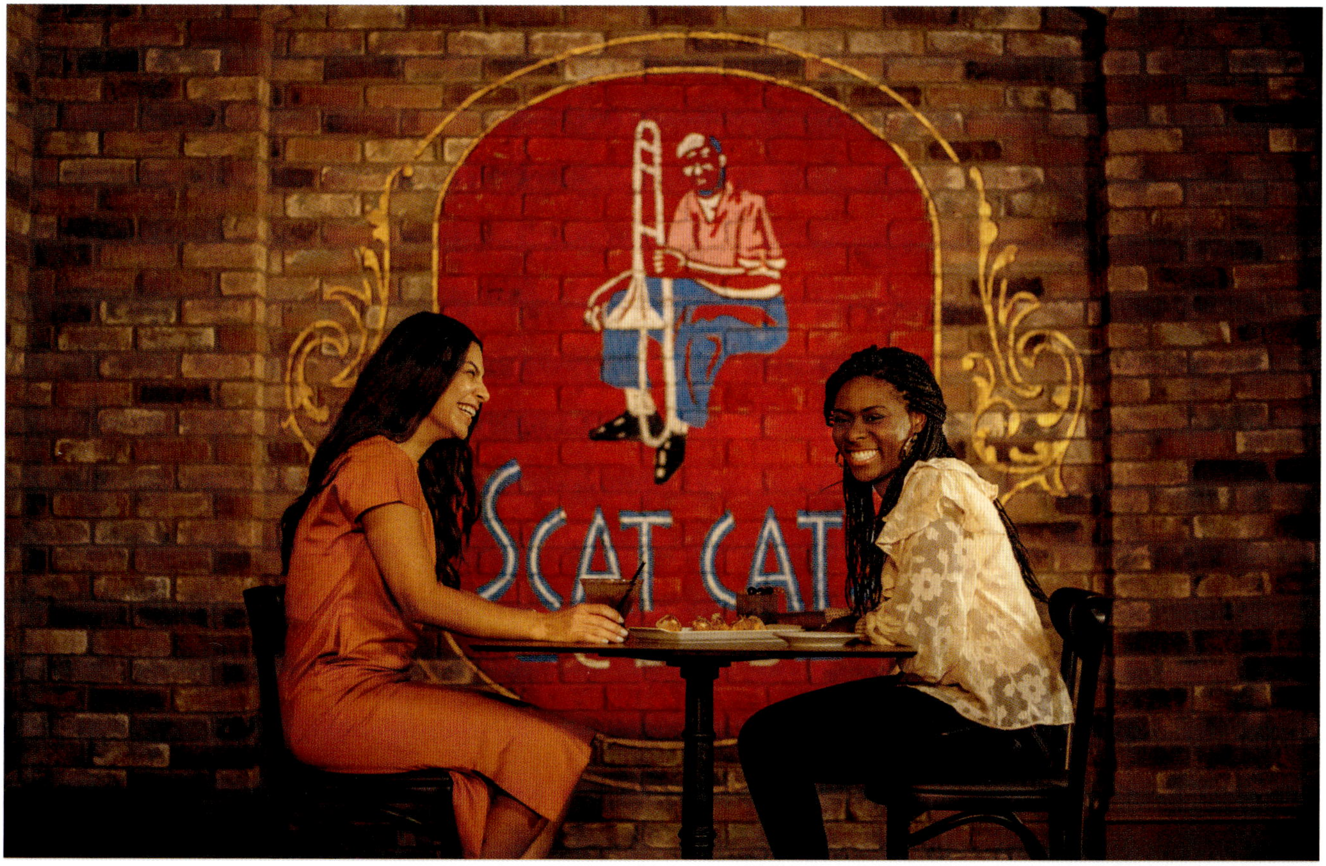
SCAT CAT

PIÑA COLADA BREAD PUDDING

This dessert, with fresh pineapple, coconut milk, and coconut rum, will take you back to a sunny day sipping cocktails on the beach.

SERVES 12

FROM BEYOND THE DISNEY PARKS

PINEAPPLE BREAD PUDDING

10 slices white bread

½ cup fresh pineapple, finely chopped

2 tablespoons unsalted butter, melted

2 cups whole or 2 percent milk

6 large eggs, beaten

½ cup heavy cream

1 cup sugar

4 tablespoons coconut milk

2 tablespoons coconut rum, optional

VANILLA-RUM SAUCE

2 large pasteurized egg yolks

2 teaspoons cornstarch

1 cup plus 2 tablespoons whole or 2 percent milk, divided

2 tablespoons sugar, divided

1 teaspoon vanilla extract

1 tablespoon coconut rum

FOR PINEAPPLE BREAD PUDDING

1   Preheat broiler to 450°F. Cut bread into 1-inch cubes, spread on a cookie sheet, and broil until golden brown. Remove from broiler and reduce oven temperature to 350°F.

2   Combine toasted bread cubes and chopped pineapple in a large bowl, mixing thoroughly. Then spread bread mixture into a 13 × 9 × 2–inch baking pan. Drizzle with melted butter.

3   Warm milk in a medium saucepan over medium heat; do not boil. Whisk in eggs, heavy cream, sugar, coconut milk, and rum (if using). Remove custard from heat.

4   Pour custard over bread mixture. Use a fork to press bread down into the liquid until well soaked. Bake for 35 to 40 minutes, or until pudding springs back in the center when pressed with a fingertip.

FOR VANILLA-RUM SAUCE

1   Combine egg yolks, cornstarch, 2 tablespoons milk, and 1 tablespoon sugar in a small mixing bowl, stirring until smooth.

2   Combine 1 cup milk, remaining 1 tablespoon sugar, and vanilla in a small saucepan over medium heat. Bring to a boil.

OPPOSITE, BOTTOM: The *Disney Dream* sailing through Norway, 2023

3 Whisk egg yolk mixture into boiling milk mixture, and then immediately pour into a bowl in an ice bath to prevent curdling. Add rum and whisk thoroughly.

TO ASSEMBLE & SERVE

Cut warmed Pineapple Bread Pudding into 12 squares. Drizzle each piece with Vanilla-Rum Sauce before serving.

MALASADAS

A popular treat with the locals in Hawai'i, malasadas are essentially a sugar-dusted donut without a hole, fried until golden brown on the outside and light and fluffy on the inside. Because malasadas are best when eaten hot, make the passion fruit curd well ahead of time so it's ready to go.

MAKES 17 MALASADAS

FROM BEYOND THE DISNEY PARKS

FOR MALASADAS

1. Combine water, yeast, and 1 ½ teaspoons sugar. Stir until yeast dissolves, and set aside for 3 minutes. Sift all-purpose flour, bread flour, and salt into a large bowl.

2. Add yeast mixture, eggs, milk, and pinch of nutmeg to flour. Beat with an electric mixer on low speed. With mixer running, add melted butter. Mix 2 minutes on low speed until ingredients are combined.

3. Increase mixer speed to medium and beat until dough no longer sticks to the side of the bowl and is soft and smooth. Cover bowl with a clean kitchen towel, and set aside for 45 minutes.

4. When ready, punch dough down. With lightly oiled fingers, pinch off pieces about the size of golf balls. Place the dough balls on greased baking sheets.

5. Cover dough balls with a clean kitchen towel and set aside in a warm place for about 15 minutes. Pour enough oil to reach 3 inches up sides of a deep pot, and with caution, heat oil to 325°F.

6. Working in small batches, carefully fry malasadas until golden brown. Combine remaining ¾ cup sugar and cinnamon in a shallow bowl. Roll hot malasadas in cinnamon-sugar mixture. Serve hot with Passion Fruit Curd.

MALASADAS

⅓ cup warm water

1 tablespoon plus 1 ½ teaspoons instant yeast

¾ cup plus 1 ½ teaspoons sugar, divided

1 cup all-purpose flour

1 ½ cups bread flour

½ teaspoon salt

2 large eggs, beaten

6 tablespoons whole or 2 percent milk

Pinch nutmeg

4 tablespoons unsalted butter, melted

Vegetable oil, for frying

2 teaspoons ground cinnamon

ABOVE: The garden overview toward the lobby building and northwest tower

FOR PASSION FRUIT CURD

1 Whisk together eggs, sugar, unsweetened passion fruit purée (or sweetened purée plus lemon juice), and cornstarch in a heatproof bowl set over a pan of simmering water. Stir until combined and slightly thickened.

2 Whisk in butter, one cube at a time. Cook, whisking frequently, until mixture thickens and coats the back of a spoon, about 5 to 7 minutes.

3 Remove from heat immediately. Cool to room temperature, then place a piece of plastic wrap directly on surface of curd and refrigerate until cold.

PASSION FRUIT CURD

6 large pasteurized eggs

1 cup sugar

⅔ cup unsweetened passion fruit purée; or ⅔ cup sweetened passion fruit purée plus 2 tablespoons lemon juice

1 tablespoon cornstarch

½ cup unsalted butter, cubed

CHAPTER SIX
Creamy & Frozen Confections

ANY OF THESE ICY CONCOCTIONS would be a perfect ending for a home party themed to *Frozen* (2013). We like to think that Anna and Elsa in particular would love any of the creamy chocolate desserts offered here, while summer-preoccupied Olaf might be partial to the Coconut–Key Lime Sundae that debuted at the EPCOT International Food & Wine Festival the same year as the film's release.

DARTH BY CHOCOLATE

REMEMBERED FROM GALACTIC GRILL

This whimsical Disneyland dessert is inspired by *Star Wars* and served at the Galactic Grill in Tomorrowland, near the popular Star Tours – The Adventures Continue attraction. With layers of cake, mousse, cookies, and ganache, what's not to love in this over-the-top chocolate sweet?

MAKES 12 (1⅛-CUP) SERVINGS

FROM THE DISNEYLAND RESORT

RED VELVET CAKE

1 (16-ounce) box red velvet cake mix

DARK CHOCOLATE MOUSSE

2½ cups semisweet chocolate chips

3 (¼-ounce) packages powdered gelatin

6 tablespoons cold water

3 tablespoons milk

5 large pasteurized egg yolks

3 cups heavy cream

FOR RED VELVET CAKE

Prepare in a 9 × 13–inch pan according to package directions. Let cool completely, and set aside.

FOR DARK CHOCOLATE MOUSSE

1 Heat chocolate in a double boiler over medium heat. Stir occasionally until melted, and then set aside. Combine gelatin and cold water in a small bowl, and let it rest for 5 minutes.

2 Bring milk to a boil in a small saucepan. Turn off heat and add gelatin mixture, stirring until very smooth.

3 Beat egg yolks in a small bowl, and slowly pour ⅓ cup of the hot milk-gelatin mixture into the egg yolks, stirring constantly. Then pour entire egg yolk mixture into the saucepan with milk.

4 Heat over medium-low heat, stirring constantly for 2 to 3 minutes, until hot but not boiling. Stir the egg yolk mixture into the melted chocolate. Cool for 20 minutes.

5 Whip the heavy cream using an electric mixer until soft peaks form. Slowly add warm chocolate to the whipped cream, a third at a time, folding gently until well mixed. Chill for at least 4 hours in the refrigerator.

ABOVE: A view of the fireworks from around the Galactic Grill in Tomorrowland at Disneyland

FOR CHOCOLATE SPONGE

1. Preheat oven to 350°F. Grease a 15 × 10–inch baking pan and line with parchment paper. Melt chocolate with water in a small saucepan over low heat, stirring constantly. Cool for 20 minutes, until lukewarm.

2. Beat egg yolks, salt, and ⅓ cup sugar with an electric mixer on medium speed for 5 minutes, until thick and pale.

3. Fold melted chocolate into egg yolk mixture. Transfer to a medium bowl. Whip egg whites with an electric mixer until soft peaks form. Add remaining ⅓ cup sugar and beat until stiff peaks form.

4. Fold a third of the egg whites into the chocolate mixture. Fold in remaining egg whites until well blended. Spread in prepared pan and bake for 15 to 18 minutes, until the top is dry to the touch.

5. Place pan on a cooling rack and cover the top of the cake with a damp paper towel for 5 minutes. Remove paper towel and cool completely.

6. Loosen the edges of the cake using a knife. Sift cocoa powder over the top of the cake. Flip onto a large cutting board and remove parchment paper.

CHOCOLATE SPONGE

6 ounces bittersweet chocolate, chopped

3 tablespoons water

6 large eggs, separated

¼ teaspoon salt

⅔ cups sugar, divided

1 tablespoon unsweetened cocoa powder

RECIPE CONTINUES ON NEXT PAGE

DARTH BY CHOCOLATE

(CONTINUED)

FOR CHOCOLATE GANACHE

1 Place chocolate chips in a medium bowl. Heat heavy cream in a saucepan over medium heat until it just begins to boil. Pour over chocolate and let sit for 2 minutes.

2 Add butter and slowly stir, beginning in the center and slowly incorporating the cream around the sides of the bowl. Set aside.

TO ASSEMBLE & SERVE

1 Cut the Red Velvet Cake into 12 (2-inch) circles using a round cookie cutter. Place each circle in the bottom of a 9-ounce clear plastic cup. Gently press cake to 1-inch thickness, making sure it is a tight fit in the bottom of the cup.

2 Pour 2 tablespoons of Chocolate Ganache on top of each piece of Red Velvet Cake. Set in refrigerator to chill for 15 minutes.

3 Sprinkle ⅓ cup crushed chocolate sandwich cookies on top of the Chocolate Ganache. Fill a piping bag fitted with a large round tip with Dark Chocolate Mousse. Pipe a ½-inch-thick layer of mousse into each cup.

4 Use a 3½-inch cookie cutter to cut the Chocolate Sponge into 12 circles. Place circles on top of the mousse and press gently to tightly fit in each cup. Top sponge cake with 1 tablespoon ganache.

5 Pipe a rosette of mousse on top of the Chocolate Ganache. Then place a Darth Vader decoration and lightsaber on top of the rosette.

6 Add additional crushed chocolate sandwich cookies behind the decorations. Sprinkle miniature chocolate chips in front of the decorations.

CHOCOLATE GANACHE

1¼ cups semisweet chocolate chips

1¼ cups heavy cream

½ tablespoon unsalted butter

TOPPINGS

1 (14-ounce) box chocolate sandwich cookies, crushed

12 edible Darth Vader decorations (chocolates often found at online shops)

12 edible lightsaber decorations (candies often found at online shops)

Miniature chocolate chips

OPPOSITE: The open terrace seating of Galactic Grill in Tomorrowland at Disneyland, 2024

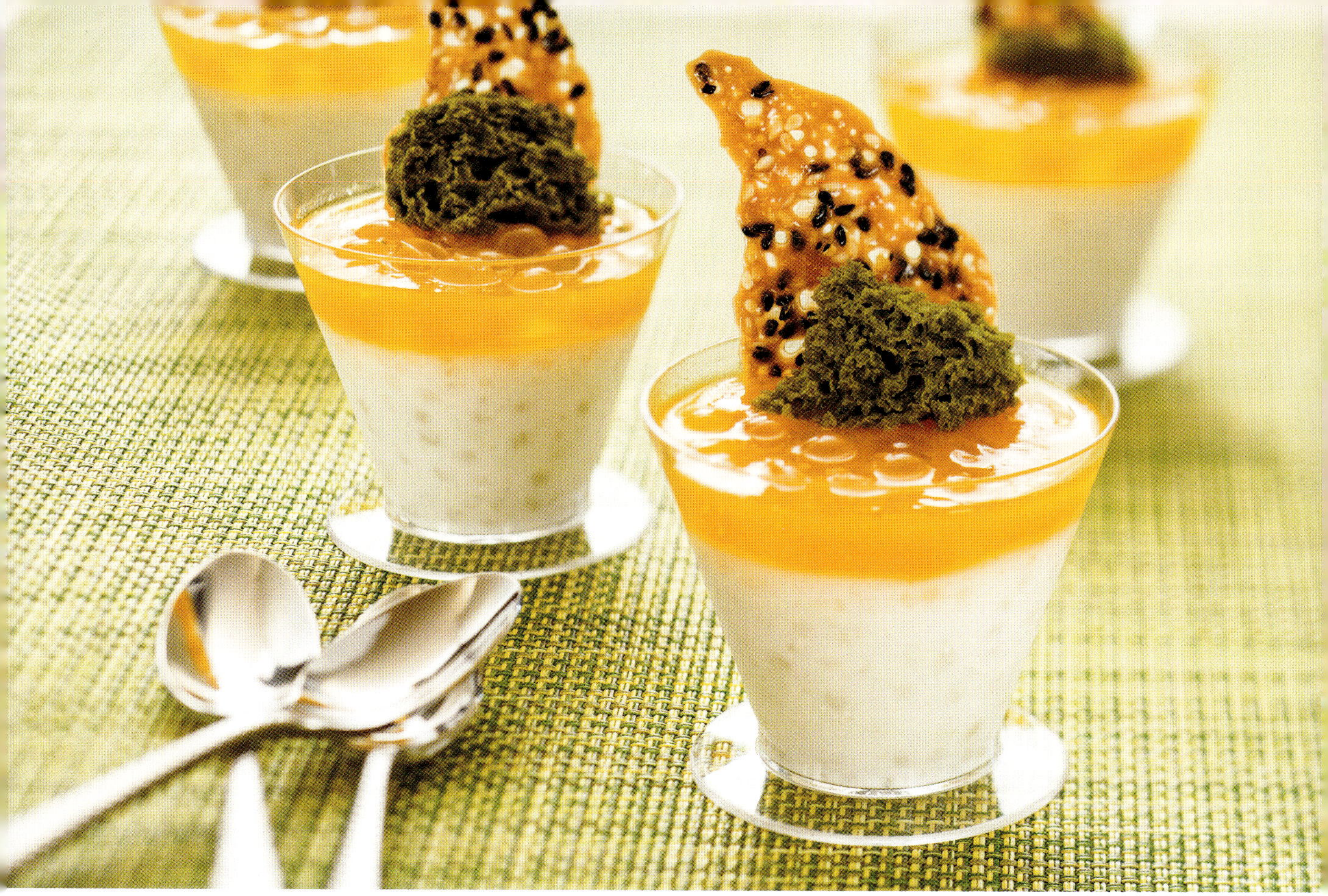

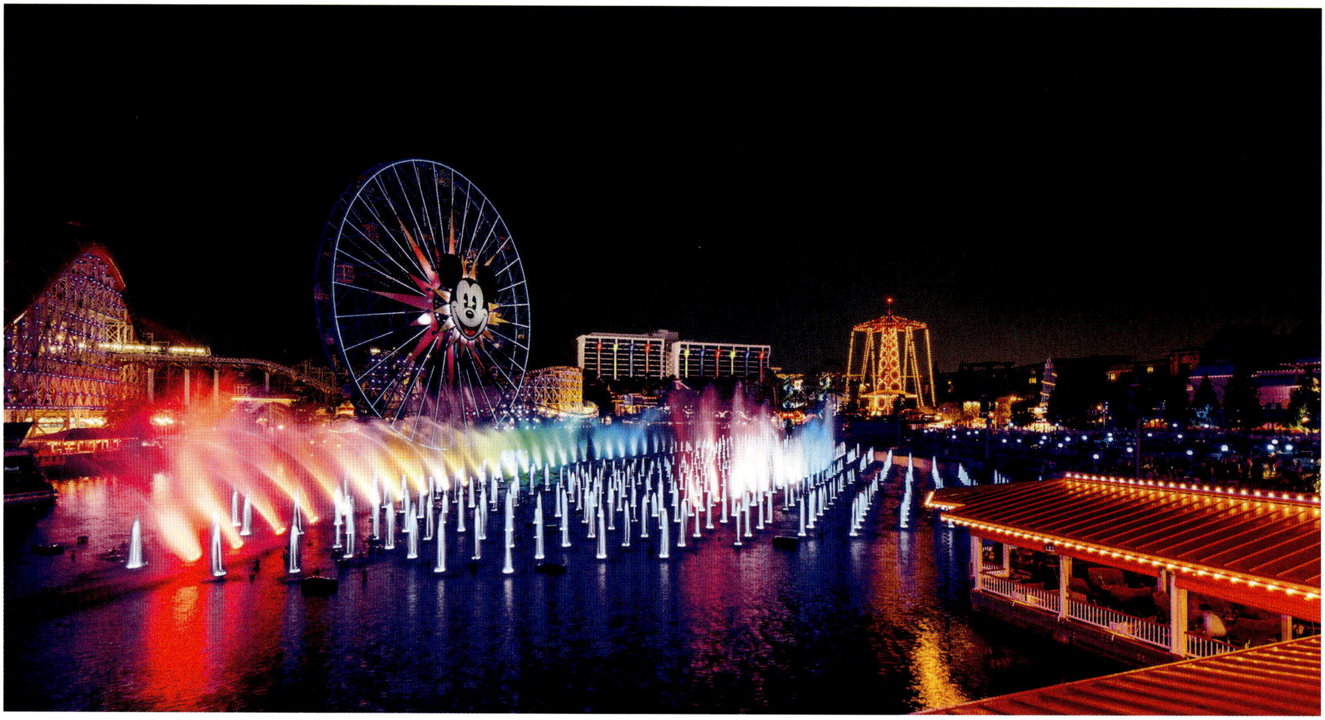

COCONUT-MANGO POSSET (TAPIOCA)

FESTIVAL DEBUT: 2017 · SEAFOOD . . . SUSTAINED FESTIVAL MARKETPLACE

Posset is an old-fashioned word for a chilled pudding; in this recipe it's coconut tapioca topped with a tart mango purée with lychee pearls. Your homemade version might skip the matcha micro sponge and even the sesame tuile (though it adds a fun crunch).

SERVES 8

FROM THE DISNEYLAND RESORT

COCONUT TAPIOCA

½ cup water

⅓ cup small tapioca pearls

6 tablespoons sugar, divided

1¾ cups coconut milk

1½ cups whole or 2 percent milk

SESAME TUILE

¾ cup dry Florentine mix

1 teaspoon black sesame seeds

1 teaspoon sesame seeds

COCONUT-MANGO TAPIOCA

4 cups frozen mango, thawed

Coconut Tapioca, cooled

FOR COCONUT TAPIOCA

1   Combine water, tapioca pearls, and 3 tablespoons sugar in a small bowl. Cover, and let it rest for 2 hours at room temperature.

2   Pour coconut milk, whole milk, and remaining 3 tablespoons sugar into a medium saucepan. Drain any excess liquid from tapioca pearls and add pearls to milk mixture.

3   Cook over high heat, stirring constantly, for 8 to 10 minutes, until pearls are tender but milk is not yet absorbed. Evenly divide mixture among 8 (6-ounce) ramekins. Refrigerate until ready to serve.

FOR SESAME TUILE

Preheat oven to 350°F. Line a baking sheet with parchment paper or a silicone baking mat. Stir Florentine mix and all sesame seeds together in a small bowl. Spread over prepared baking sheet. Bake for 6 to 7 minutes, until golden brown. Cool for 30 minutes.

FOR COCONUT-MANGO TAPIOCA

Place thawed mango in blender or food processor. Purée until smooth. Then evenly spoon over the Coconut Tapioca in each ramekin. Refrigerate until ready to serve.

OPPOSITE, BOTTOM: A view of the nighttime spectacular from Pixar Pier at Disney California Adventure

RECIPE CONTINUES ON NEXT PAGE

COCONUT-MANGO POSSET (TAPIOCA)

FOR MATCHA MICRO SPONGE

1. Place egg whites in a large microwave-safe bowl. Mix sugar, almond flour, and matcha powder in a small bowl.

2. Add dry ingredients to egg whites and purée with an immersion blender until very smooth. Microwave for 1 minute, until sponge is set. Cool for 3 to 5 minutes. Tear into small pieces.

TO ASSEMBLE & SERVE

1. Drop 5 lychee pearls on one side of each ramekin of Coconut-Mango Tapioca. Place pieces of Matcha Micro Sponge on the other side of each ramekin.

2. Break Sesame Tuile into 8 pieces and place 1 piece on each ramekin, between the lychee pearls and sponge.

MATCHA MICRO SPONGE

5 large egg whites

2 tablespoons sugar

2 tablespoons almond flour

¾ teaspoon matcha powder

TOPPING

½ cup lychee popping dessert pearls

COCONUT-LIME SEMIFREDDO
WITH STRAWBERRY-CITRUS SOUP

REMEMBERED FROM NAPA ROSE

Start a day early to make this rich, elegant dessert, as the semifreddo needs hours to completely freeze (even though semifreddo means "half-frozen" in Italian) and the soup takes several hours to meld the flavors and cool.

SERVES 10

FROM THE DISNEYLAND RESORT

FOR MACADAMIA NUT CRUST

1. Preheat oven to 325°F. Spread nuts on baking sheet and toast until light golden brown, about 5 to 10 minutes, gently tossing once halfway through, and set aside.

2. Remove from oven and grind nuts in a food processor. Add cereal and sugar; process until finely ground and crumbly. Transfer to a mixing bowl and mix in melted butter, and set aside.

FOR COCONUT-LIME SEMIFREDDO

1. Bring cream and milk to a low boil in a small saucepan over medium-low heat. Whisk together egg yolks and sugar in a medium bowl.

2. Once cream comes to a boil, slowly drizzle in a steady stream into egg yolk–sugar mixture, whisking vigorously.

3. Once milk mixture is added to yolk mixture, return entire mixture to pan over very low heat while stirring constantly with a rubber spatula. Mixture will thicken slightly.

4. Once mixture coats back of rubber spatula, remove from heat and add white chocolate. Let chocolate sit for 1 minute, then gently stir to combine. Cool.

MACADAMIA NUT CRUST

½ cup raw macadamia nuts

4 tablespoons crispy rice cereal

2 tablespoons sugar

2 tablespoons unsalted butter, melted

COCONUT-LIME SEMIFREDDO

4 tablespoons heavy cream

4 tablespoons milk

4 large pasteurized egg yolks

1 tablespoon sugar

6 tablespoons chopped white chocolate or white chocolate chips

2 cups full-fat unsweetened coconut milk

½ cup sweetened condensed milk

1 teaspoon lime zest

¾ cup raw macadamia nuts, toasted and finely ground

¾ cup heavy cream, whipped to soft peaks

RECIPE CONTINUES ON NEXT PAGE

COCONUT-LIME SEMIFREDDO
WITH STRAWBERRY-CITRUS SOUP

(CONTINUED)

5 Stir in coconut milk, sweetened condensed milk, and lime zest. Cover and refrigerate until chilled, about 2 to 4 hours. Remove from refrigerator and fold in toasted nuts, then whipped cream.

6 Line inside of a 9 × 5 × 2¾–inch loaf pan with plastic wrap on all 4 sides (which makes it easy to remove semifreddo after freezing). Pour semifreddo into prepared pan and freeze until semisolid, about 4 hours.

7 Spread Macadamia Nut Crust on top (which will be the bottom of the semifreddo once flipped) and lightly press down crust. Freeze overnight. When ready to serve, unmold semifreddo with crust on bottom.

FOR STRAWBERRY-CITRUS SOUP

1 Bring strawberries, water, sugar, and raspberries to a boil in a medium saucepan. Turn off heat, cover, and let sit for several hours at room temperature.

2 Strain mixture, reserving liquid and discarding pulp. Stir in lime juice and diced strawberries. Refrigerate until ready to serve.

TO SERVE

Pour a small pool of the Strawberry-Citrus Soup into 10 shallow serving bowls. Cut the Coconut-Lime Semifreddo into 10 even slices, and add 1 slice to each serving bowl. If desired, garnish with strawberries.

STRAWBERRY-CITRUS SOUP

⅔ cup sliced strawberries

½ cup water

4 tablespoons sugar

4 tablespoons raspberries

4 tablespoons fresh lime juice

⅓ cup diced strawberries

GARNISH

Fresh strawberries, sliced, optional

WHITE CHOCOLATE–JASMINE TEA MOUSSE
WITH LEMON-LIME CURD & HONEY-OAT CRISP

Slow-witted Gus and quick-witted Jaq are a little like the yin and yang of this dessert—also known as Gus and Jaq's Favorite on the menu at Cinderella's Royal Table—with the tart curd and crisp topping as counterpoints to the mellow mousse.

SERVES 8

FROM THE WALT DISNEY WORLD RESORT

WHITE CHOCOLATE–JASMINE TEA MOUSSE

2 cups heavy cream, divided

1 tablespoon loose-leaf jasmine tea

4 large pasteurized egg yolks

3 tablespoons sugar

8 ounces white chocolate

FOR WHITE CHOCOLATE–JASMINE TEA MOUSSE

1 Heat ¾ cup cream and jasmine tea in a small saucepan over medium heat until hot but not boiling. Turn off heat and let tea steep for 3 minutes. Strain through a sieve and set aside.

2 Whisk together egg yolks and sugar in a medium saucepan until well blended. Slowly add warm cream-tea mixture to egg yolk–sugar mixture, whisking constantly until combined.

3 Cook over medium-low heat, stirring constantly for 5 to 7 minutes, until mixture begins to bubble and thicken. Strain custard through a sieve into a large bowl.

4 Melt white chocolate in a double boiler or heatproof bowl placed over a pan of simmering water, stirring frequently until melted.

5 Pour melted white chocolate into custard, stirring until mixture is smooth. Refrigerate for at least 4 hours, up to 2 days.

6 Before serving, whip remaining 1 ¼ cups heavy cream with an electric mixer until medium-stiff peaks form.

7 Whisk a quarter of the whipped cream into the white chocolate–jasmine tea custard. Fold in remaining cream until combined.

FOR LEMON-LIME CURD

1 Heat water in double boiler or saucepan for 3 minutes. Combine sugar and egg yolks in top of double boiler or heatproof bowl. Place over simmering water and whisk for 1 minute.

2 Add lemon and lime juice and cook, whisking constantly for 6 to 8 minutes, until mixture thickens. Then remove from heat and add butter, one cube at a time, stirring until fully melted before adding next cube.

3 Pour into a clean bowl. Place plastic wrap directly on top of curd to prevent skin from forming. Refrigerate for at least 4 hours, up to 2 days.

FOR HONEY-OAT CRISP

1 Preheat oven to 325°F. Line a baking sheet with parchment paper. Mix all ingredients together in a medium bowl until completely coated with butter.

2 Spread on parchment paper–lined baking sheet. Bake for 10 to 12 minutes, until golden brown and toasted. Cool for 15 minutes, then crumble into smaller pieces.

TO ASSEMBLE & SERVE

Place 1 tablespoon Lemon-Lime Curd on the bottom of a plate. Scoop about an eighth of the White Chocolate–Jasmine Tea Mousse on top of the curd. Drizzle with honey and top with Honey-Oat Crisp.

LEMON-LIME CURD

1 cup sugar

6 large pasteurized egg yolks

⅓ cup fresh lemon and lime juice (from about 3 lemons and 1 lime)

½ cup unsalted butter, cubed

HONEY-OAT CRISP

4 tablespoons brown sugar

4 tablespoons sugar

½ cup all-purpose flour

¼ teaspoon baking soda

¼ teaspoon baking powder

⅓ cup steel-cut oats

¼ teaspoon salt

6 tablespoons unsalted butter, melted

1 ½ teaspoons honey, plus more for garnish

ESPRESSO-CARAMEL CREAM

REMEMBERED FROM HOLLYWOOD BROWN DERBY

An indulgent combination of two favorite flavors, espresso and caramel, makes this a rich ending for any meal.

SERVES 8

FROM THE WALT DISNEY WORLD RESORT

FOR ESPRESSO CREAM

1. Sprinkle gelatin over espresso in a medium bowl and let stand 5 to 10 minutes. Heat cream and sugar in a medium saucepan over medium heat, stirring occasionally.

2. Once sugar dissolves and cream starts to simmer, remove from heat. Then pour warm cream mixture over gelatin and whisk until gelatin completely dissolves.

3. Fill 8 (8-ounce) glasses each half full with the Espresso Cream and refrigerate until chilled, about 2 hours.

FOR CARAMEL CREAM

1. Sprinkle gelatin over water in a medium bowl and let stand 5 to 10 minutes. Heat cream and caramel in a medium saucepan over medium heat, stirring occasionally until it starts to simmer.

2. Remove from heat, pour warm cream mixture over gelatin, and whisk until gelatin completely dissolves.

3. Fill glasses the rest of the way with Caramel Cream and refrigerate until chilled, about 2 hours. (Note our photographed glasses were topped with whipped cream and a generous sprinkle of cocoa for added flair.)

ESPRESSO CREAM

2 (¼-ounce) packages powdered gelatin

6 tablespoons cold espresso

4 cups heavy cream

½ cup sugar

CARAMEL CREAM

2 (¼-ounce) packages powdered gelatin

6 tablespoons cold water

3 cups heavy cream

1 cup caramel sauce

Fresh heavy cream, unsweetened cocoa powder, or other optional garnishes

ABOVE: Outside the Hollywood Brown Derby Lounge, 2013

AVOCADO PUDDING
(POTTED CHOCOLATE)

FESTIVAL DEBUT: 2019 · TROWEL & TRELLIS OUTDOOR KITCHEN

Made with almond milk and ripe avocados, this treat is a dairy-free alternative to traditional chocolate pudding. The matcha makes a cute topping, but the pudding is delicious on its own.

SERVES 6

FROM THE WALT DISNEY WORLD RESORT

FOR POMEGRANATE CHIA SEEDS

Whisk pomegranate juice and chia seeds together in a small bowl. Then cover and refrigerate overnight.

FOR MATCHA CRUMB

1 Preheat oven to 300°F. Line a baking sheet with parchment paper or a silicone baking mat. Then combine sugar, flour, and green tea powder in a medium mixing bowl.

2 Cut vegan butter substitute into small pieces and mix into green tea powder mixture. Mix with hands until it resembles sand. Spread on prepared baking sheet and bake for 10 minutes. Cool until ready to serve.

FOR CHOCOLATE-AVOCADO PUDDING

Combine avocado, almond milk, maple syrup, cocoa powder, vanilla, and salt in a blender. Blend on medium speed until smooth, scraping down the sides as needed, and set aside until ready to serve.

TO ASSEMBLE & SERVE

Evenly divide Chocolate-Avocado Pudding among 6 jars. Place a thin layer of the Pomegranate Chia Seeds on top of the pudding. Sprinkle with Matcha Crumb. Then garnish with 3 to 4 pomegranate seeds and an edible flower on top of each jar.

POMEGRANATE CHIA SEEDS

4 tablespoons pomegranate juice

2 tablespoons chia seeds

MATCHA CRUMB

1 cup sugar

1 cup gluten-free flour

2 tablespoons green tea powder

½ cup vegan butter substitute

CHOCOLATE-AVOCADO PUDDING

2 ripe avocados

1 cup unsweetened almond milk

¾ cup maple syrup

¾ cup unsweetened cocoa powder

1 teaspoon vanilla extract

⅛ teaspoon salt

TOPPING

Pomegranate seeds

Edible flowers

OPPOSITE, BOTTOM: Topiary of Mirabel Madrigal, and her sister Luisa, at the 2023 EPCOT International Flower & Garden Festival

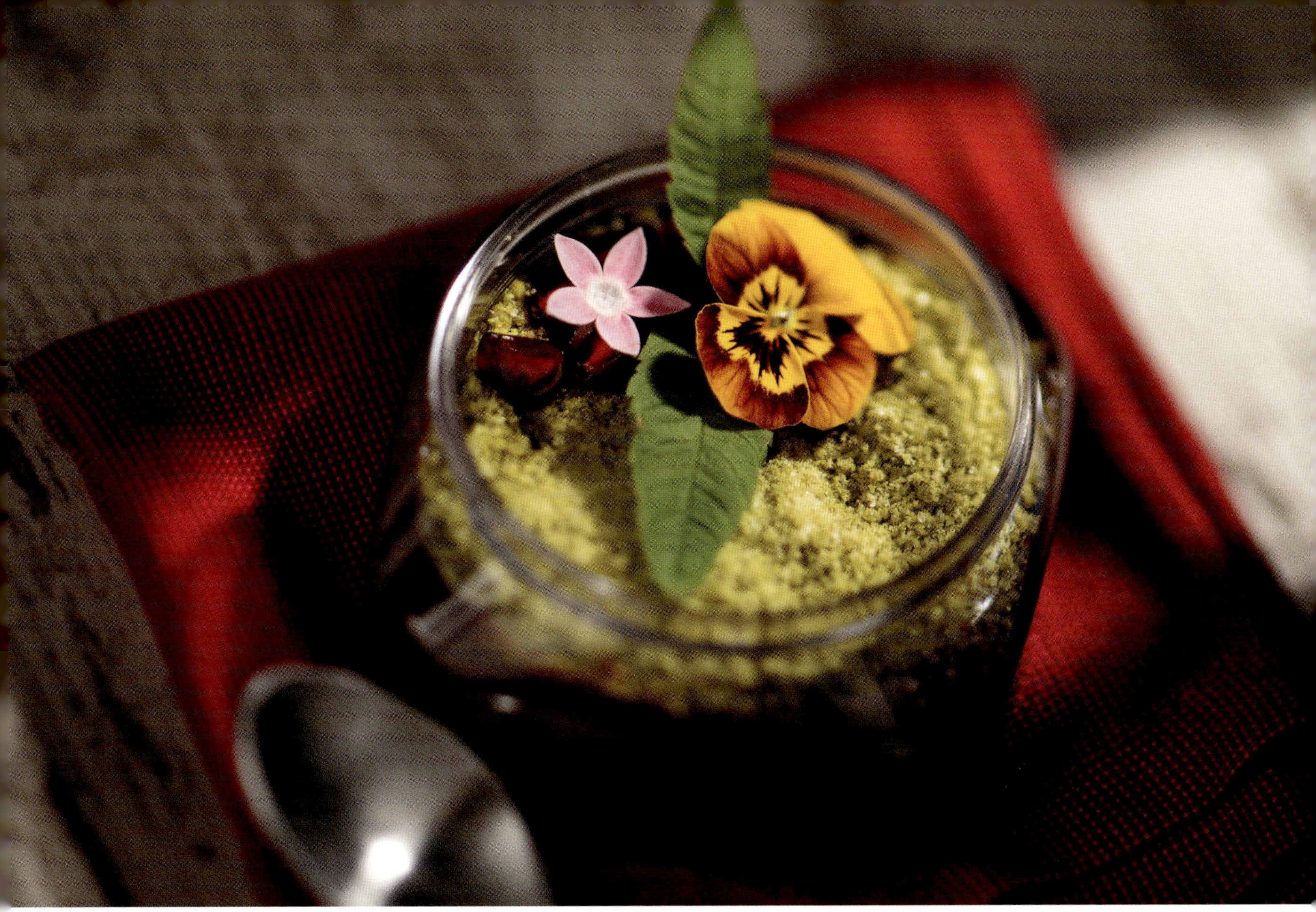

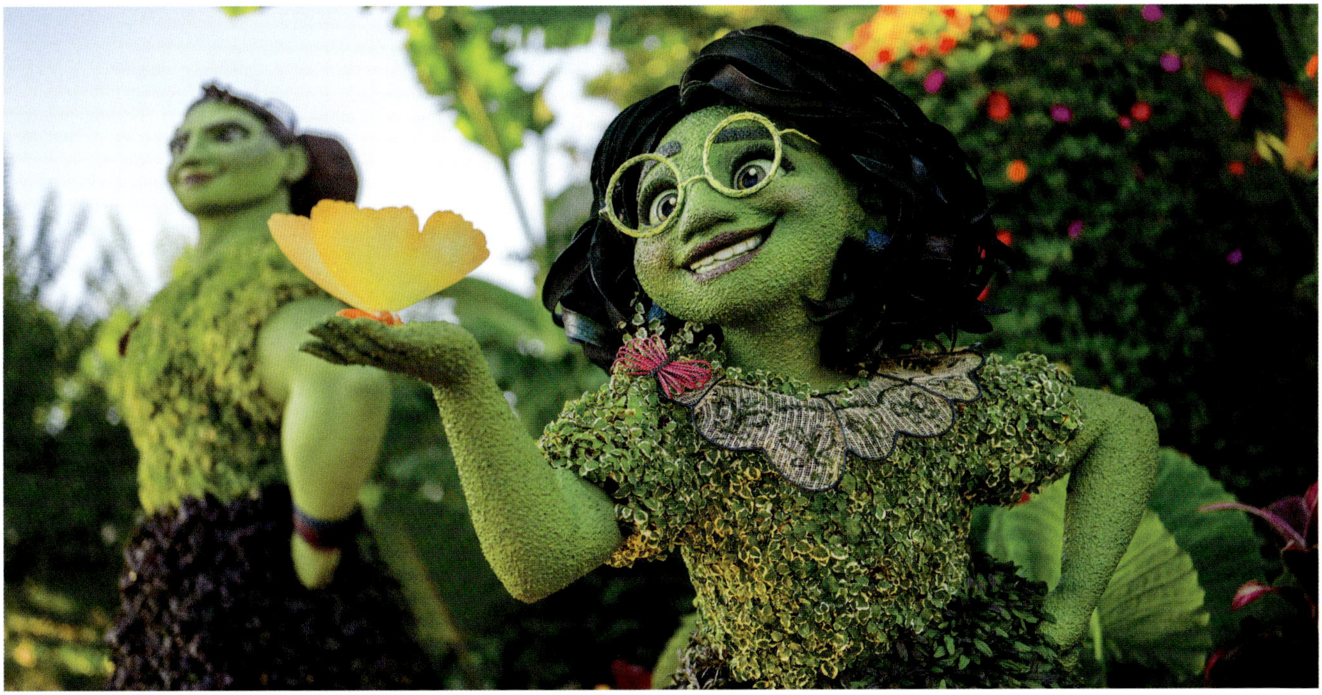

LEMON CUSTARD VERRINE
WITH BLUEBERRY COMPOTE

FESTIVAL DEBUT: 2012 · DESSERTS & CHAMPAGNE GLOBAL MARKETPLACE

A verrine is a grown-up version of a parfait, and this rich lemon custard could also be called a lemon curd. Be sure to whisk it well before stirring in the butter. Both the blueberries and the custard need time to cool before building the dessert.

SERVES 6

FROM THE WALT DISNEY WORLD RESORT

LEMON CURD

10 large pasteurized egg yolks

1 cup sugar

8 large lemons, zested and juiced (about ⅔ cup juice)

1 cup unsalted butter, chilled and cubed

BLUEBERRY COMPOTE

2¼ cups blueberries, washed and drained, divided

⅓ cup sugar

⅓ cup water

FOR LEMON CURD

1. Fill a medium saucepan with a few inches of water and place over medium-high heat. Combine egg yolks and sugar in a heatproof bowl slightly bigger than the saucepan.

2. Place bowl on top of saucepan. Whisk yolks 1 minute, then add lemon zest and juice. Whisk 6 to 8 minutes, or until mixture thickens.

3. Remove from heat and add butter, one cube at a time and stirring until fully melted before adding the next piece. Cool.

FOR BLUEBERRY COMPOTE

Heat 1¼ cups blueberries, sugar, and water in medium saucepan over medium heat, stirring occasionally, 8 to 10 minutes, or until berries burst. Stir in remaining blueberries and cook for 5 to 6 minutes until thickened. Pour into shallow container and cover with plastic wrap. Cool.

ABOVE: A sunny view of La Crêperie de Paris in the France pavilion at EPCOT, with the Disney Skyliner gondolas in the distance

FOR PIECRUST CRUMBLES

1. Preheat oven to 375°F. Mix cinnamon and sugar in a small bowl, and set aside. Place pie dough on 10-inch pizza pan. Brush pie dough with melted butter and sprinkle with cinnamon-sugar mixture.

2. Bake for 10 to 12 minutes or until light golden brown. Cool. Crumble with hands. Spread crumbles evenly and bake for 5 to 7 minutes until golden brown.

TO ASSEMBLE & SERVE

Evenly fill bottom of 6 individual 4¼-inch ramekins or one trifle bowl with Blueberry Compote. Layer Lemon Curd on top of compote. Garnish with Piecrust Crumbles.

PIECRUST CRUMBLES

1 teaspoon cinnamon

3 tablespoons sugar

1 (9-inch) rolled ready-to-bake piecrust

2 tablespoons unsalted butter, melted

WARM CHOCOLATE PUDDING
WITH IRISH CREAM CUSTARD SAUCE

FESTIVAL DEBUT: 2015 · IRELAND GLOBAL MARKETPLACE

Start by making the Irish Cream Custard Sauce so it can cool while the cakes bake. And be sure not to overbake the pudding cakes so that you have a warm liquid core.

SERVES 6

FROM THE WALT DISNEY WORLD RESORT

IRISH CREAM CUSTARD SAUCE

2 large pasteurized egg yolks

1 tablespoon cornstarch

4 tablespoons sugar, divided

1 cup milk

½ cup Irish cream liqueur

WARM CHOCOLATE PUDDING

8 ounces semisweet chocolate, chopped

1 cup unsalted butter

5 large egg yolks

4 large eggs

¾ cup sugar

⅓ cup all-purpose flour, sifted

FOR IRISH CREAM CUSTARD SAUCE

1   Whisk together the egg yolks, cornstarch, and 2 tablespoons sugar in a medium bowl, and set aside.

2   Combine the milk and the remaining sugar. Bring to a boil over medium heat, stirring constantly. Slowly pour the hot milk and sugar into the egg yolk mixture, whisking the egg yolks constantly to temper.

3   Pour back into saucepan. Cook over medium heat, whisking constantly, for 2 minutes, until custard thickens.

4   Once thickened, pour custard into a medium bowl set in an ice bath. Whisk in Irish cream liqueur and cool while warm chocolate pudding is baking.

FOR WARM CHOCOLATE PUDDING

1   Preheat oven to 375°F. Lightly butter the bottom and sides of 6 (6-ounce) ramekins. Lightly dust with sugar, shaking out any extra.

2   Melt the chocolate and butter in a double boiler or heatproof bowl on top of a saucepan of simmering water, stirring until smooth. Remove from heat and cool for 10 minutes.

OPPOSITE, BOTTOM: Guests of the 2013 EPCOT International Food & Wine Festival enjoy the offerings of the Ireland Global Marketplace.

3 Beat egg yolks and whole eggs together in a large bowl. Add sugar and whisk for 2 minutes, until sugar is fully incorporated.

4 Fold in melted chocolate. Fold in sifted flour, mixing until smooth. Evenly divide among prepared ramekins.

5 Place ramekins on a baking sheet and bake for 23 to 25 minutes, until the sides of the cakes are set and the middles are still soft. Do not overbake.

6 Cut around the sides of each cake with a knife to loosen from the ramekins. Invert onto a plate. Pour 2 to 3 tablespoons of custard sauce on top of warm pudding before serving.

PEANUT BUTTER-WHITE CHOCOLATE MOUSSE

FESTIVAL DEBUT: 2016 · *THE CHEW* EARTH EATS GLOBAL MARKETPLACE

A shot glass is the perfect portion of this rich combo of peanut butter, white chocolate, and candied peanuts.

SERVES 12

FROM THE WALT DISNEY WORLD RESORT

FOR CANDIED PEANUTS

1. Place all ingredients in a large sauté pan. Cook over medium heat, stirring frequently, until sugar is melted. Cook for an additional 5 to 7 minutes, until peanuts are golden and liquid evaporates.

2. Pour onto a silicone baking mat and top with additional coarse salt. Cool for 10 minutes. Chop candied peanuts into large pieces and set aside.

FOR WHITE CHOCOLATE MOUSSE

1. Place white chocolate chips in a medium heatproof bowl. Whisk together ½ cup heavy cream, egg yolks, and sugar in a small saucepan.

2. Cook over medium heat, whisking constantly for 3 to 5 minutes, until mixture thickens. Strain over white chocolate chips and let sit for 3 minutes.

3. Stir until white chocolate is smooth. Cool for 10 minutes. When ready, whip remaining 2 cups heavy cream, vanilla, and salt in the bowl of an electric mixer until stiff peaks form.

CANDIED PEANUTS

2 cups unsalted peanuts

½ cup light brown sugar

½ cup sugar

1 teaspoon coarse salt, plus more to taste

⅓ cup water

WHITE CHOCOLATE MOUSSE

11 ounces white chocolate chips

2½ cups heavy cream, divided

4 large pasteurized egg yolks

4 tablespoons sugar

1 teaspoon vanilla extract

1 teaspoon coarse salt

FOR PEANUT BUTTER MOUSSE

Whip heavy cream in the bowl of an electric mixer for 4 minutes, or until soft peaks form. Add peanut butter and whip for 1 to 2 minutes. Add sugar and vanilla and whip for 2 minutes, until stiff peaks form, and set aside.

TO ASSEMBLE & SERVE

1 Layer White Chocolate Mousse in bottom of each shot glass (a piping bag or large zip-top bag with a snipped corner makes it easier).

2 Top with equal amount of Peanut Butter Mousse. Repeat with layers until glass is full. Refrigerate until ready to serve. Top with Candied Peanuts to serve.

PEANUT BUTTER MOUSSE

2 cups heavy cream

1 cup creamy natural peanut butter

4 tablespoons sugar

½ teaspoon vanilla extract

OPPOSITE: Guests enjoy a snack in a doorway of Souk-Al-Magreb at the Morocco pavilion at EPCOT.

BANANA-ALMOND SOFT-SERVE SUNDAE WITH FRESH BERRIES & CRUNCHY CHOCOLATE OATS

FESTIVAL DEBUT: 2017 · THE ALMOND ORCHARD GLOBAL MARKETPLACE

This dairy-free version of a sundae starts with almond milk, with streusel for a satisfying crunch. And you can use any seasonal berries in the compote or just top with your favorite fresh berries.

SERVES 6

FROM THE WALT DISNEY WORLD RESORT

FOR CHOCOLATE, ALMOND & OAT STREUSEL

1. Preheat oven to 350°F. Toast oats and almonds on a baking sheet for 5 to 7 minutes, stirring once, until brown. Cool for 30 minutes.

2. Preheat oven to 300°F. Beat egg whites in a medium bowl. Add toasted oats and almonds and stir until coated. Stir in powdered sugar.

3. Place on a baking sheet and cook for 10 minutes until dry. Cool for 10 minutes. Add cocoa powder and place in a fine-mesh strainer to remove any excess cocoa powder, and set aside.

FOR MIXED-BERRY COMPOTE

Combine blackberries, raspberries, blueberries, lemon juice, and sugar in a small saucepan. Cook over medium heat for 5 minutes, until sugar is dissolved and liquid begins to simmer. Then in a separate small bowl, stir the orange juice and cornstarch. When ready, add juice mixture to the simmering berries and cook over medium-low heat for 3 minutes, until compote begins to thicken. Then cool for 30 minutes, until room temperature. To finish, gently fold in strawberries, and set aside.

CHOCOLATE, ALMOND & OAT STREUSEL

½ cup old-fashioned oats

½ cup slivered almonds

2 large egg whites

4 tablespoons powdered sugar

2 tablespoons unsweetened cocoa powder

MIXED-BERRY COMPOTE

½ cup blackberries

½ cup raspberries

½ cup blueberries

1 tablespoon lemon juice

½ cup sugar

3 tablespoons orange juice

1 tablespoon cornstarch

½ cup quartered strawberries

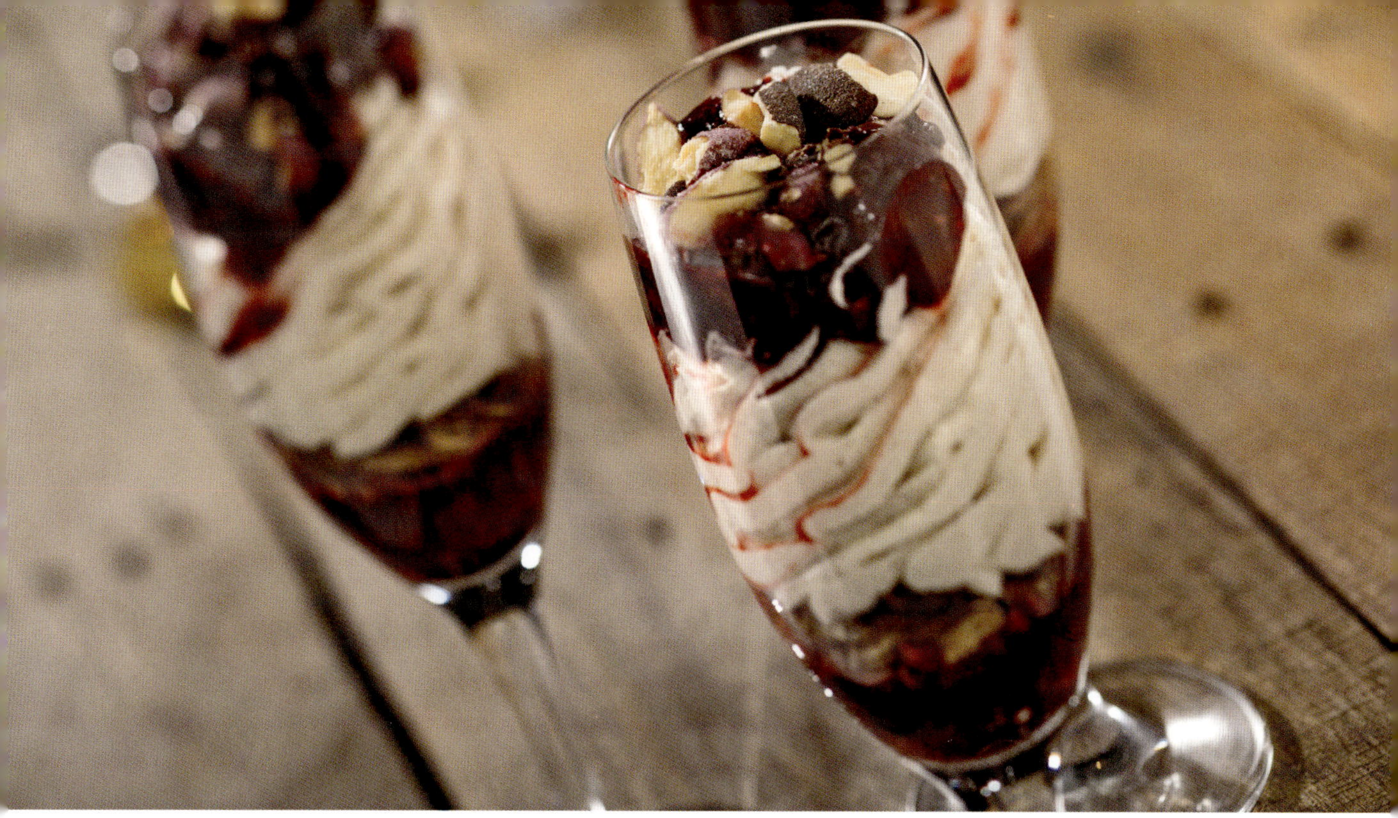

FOR BANANA SUNDAE BASE

1 Combine almond milk and sugar in a small saucepan. Cook over medium heat, stirring occasionally for 5 minutes, until sugar is dissolved. Remove from heat and stir in vanilla extract. Chill syrup in refrigerator for 1 hour, until cool.

2 Place peeled bananas and cooled almond milk syrup in a blender and purée until smooth.

3 Pour into an ice cream machine and churn for 20 minutes, until thick. Serve immediately or store in freezer until ready to use.

TO ASSEMBLE & SERVE

Place 2 tablespoons of Chocolate, Almond & Oat Streusel in a bowl. Top with ½ cup Banana Sundae Base, 4 tablespoons Mixed-Berry Compote, and 1 additional tablespoon of the streusel.

BANANA SUNDAE BASE

½ cup almond milk

½ cup sugar

1 tablespoon vanilla extract

6 large bananas, peeled

CHOCOLATE PICANTE

FESTIVAL DEBUT: 2017 · FLAVORS FROM FIRE GLOBAL MARKETPLACE

The "picante" (heat) in the chocolate mousse comes from smoked paprika, with layers of orange-scented cake that make a spicy-sweet combination. Paprika will lose its flavor over time; take a quick sniff, and if it doesn't smell like anything, it's time for a fresh jar. For a little extra heat, add a sprinkle of chili flakes!

MAKES 24 SMALL-GLASS SERVINGS

FROM THE WALT DISNEY WORLD RESORT

CHOCOLATE MOUSSE WITH SMOKED PAPRIKA
Makes about 4 cups

4 large pasteurized egg yolks

4 tablespoons sugar, divided

2 cups heavy cream, divided

8 ounces bittersweet chocolate, melted

1 teaspoon vanilla extract

1 teaspoon smoked paprika

ORANGE ZEST CAKE

1 box yellow cake mix

Zest of 1 orange

SIMPLE SYRUP

1 cup sugar

1 cup water

FOR CHOCOLATE MOUSSE WITH SMOKED PAPRIKA

1. Whisk together egg yolks, 2 tablespoons sugar, and ¾ cup heavy cream in a medium saucepan. Cook over medium-low heat for 3 to 4 minutes.

2. Remove from heat and whisk in melted chocolate and vanilla. Strain into bowl and refrigerate until cool.

3. Beat remaining heavy cream and sugar until stiff peaks form. Stir into cooled chocolate mixture with a rubber spatula. Stir in vanilla and paprika. Cover and chill.

FOR ORANGE ZEST CAKE

1. Cover a half-sheet cake pan (13 × 18-inch) with parchment paper, and set aside. Make batter according to package directions. Stir in orange zest.

2. Spread in prepared pan and bake for 20 minutes, or until a toothpick inserted in the center comes out clean. Remove from oven and cool.

FOR SIMPLE SYRUP

Stir together sugar and water in a saucepan; bring to a simmer over medium heat, stirring until sugar dissolves. Increase heat and bring to a boil; reduce heat to medium and simmer 3 minutes. Transfer to a bowl and thoroughly chill.

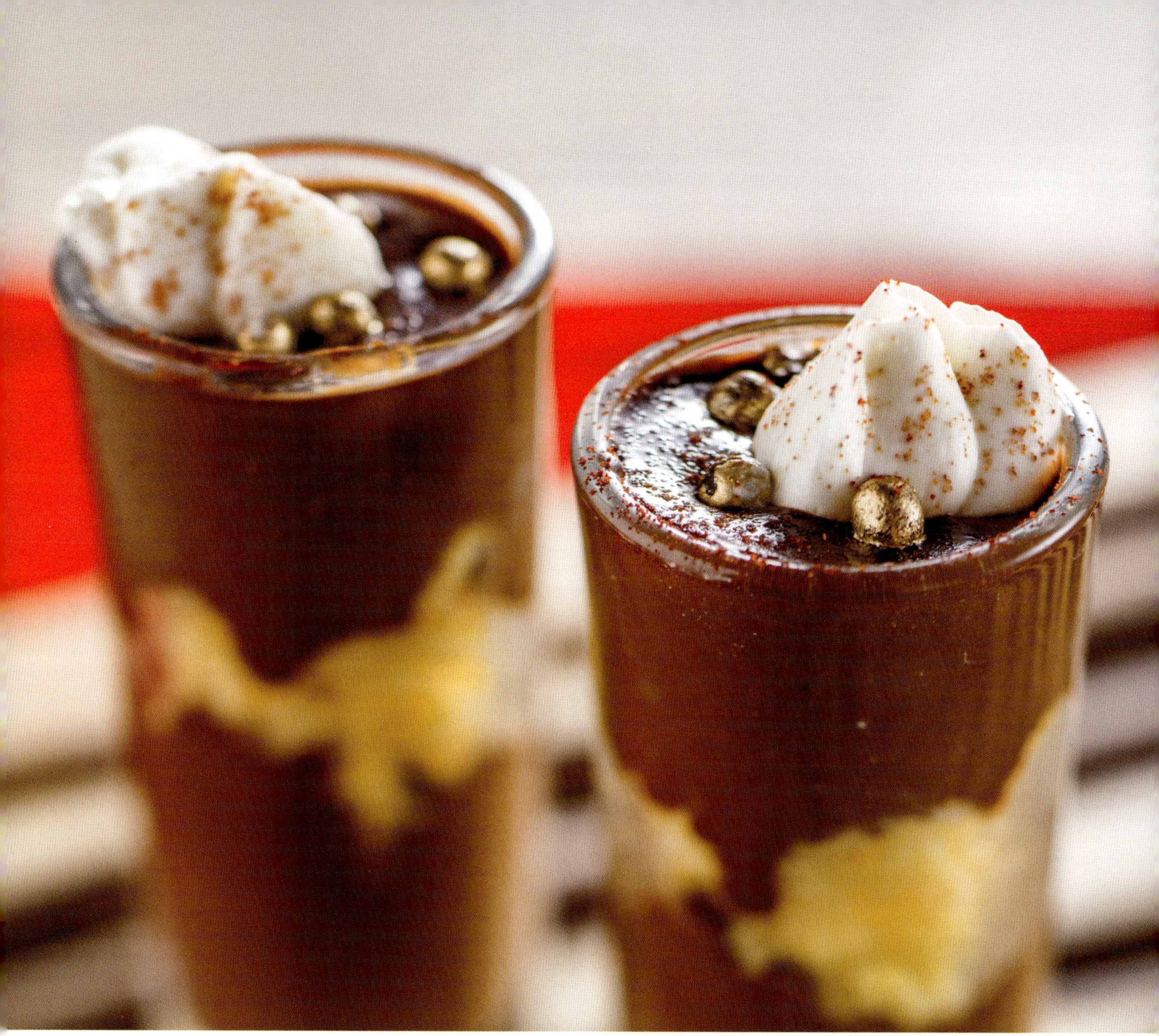

TO ASSEMBLE & SERVE

Drizzle Simple Syrup over the Orange Zest Cake. Cut cake into 24 slices to fit into 24 small dessert glasses. For each serving, layer the Chocolate Mousse with Smoked Paprika, then cake, then mousse again. (Note our photographed glasses were topped with gold crisp pearls, whipped cream, and a sprinkle of more paprika for added flair.)

OPPOSITE: Guests out and about in the Mexico pavilion at EPCOT

DECONSTRUCTED PAVLOVA

FESTIVAL DEBUT: 2019 · AUSTRALIA GLOBAL MARKETPLACE

One of the favorite desserts from the Australia Global Marketplace, this is an easier version of a classic Pavlova, with light pastry cream, fresh fruit, and crunchy meringue cookies.

MAKES 12 PAVLOVAS

FROM THE WALT DISNEY WORLD RESORT

MERINGUE KISSES

4 tablespoons meringue powder

¾ cup water

½ cup sugar

2 teaspoons vanilla extract

PASTRY CREAM

1 large pasteurized egg

2 large pasteurized egg yolks

4 tablespoons cornstarch

⅓ cup plus 4 tablespoons sugar, divided

2 cups whole or 2 percent milk

2 tablespoons unsalted butter

1 teaspoon vanilla extract

FOR MERINGUE KISSES

1. Preheat oven to 250°F. Line two baking sheets with parchment paper. In a mixer fitted with whisk attachment, whip meringue powder and water on high speed until soft peaks form.

2. Reduce to low speed and slowly add sugar. Increase to high speed and whip until stiff peaks form. Then add vanilla and whip until combined. When ready, transfer to a piping bag fitted with a large star tip. Pipe 24 meringues onto prepared baking sheets, spacing 1 inch apart.

3. Bake for 50 to 60 minutes, until meringues are firm and crisp. Cool completely before removing from parchment. Store in airtight container until ready to serve.

FOR PASTRY CREAM

1. Whisk egg, egg yolks, cornstarch, and ⅓ cup sugar together in a medium mixing bowl until smooth, and set aside.

2. Combine milk and remaining 4 tablespoons sugar in a medium saucepan. Bring to a simmer over medium heat. Slowly pour half of the simmering milk mixture into the egg and cornstarch mixture, stirring constantly.

3. Pour egg mixture into saucepan with remaining milk. Whisk constantly until pastry cream thickens. Remove from heat. Stir in butter and vanilla extract.

4 Pour into a medium bowl. Cover with plastic wrap directly on top of pastry cream. Refrigerate at least 4 hours.

FOR MACERATED CITRUS BERRIES

Place berries in a large bowl. Sprinkle sugar over berries and add orange juice and zest. Stir to combine. Cover and refrigerate for at least 1 hour, up to 2 days.

TO ASSEMBLE & SERVE

Spread 2 to 3 tablespoons of Pastry Cream on the bottom of a plate. Then place 3 tablespoons of the Macerated Citrus Berries on top of the cream. Top with 2 Meringue Kisses, and garnish with mint.

MACERATED CITRUS BERRIES

2 cups assorted berries

2 tablespoons sugar

1 orange, juiced and zested

GARNISH

Fresh mint leaves

PLANT-BASED GUAVA MOUSSE ON A SUGAR COOKIE

FESTIVAL DEBUT: 2022 · SHIMMERING SIPS GLOBAL MARKETPLACE

The taste of guava is a tangy cross between a pear and a strawberry and makes a light and refreshing combination with the crunch of the sugar cookie in this recipe. Add plant-based whipped cream, and it's a fancy finale.

MAKES 12 SERVINGS

FROM THE WALT DISNEY WORLD RESORT

FOR PLANT-BASED GUAVA MOUSSE

1 Place white chocolate in a medium bowl, and set aside. Then stir sugar and agar-agar together in a small bowl, and set aside.

2 Heat guava pulp in a small saucepan over medium-high heat until simmering. Add agar-agar-sugar mixture and whisk constantly until dissolved.

3 Pour simmering mixture over white chocolate. Let it rest for 2 minutes, then stir until white chocolate is smooth. Cool at room temperature for 30 minutes.

4 While guava mixture is cooling, whip dairy-free whipping cream in the bowl of an electric mixer fitted with a whisk attachment until soft peaks form.

5 Fold whipped cream into cooled guava mixture. Then spread into twelve 1½ × 4½ × 1–inch rectangular silicone molds and freeze for at least 4 hours.

6 If you want an extra-glossy finish, spray pink and orange aerosol food coloring on the frozen mousse before placing on each cookie in the To Assemble & Serve step.

PLANT-BASED GUAVA MOUSSE

2½ cups plant-based white chocolate chips

1 tablespoon sugar

1½ teaspoons agar-agar

1 cup guava pulp

1½ cups dairy-free whipping cream

Pink and orange aerosol food coloring, optional

OPPOSITE: Guests around World Showcase at EPCOT watch Luminous The Symphony of Us, 2024.

FOR PLANT-BASED SUGAR COOKIE

1. Cream sugar and plant-based butter substitute in the bowl of an electric mixer fitted with a paddle attachment until fluffy. Add egg substitute and vanilla extract.

2. Beat on low speed for 1 minute, until egg substitute is fully incorporated. Slowly add salt, all-purpose flour, and cake flour and mix until fully incorporated.

3. Roll dough into a ball and flatten into a disk. Wrap in plastic wrap and refrigerate for 30 minutes.

4. Preheat oven to 325°F. Line a baking sheet with parchment paper, and set aside. Dust a large cutting board with flour. Remove dough from refrigerator and roll to ¼-inch thick.

5. Cut into 12 (1½ × 4½–inch) rectangles and place on prepared baking sheet. Bake for 12 to 15 minutes, until golden brown. Cool completely before serving.

FOR COCONUT WHIPPED CREAM

Whip dairy-free whipping cream and coconut milk in the bowl of an electric mixer fitted with a whisk, on high speed until stiff peaks form. Transfer to a piping bag with a pastry tip. Refrigerate until ready to serve.

FOR TOASTED COCONUT

Preheat oven to 300°F. Place shredded coconut on a small baking sheet. Bake, stirring every 2 minutes, for 8 to 10 minutes, until golden brown.

TO ASSEMBLE & SERVE

Remove Plant-Based Guava Mousse from silicone molds. Place mousse on top of Plant-Based Sugar Cookies, then pipe a ribbon of Coconut Whipped Cream down the center of each dessert. Top with Toasted Coconut.

PLANT-BASED SUGAR COOKIE

½ cup sugar

½ cup plant-based butter substitute, softened

⅓ cup liquid egg substitute

½ teaspoon vanilla extract

¼ teaspoon salt

1 cup all-purpose flour

1 cup cake flour

COCONUT WHIPPED CREAM

½ cup dairy-free whipping cream

4 tablespoons coconut milk

TOASTED COCONUT

1 cup shredded coconut

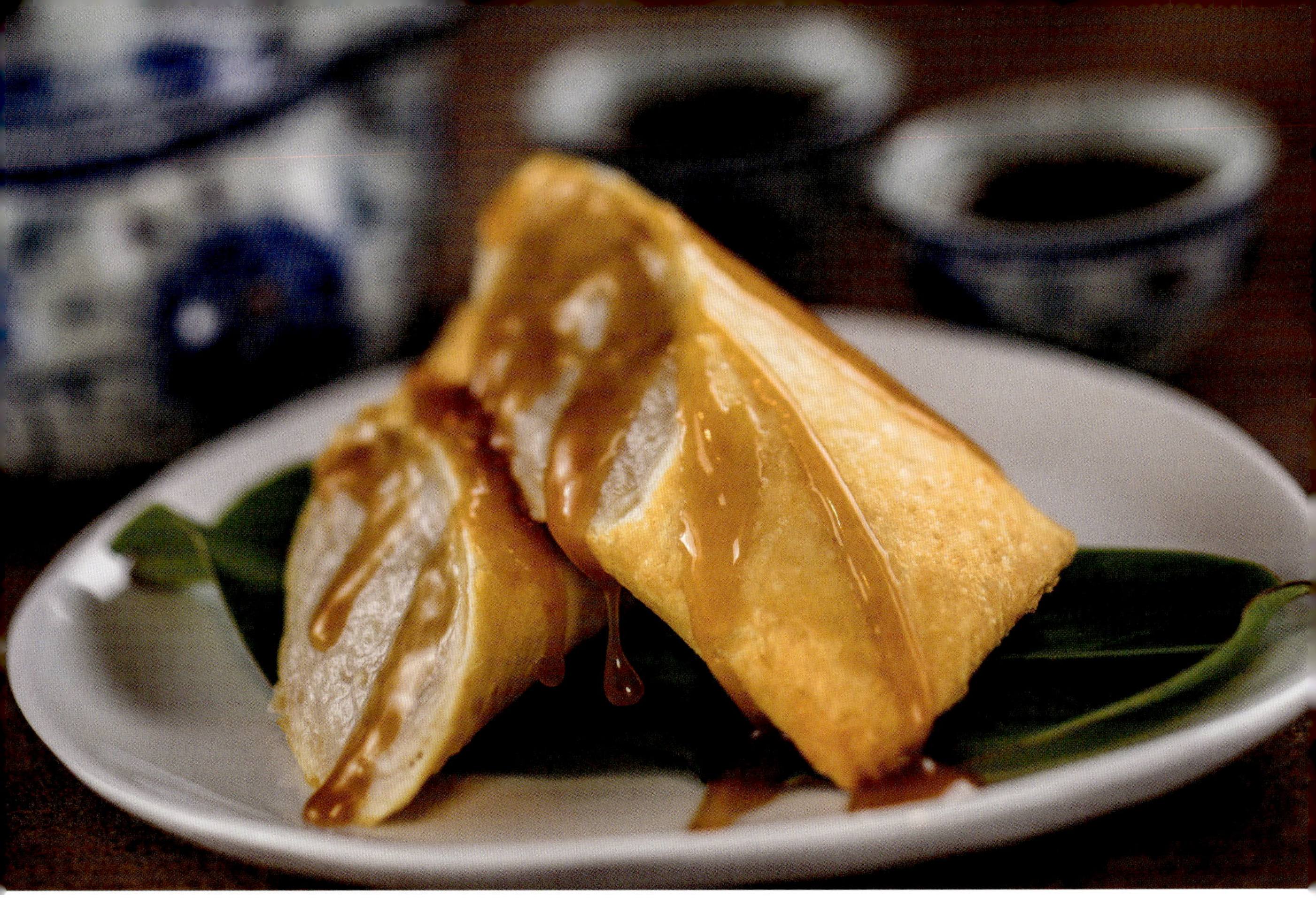

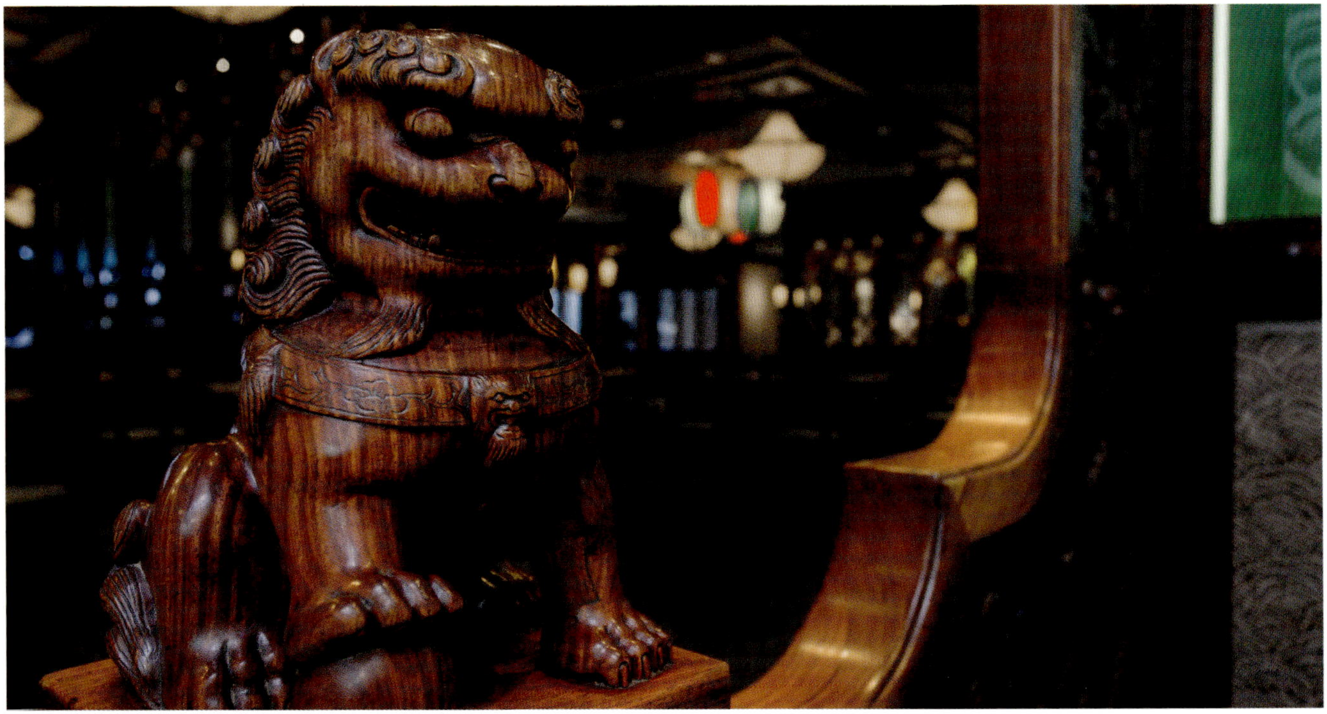

BANANA EGG ROLLS

REMEMBERED FROM NINE DRAGONS RESTAURANT

Nine Dragons Restaurant has been a favorite in World Showcase at EPCOT since 1985 and features Chinese cuisine from many provinces. This "egg roll" uses a flour tortilla for a deep-fried sweet—serve it hot with ice cream or a drizzle of store-bought caramel sauce.

SERVES 6

FROM THE WALT DISNEY WORLD RESORT

BANANA FILLING

8-ounce package cream cheese, softened

¾ cup sugar

½ teaspoon salt

½ teaspoon banana essence

6 medium bananas, peeled and diced

EGG ROLLS

Oil, for frying

12 flour tortillas

TOPPINGS

Ice cream

Caramel sauce

FOR BANANA FILLING

1   Place cream cheese in the bowl of an electric mixer fitted with a paddle attachment and beat until smooth. Slowly add sugar, salt, and banana essence and cream until fluffy. Then fold in diced bananas.

2   Prepare a double boiler or heat-safe bowl over a pot of simmering water. Pour banana filling into double boiler and cook for 10 minutes, until it begins to bubble.

3   Pour into a medium bowl and cool to room temperature. Refrigerate for 8 hours, until set.

FOR EGG ROLLS

1   With caution, preheat oil in deep fryer to 350°F. Place flour tortilla on a clean surface. Spoon 4 tablespoons banana filling near bottom edge of tortilla.

2   Roll banana filling in the tortilla one roll, then fold in edges and continue rolling. Seal edges with a small amount of water. Repeat with remaining tortillas.

3   When ready, carefully fry for 6 minutes, or until golden brown. Drain on paper towels.

TO SERVE

Cut 2 Egg Rolls in half and place in a bowl. Place a scoop of ice cream in the center of the bowl and drizzle with caramel sauce.

OPPOSITE, BOTTOM: An entryway statue within Nine Dragons Restaurant in the China pavilion at EPCOT

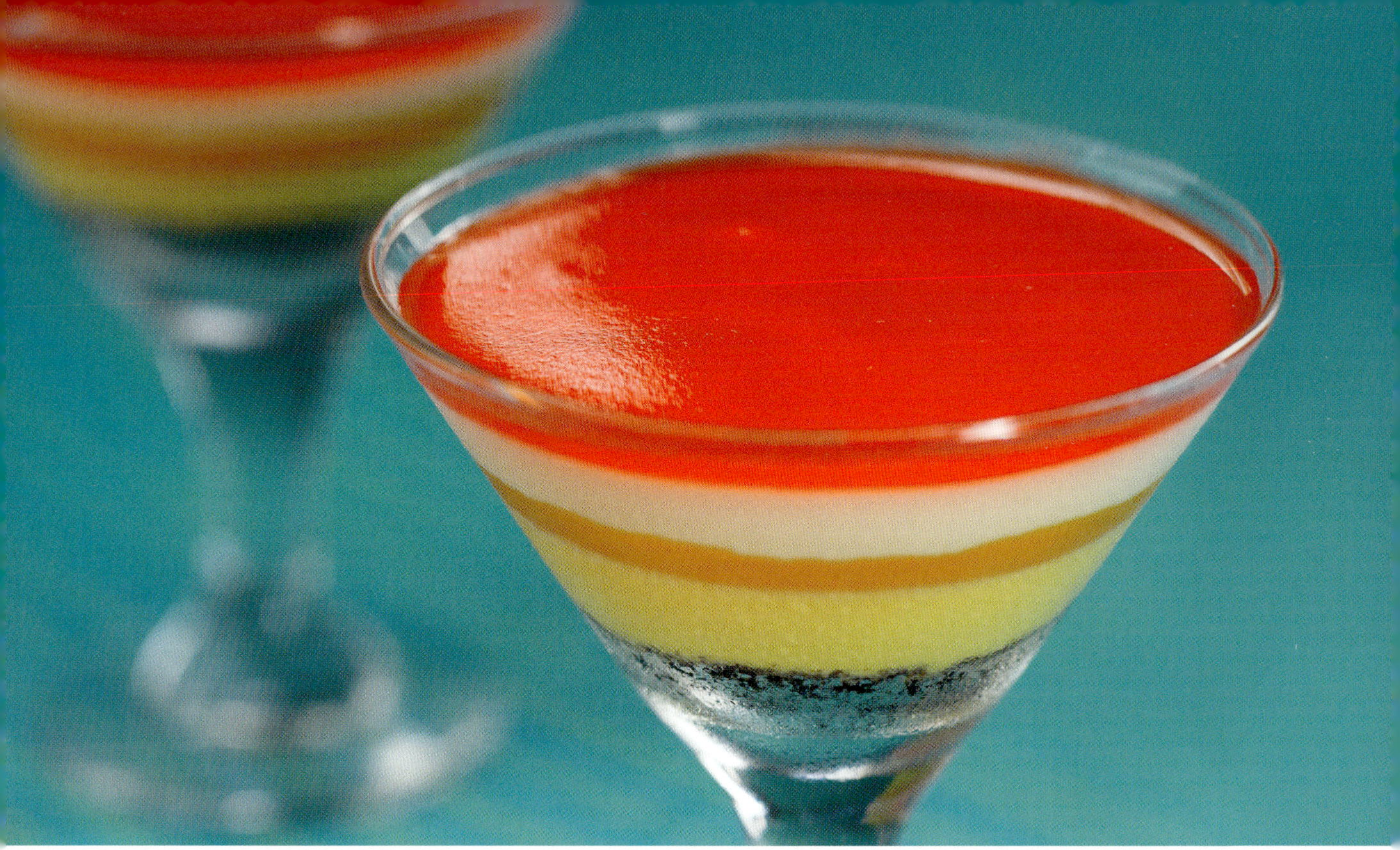

PASSION FRUIT-COCONUT PARFAIT

FESTIVAL DEBUT: 2014 · DESSERTS & CHAMPAGNE GLOBAL MARKETPLACE

A double dose of mousse—passion fruit and coconut—takes a little time and needs to be refrigerated and then frozen, but patience pays off in this elegant sweet ending.

SERVES 8

FROM THE WALT DISNEY WORLD RESORT

CHOCOLATE CRUST

1 ½ cups chocolate cookie crumbs

2 tablespoons unsalted butter, melted

FOR CHOCOLATE CRUST

Combine cookie crumbs and melted butter in a small bowl until mixture is uniform, and set aside.

FOR PASSION FRUIT MOUSSE

1 Place white chocolate chips in a heatproof bowl set over a small saucepan of simmering water, making sure bottom of bowl does not touch water.

2 Melt chocolate, stirring frequently. Remove from heat, and set aside. Sprinkle gelatin over 1 cup heavy cream in a small saucepan, and set aside for 5 minutes.

3 Heat over low heat, whisking gently until gelatin is melted. Do not allow to simmer or boil. Whisk egg yolk into melted white chocolate. Mixture will get very thick and grainy.

4 Heat passion fruit purée until simmering in a small saucepan over medium-high heat, and set aside. Pour warm cream-gelatin mixture over white chocolate mixture, whisking until smooth.

5 Add hot passion fruit purée (or juice concentrate), whisking to combine, and set aside until room temperature. Whisk remaining 1 cup heavy cream to soft peaks using an electric mixer.

6 Pour a third of the passion fruit mixture into whipped cream, gently folding to combine. Repeat with remaining passion fruit mixture, adding a third at a time and gently folding until just combined. Mixture will be liquid and will not thicken.

7 Cover with plastic wrap, pressing wrap directly on surface of mousse. Refrigerate 6 to 8 hours, or until firm.

FOR COCONUT MOUSSE

1 Place white chocolate chips in a heatproof bowl set over a small saucepan of simmering water, making sure bottom of bowl does not touch water.

2 Melt chocolate, stirring frequently. Remove from heat and set aside. Sprinkle gelatin over 1 cup heavy cream in a small saucepan, and set aside for 5 minutes.

PASSION FRUIT MOUSSE

1 cup white chocolate chips

2 (¼-ounce) packages plus 1 teaspoon powdered gelatin

2 cups heavy cream, divided

1 large pasteurized egg yolk

2 cups passion fruit purée or juice concentrate

COCONUT MOUSSE

1 cup white chocolate chips

2 (¼-ounce) packages plus 1 teaspoon powdered gelatin

2 cups heavy cream, divided

1 large pasteurized egg yolk

2 cups coconut milk

2 tablespoons coconut liqueur

1 cup sweetened shredded coconut

ABOVE: Guests dine al fresco at the Italy pavilion at EPCOT, 2024.

RECIPE CONTINUES ON NEXT PAGE

PASSION FRUIT-COCONUT PARFAIT

(CONTINUED)

3 Heat over low heat, whisking gently until gelatin is melted. Do not allow to simmer or boil. Whisk egg yolk into melted white chocolate. Mixture will get very thick and grainy.

4 Heat coconut milk until simmering in a small saucepan over medium-high heat, and set aside. Pour warm cream-gelatin mixture over white chocolate mixture, whisking until smooth.

5 Add hot coconut milk, whisking to combine, and set aside until room temperature. Whisk coconut liqueur and remaining 1 cup heavy cream to soft peaks using an electric mixer.

6 Pour a third of the coconut mixture into whipped cream, gently folding to combine. Repeat with remaining coconut mixture, adding a third at a time and gently folding until just combined. Fold in shredded coconut. Mixture will be liquid and will not thicken.

7 Cover with plastic wrap, pressing wrap directly on surface of mousse. Refrigerate until firm, 6 to 8 hours.

FOR TROPICAL FRUIT GLAZE

Combine fruit purée (or juice concentrate) and gelatin in a small saucepan; heat, stirring, until gelatin melts. Add a few drops of red food coloring, if desired.

TO ASSEMBLE & SERVE

1 Place cookie crumb mixture in the bottom of a 9-inch trifle dish, pressing until flat. Spoon 2 cups Passion Fruit Mousse over cookie crust.

2 Freeze 30 minutes until top is firm. Pour ½ cup fruit glaze on top. Freeze 30 minutes or until firm. Spread 2 cups Coconut Mousse atop glaze.

3 Freeze 30 minutes until top is firm. Pour remaining ½ cup glaze on top. Refrigerate 1 hour before serving.

TROPICAL FRUIT GLAZE

1 cup pre-blended tropical fruit purée or juice concentrate (recommended fruits include banana, guava, lime, lychee, mango, and passion fruit)

Half of a (¼-ounce) package powdered gelatin

Red food coloring, optional

ABOVE: A view of a FriendShip boat gliding along World Showcase Lagoon from the Italy pavilion at EPCOT, 2022

MAPLE CRÈME BRÛLÉE

Here's a classic with a dash of pure maple extract. If you don't have a kitchen torch, you can broil just until the sugar starts to caramelize, then chill until the topping hardens.

SERVES 6

FROM THE WALT DISNEY WORLD RESORT

1 Preheat oven to 325°F. Place 6 (¾-cup) custard ramekins in a large roasting pan. Then combine cream, milk, and sugar in a medium saucepan over medium heat.

2 Slowly bring mixture to a simmer, whisking constantly to dissolve sugar. When sugar is dissolved, stir every few minutes while the mixture is heating to avoid scalding.

3 When small bubbles appear around the edges, remove milk mixture from heat. Whisk egg yolks and maple extract together in a large bowl.

4 Slowly add hot cream mixture to egg yolk mixture, whisking constantly. Then divide among custard cups in pan, and pour enough hot water into roasting pan to come halfway up sides of custard cups.

5 Bake custard until center moves only slightly when cups are gently shaken, about 55 minutes. Remove custard cups from pan. Refrigerate until thoroughly cool.

6 Sprinkle 2 teaspoons sugar evenly over each custard. Working with one custard at a time, hold kitchen torch so that flame is 2 inches above surface.

7 Direct flame so that sugar melts and browns, about 2 minutes. (If you don't have a kitchen torch, place ramekins on small baking sheet in preheated broiler. Broil until sugar just starts to caramelize, rotating sheet for even browning, about 2 minutes; then chill until topping hardens, about 2 hours.) Garnish with blackberry preserves and tuile.

2¾ cups heavy cream

½ cup whole or 2 percent milk

½ cup plus 2 tablespoons sugar

9 large egg yolks

1½ tablespoons pure maple extract

12 teaspoons sugar for caramelized topping

Blackberry preserves, for garnish

Your favorite tuile, for garnish

COCONUT–KEY LIME SUNDAE

You'll need to plan ahead (and have an ice cream maker), but this is a dazzling finale with coconut ice cream and a dollop of white chocolate–key lime cream topped with roasted pineapple and the crunch of sea salt brittle. Every element adds pizzazz.

MAKES 8 SMALL-DISH SERVINGS

FROM THE WALT DISNEY WORLD RESORT

FOR COCONUT ICE CREAM

1. Preset oven to 350°F. Place coconut on a sheet pan and bake until golden brown, stirring once, 5 to 6 minutes.

2. Combine milk, cream, and cream of coconut in a small saucepan over low heat. Heat until steam begins to rise from the pan.

3. Remove from heat and add toasted coconut. Cover and steep 15 minutes. Strain mixture through a fine-mesh strainer into a medium bowl; discard coconut.

4. Place bowl with milk-cream mixture into a larger bowl filled with ice water. Stir until mixture is cool.

5. Pour mixture into an ice cream maker and freeze according to the manufacturer's directions. Freeze ice cream overnight.

FOR WHITE CHOCOLATE–KEY LIME CREAM

1. Place lime zest and juice into a small bowl. Sprinkle with gelatin, and set aside. Place white chocolate chips and milk in a medium bowl set over a small saucepan filled with a few inches of water.

2. Place pan over medium-high heat and bring water to a simmer. Then stir white chocolate chips and milk until white chocolate melts and mixture is uniform.

COCONUT ICE CREAM

1 cup sweetened shredded coconut

1 cup milk

1½ cups heavy cream

1 (14-ounce) can cream of coconut

WHITE CHOCOLATE–KEY LIME CREAM

1 teaspoon finely grated key lime zest

4 tablespoons fresh key lime juice

Half of a (¼-ounce) package powdered gelatin

1 cup white chocolate chips

4 tablespoons whole or 2 percent milk

¾ cup heavy cream

3   Remove bowl from saucepan and add lime-gelatin mixture until totally combined. Whip cream with an electric mixer to soft peaks. Fold whipped cream into white chocolate mixture. Refrigerate overnight.

FOR SPICED RUM–ROASTED PINEAPPLE

1   Preheat oven to 375°F. Whisk together brown sugar, rum, and orange juice. Stir in vanilla bean seeds.

2   Place pineapple quarters in a baking dish; pour brown sugar mixture over pineapple, turning to coat, and set aside for 30 minutes.

3   Roast uncovered 1 hour or until soft and golden brown. Cool pineapple in roasting liquid; refrigerate overnight. Before serving, cut into ½-inch cubes and store in roasting liquid.

SPICED RUM–ROASTED PINEAPPLE

4 tablespoons light brown sugar

4 tablespoons spiced rum

4 tablespoons orange juice

1 vanilla bean, split lengthwise, seeds scraped out and reserved

1 small pineapple, peeled, cored, and cut in quarters

RECIPE CONTINUES ON NEXT PAGE

COCONUT-KEY LIME SUNDAE

(CONTINUED)

FOR MACADAMIA-SEA SALT BRITTLE

1 Preheat oven to 350°F. Place macadamia nuts on a baking sheet; bake, stirring once, until golden, 4 to 6 minutes.

2 Line a separate baking sheet with parchment paper and spray with nonstick cooking spray, and set aside. Cool macadamia nuts to room temperature, then coarsely chop, and set aside.

3 Combine sugar, corn syrup, and water in a small saucepan over medium heat. Heat until mixture reaches 300°F on a candy thermometer, about 25 to 30 minutes.

4 When mixture reaches 300°F, stir in butter and macadamia nuts until butter melts and nuts are fully coated, 1 to 2 minutes.

5 Remove pan from heat and stir in vanilla extract and baking powder. Pour the mixture onto the prepared baking sheet, quickly spreading with an offset spatula or the back of a spoon.

6 Sprinkle with salt; set aside for at least 1 hour, or until completely hardened, then break into 8 pieces.

TO ASSEMBLE & SERVE

1 Evenly divide half of Coconut Ice Cream among 8 small dessert bowls or rocks glasses. Whip White Chocolate–Key Lime Cream to soften it. Dollop cream over ice cream.

2 Spoon 2 tablespoons Spiced Rum–Roasted Pineapple over the White Chocolate–Key Lime Cream. Then top each serving with remaining ice cream and White Chocolate–Key Lime Cream. Top each serving with a piece of Macadamia–Sea Salt Brittle.

MACADAMIA-SEA SALT BRITTLE

1 cup macadamia nuts

1 cup sugar

½ cup light corn syrup

½ cup water

1 tablespoon unsalted butter, softened

½ teaspoon vanilla extract

1 teaspoon baking powder

½ teaspoon coarse sea salt

OPPOSITE: Mickey Mouse greets guests at Topolino's Terrace – Flavors of the Riviera.

PISTACHIO MOUSSE WITH LEMON CURD & COFFEE-HAZELNUT CUSTARD

REMEMBERED FROM TOPOLINO'S TERRACE – FLAVORS OF THE RIVIERA

There are multiple steps to this elegant dessert—start with the pistachio mousse, which needs to freeze for four hours. A biscuit sans farine is simply a flourless biscuit spread on a baking sheet and cut after baking.

SERVES 12

FROM THE WALT DISNEY WORLD RESORT

BISCUIT SANS FARINE

10 large egg yolks

1 cup sugar, divided

5 large egg whites

2 tablespoons unsweetened cocoa powder

LEMON CURD

6 tablespoons lemon juice

1½ teaspoons lemon zest

½ cup sugar, divided

4 large pasteurized egg yolks

5 tablespoons unsalted butter

FOR BISCUIT SANS FARINE

1 Preheat oven to 325°F. Line baking sheet with parchment paper or a silicone baking mat. Whip 10 egg yolks and ½ cup sugar in mixer fitted with a whisk attachment until thick and pale.

2 Transfer mixture to separate bowl. Then place 5 egg whites in the bowl of an electric mixer fitted with a whisk attachment and whip until soft peaks form.

3 Slowly add remaining ½ cup sugar and whip to stiff peaks. Then fold egg yolk mixture into egg white mixture.

4 Sift cocoa powder into mixture and gently fold with spatula. Then spread into prepared baking pan and bake for 15 minutes, until biscuit begins to pull away from sides of pan. Cool completely before serving.

FOR LEMON CURD

1 Combine lemon juice, lemon zest, and 4 tablespoons sugar in double boiler and cook over simmering water until warm but not simmering.

2 Whisk the remaining 4 tablespoons sugar with the egg yolks in a medium bowl. Add half of the warm lemon mixture to the eggs, whisking constantly.

RECIPE CONTINUES ON NEXT PAGE

PISTACHIO MOUSSE WITH LEMON CURD & COFFEE-HAZELNUT CUSTARD

3 Pour egg mixture into remaining lemon mixture in double boiler and whisk constantly until thickened. Remove lemon curd from heat and allow to cool for 20 minutes.

4 Cut butter into 1-tablespoon pieces and whisk into lemon curd. Cover with plastic wrap and refrigerate for 4 hours, until set.

FOR COFFEE-HAZELNUT CUSTARD

1 Place hazelnuts in food processor and pulse until finely ground. Bloom gelatin in water in a small bowl for 5 minutes.

2 Combine milk and espresso in a small saucepan. Bring to simmer over medium heat.

3 Whisk egg yolk and sugar together in a small bowl. Add to simmering milk mixture and whisk until slightly thickened. Add gelatin and whisk until dissolved.

4 Place milk chocolate and ground hazelnuts in medium bowl. Pour milk-espresso mixture over chocolate and nuts, and stir until combined. Let it rest at room temperature for 15 minutes.

5 Place heavy cream in the bowl of an electric mixer fitted with a whisk attachment. Whip to soft peaks. Fold heavy cream into custard mixture. Allow to set in refrigerator.

FOR PISTACHIO MOUSSE DOMES

1 Bloom gelatin in water in a small bowl for 5 minutes. Then combine milk, vanilla extract, and pistachio paste in a small saucepan, and bring to simmer over medium heat.

2 Whisk egg yolks and sugar together in a small bowl. Add to simmering milk mixture and whisk until slightly thickened. Add gelatin.

COFFEE-HAZELNUT CUSTARD

¾ cup hazelnuts

Half of a (¼-ounce) package powdered gelatin

2 tablespoons cold water

2 tablespoons milk

2 tablespoons espresso

1 large pasteurized egg yolk

1 tablespoon sugar

4 tablespoons heavy cream

1 cup milk chocolate chips

PISTACHIO MOUSSE DOMES

1 (¼-ounce) package powdered gelatin

4 tablespoons water

¾ cup milk

1 teaspoon vanilla extract

1½ tablespoons pistachio paste

2 large pasteurized egg yolks

⅓ cup sugar

¾ cup heavy cream

Lemon Curd

Coffee-Hazelnut Custard

3 Pour mixture into a medium bowl and cool for 15 minutes at room temperature. Then place heavy cream in the bowl of an electric mixer fitted with a whisk attachment. Whip to soft peaks.

4 Fold heavy cream into pistachio mixture. Spoon 2 tablespoons of pistachio mousse into 2-inch silicone dome molds.

5 Spoon 1 tablespoon reserved Lemon Curd and 1 tablespoon Coffee-Hazelnut Custard into each mold. Then fill the rest of the mold with pistachio mousse. Freeze for 4 hours, until solid.

FOR CHERRY REDUCTION

Place cherry juice, sugar, vanilla extract, and red wine in a small saucepan. Bring to simmer over medium heat. Reduce heat and continue simmering until liquid is reduced by half. Fold in cherries. Refrigerate until ready to serve.

TO ASSEMBLE & SERVE

Cut cooled Biscuit Sans Farine using 2-inch circle cutter. Place each circle on a plate and top with a Pistachio Mousse Dome and a drizzle of Cherry Reduction.

CHERRY REDUCTION

½ cup cherry juice

4 tablespoons sugar

1 teaspoon vanilla extract

4 tablespoons red wine

1½ cups frozen cherries, thawed

PANNA "CARPA"

The sophisticated interior of Flying Fish pays homage to the golden era of seaside boardwalk dining. This delicate Panna "Carpa" was the seafood restaurant's take on a classic chilled panna cotta in a "pool" of strawberry consommé. It's a great one to make ahead of time and assemble just before serving.

SERVES 6

FROM THE WALT DISNEY WORLD RESORT

FOR BUTTERMILK PANNA COTTA

1. Add the buttermilk to a medium bowl. Sprinkle gelatin over buttermilk and set aside. Heat cream, milk, and sugar in a medium saucepan over medium heat, stirring occasionally.

2. Once sugar dissolves and liquid is steaming, remove from heat. Then carefully pour hot cream mixture over buttermilk and gelatin, whisking to combine. Whisk in vanilla.

3. Evenly divide mixture between silicone molds of your choice. A silicone muffin mold will work for this recipe. Chill until set, at least 4 hours or overnight. For easier removal from molds, after they are chilled, place in freezer for 4 to 6 hours.

FOR STRAWBERRY CONSOMMÉ

1. Trim tops off strawberries and cut into quarters. Place strawberries, raspberries, sugar, lime zest, lime juice, and salt in the top of a double boiler.

2. Cover and cook over simmering water until the berries look pale, about 2 hours. Strain, reserving the juice and discarding fruit pulp. Refrigerate until ready to serve.

BUTTERMILK PANNA COTTA

½ cup buttermilk

1 (¼-ounce) package powdered gelatin

2 cups heavy cream

½ cup whole or 2 percent milk

¾ cup sugar

½ teaspoon vanilla

STRAWBERRY CONSOMMÉ

2 cups fresh strawberries

¾ cup fresh raspberries

½ cup sugar

1 lime, zested and juiced

⅛ teaspoon salt

ABOVE: Beautiful and bubbly ceiling fixtures at Flying Fish

FOR CHOCOLATE "FIN" GARNISH

1 Melt chocolate chips in a microwave-safe bowl on low heat for 30 seconds. Stir and microwave on low for additional 10-second increments if necessary to melt. Do not overheat.

2 Place a dollop of chocolate about the size of a nickel on a piece of parchment paper. Using the back of a spoon, spread the chocolate in an upward, across, and down motion to resemble a fin. (Fins can be remelted to reshape if necessary.)

3 Sprinkle each fin with sea salt before chocolate sets. Fins can be refrigerated to set, if desired.

TO ASSEMBLE & SERVE

1 Pop Buttermilk Panna Cotta out of silicone mold and place in a shallow serving dish. Allow several minutes to let it thaw, if frozen.

2 Peel the Chocolate "Fin" Garnish off parchment, and set aside. Pour Strawberry Consommé around bottom of panna cotta. Just before serving, stick a fin garnish in top of the panna cotta.

CHOCOLATE "FIN" GARNISH

4 tablespoons chocolate chips

¼ teaspoon sea salt flakes

ROASTED WHITE CHOCOLATE BUDINO

Roasting the chocolate for this version of the creamy Italian custard is worth the time it takes, adding hints of butterscotch and toasted marshmallow. You can buy amaretti cookies or make them ahead of time.

SERVES 6

FROM THE WALT DISNEY WORLD RESORT

FOR BUDINO

1. Preheat oven to 250°F. Place white chocolate chips in a shallow baking dish. Bake for 10 minutes and stir. Cook for an additional 30 to 60 minutes, stirring every 10 minutes. Color should be medium caramel.

2. Using a rubber spatula, scrape chocolate into a medium bowl. Then sprinkle gelatin over 4 tablespoons milk in a separate small bowl.

3. Combine remaining ¾ cup milk, heavy cream, and corn syrup in a saucepan and bring to a boil. Remove from heat and mix in the gelatin-milk mixture, whisking until fully dissolved.

4. Pour hot cream mixture over roasted chocolate, whisking to combine. Divide evenly between 6 serving glasses. Refrigerate until set, at least 2 hours. (Note our photographed glasses were topped with whipped cream and a maraschino cherry for added flair.)

FOR AMARETTI COOKIES

1. Preheat oven to 325°F. Line two baking sheets with parchment paper. Beat almond paste with an electric mixer until crumbly.

2. Beat in egg whites until mixture is smooth. Sift in powdered sugar and all-purpose flour, beating until just combined, about 1 minute.

BUDINO

1¾ cups white chocolate chips

1 (¼-ounce) package powdered gelatin

1 cup whole or 2 percent milk, divided

1 cup plus 1 tablespoon heavy cream

1 teaspoon light corn syrup

AMARETTI COOKIES
Makes 30 cookies

½ cup plus 3 tablespoons almond paste

2 large egg whites

¾ cup plus 1 tablespoon powdered sugar

2 tablespoons all-purpose flour

½ cup plus 1 tablespoon almond flour

3 Stir in almond flour with a wooden spoon. (Dough will be sticky.) Then scoop rounded teaspoons of dough onto prepared baking sheets, about 2 inches apart. Use water to lightly wet scoop before working with dough.

4 Bake until cookies rise, crack slightly, and are golden brown, about 12 to 15 minutes. Remove from oven and cool completely before removing from baking sheet with a thin metal spatula. Store in an airtight container.

RASPBERRY GELATO (DAIRY-FREE)

This recipe goes all the way back to 2006 and stays in rotation for an easy light dessert with just five ingredients. We love serving it in a martini glass with fresh mint and a splash of Champagne.

SERVES 4-6

FROM THE WALT DISNEY WORLD RESORT

1. In a medium saucepan, heat the sugar and spring water until the sugar dissolves. Remove from heat and cool.

2. In a blender or food processor, purée the raspberries, and then strain the seeds and transfer purée to small mixing bowl. (If using store-bought raspberry purée, place purée directly in small mixing bowl.) Then add the sugar syrup along with the lemon juice and raspberry-blackberry liqueur. Refrigerate until cold.

3. Pour the cold mixture into an ice cream maker. Fill the machine only halfway, as the mixture will expand as it freezes. Freeze according to ice cream maker instructions.

1 cup sugar

½ cup spring water

4 cups fresh or frozen raspberries, or 1 cup raspberry purée

Juice of ½ lemon

2 tablespoons raspberry-blackberry liqueur

ABOVE: A view of Disney's Beach Club Resort from the Stormalong Bay pool area it shares with its neighbor, Disney's Yacht Club Resort

HAUPIA WITH MANGO COMPOTE

This coconut pudding is a classic taste of the Hawaiian Islands, often served at luaus. It's the perfect dessert to make when mangoes are in season, pairing the creamy coconut with the succulent, sweet mango fruit.

SERVES 4

FROM BEYOND THE DISNEY PARKS

HAUPIA

1 (14½-ounce) can coconut milk, divided

6 tablespoons cornstarch

⅓ cup water

4 tablespoons sugar

3 tablespoons shredded coconut, toasted

MANGO COMPOTE

1 mango, peeled, cut away from pit, and diced small

1 small lime, washed

1 teaspoon orange blossom honey, heated until thin

GARNISH

4 large marshmallows, toasted, optional

Zest of 1 small lime, washed, optional

FOR HAUPIA

1. Combine ½ cup coconut milk and cornstarch in a small bowl, stirring until smooth. Set aside. Combine remaining coconut milk, water, and sugar in a small saucepan over medium heat. Stir until sugar is dissolved.

2. Drizzle cornstarch mixture slowly into saucepan, whisking constantly. Cook, whisking vigorously (do not let boil) until mixture is very thick and no longer tastes floury, 4 to 6 minutes.

3. Pour into 4 (½-cup) ramekins; cover with plastic wrap, pressing plastic wrap directly onto surface of coconut milk mixture. Refrigerate 2 hours. Garnish with toasted coconut.

FOR MANGO COMPOTE

Place diced mango in a medium bowl. (Note that mangoes have a hard oblong pit that runs through the narrow center. To easily cube the fruit, cut each round "cheek" away from pit, score with a paring knife, and cut fruit away from peel.) Then zest lime into a bowl, and stir to combine. When ready, stir in honey. Serve Mango Compote with Haupia. If desired, top each glass with a toasted marshmallow and a sprinkle of lime zest. (The marshmallow in our photograph was carefully trimmed to create straight lines.)

ABOVE: Playful Goofy poses with a young guest in the gardens of Aulani, A Disney Resort & Spa.

CHAPTER SEVEN
Drinks

LIFTING YOUR GLASS FOR A TOAST IS encouraged during the jubilant popping of Champagne corks during the "Be Our Guest" number in *Beauty and the Beast* (1991), which perfectly conveys the joys of celebrating together. The beverages in this chapter range from a crisp martini like you might find at a fancy establishment such as Gusteau's from Disney and Pixar's 2007 classic *Ratatouille*, to a Peanut Butter & Jelly Milkshake, which combines ingredients as perfectly as the pairing of Mickey Mouse and Minnie Mouse. There's a little something for any kind of celebration.

DOUBLE PEAR MARTINI

Cocktails at Carthay Circle Lounge are handcrafted by mixologists with attention to detail, including unique glassware, gourmet garnishes, and drink-specific ice. This one is pure elegance in a cocktail glass with the subtle sweetness of pears and a splash of lime for brightness.

SERVES 1

FROM THE DISNEYLAND RESORT

1 ounce vodka

1 ounce pear-flavored vodka

1 ounce pear nectar

½ ounce fresh lime juice

¼ ounce (1 pump) Monin® Agave Organic Nectar

1 Tamaya Chilean wild baby pear, for garnish

Mint leaf, for garnish

Combine in mixing glass, add ice, shake, and strain into martini glass. Garnish with baby pear slice and a large mint leaf on a clear pick in the glass.

BUENA VISTA STREET · DISNEY CALIFORNIA ADVENTURE

CALPICO® CONCENTRATE YOGURT-STRAWBERRY SWIRL SAKE

FESTIVAL DEBUT: 2018 · TAKUMI TABLE FOOD STUDIO

You can find CALPICO® Concentrate drink mix, a fermented milk-based drink, online. It's made from lactic acid and nonfat dry milk for a sweet flavor similar to vanilla yogurt.

SERVES 1

FROM THE WALT DISNEY WORLD RESORT

1¾ ounces sake

1½ ounces CALPICO® Concentrate drink mix

½ ounce prepared piña colada mix

½ cup ice cubes

2 tablespoons frozen diced strawberries

Add sake, CALPICO® Concentrate, piña colada mix, and ice cubes to blender; blend until smooth. Pour half of blended mixture into a chilled Champagne flute. Add a layer of strawberries, then top with remaining mixture and lightly swirl strawberries.

IRISH STOUT & IRISH CREAM MILKSHAKE

FESTIVAL DEBUT: 2018 · IRELAND GLOBAL MARKETPLACE

A little stout, a little Irish cream . . . what's not to love about this grown-up milkshake?

SERVES 2

FROM THE WALT DISNEY WORLD RESORT

½ cup vanilla ice cream

4 ounces Irish stout

4 ounces Irish cream

Cocoa powder, for garnish

Mix ice cream, Irish stout, and Irish cream in blender until smooth. Pour into serving glasses and garnish with a sprinkle of cocoa powder.

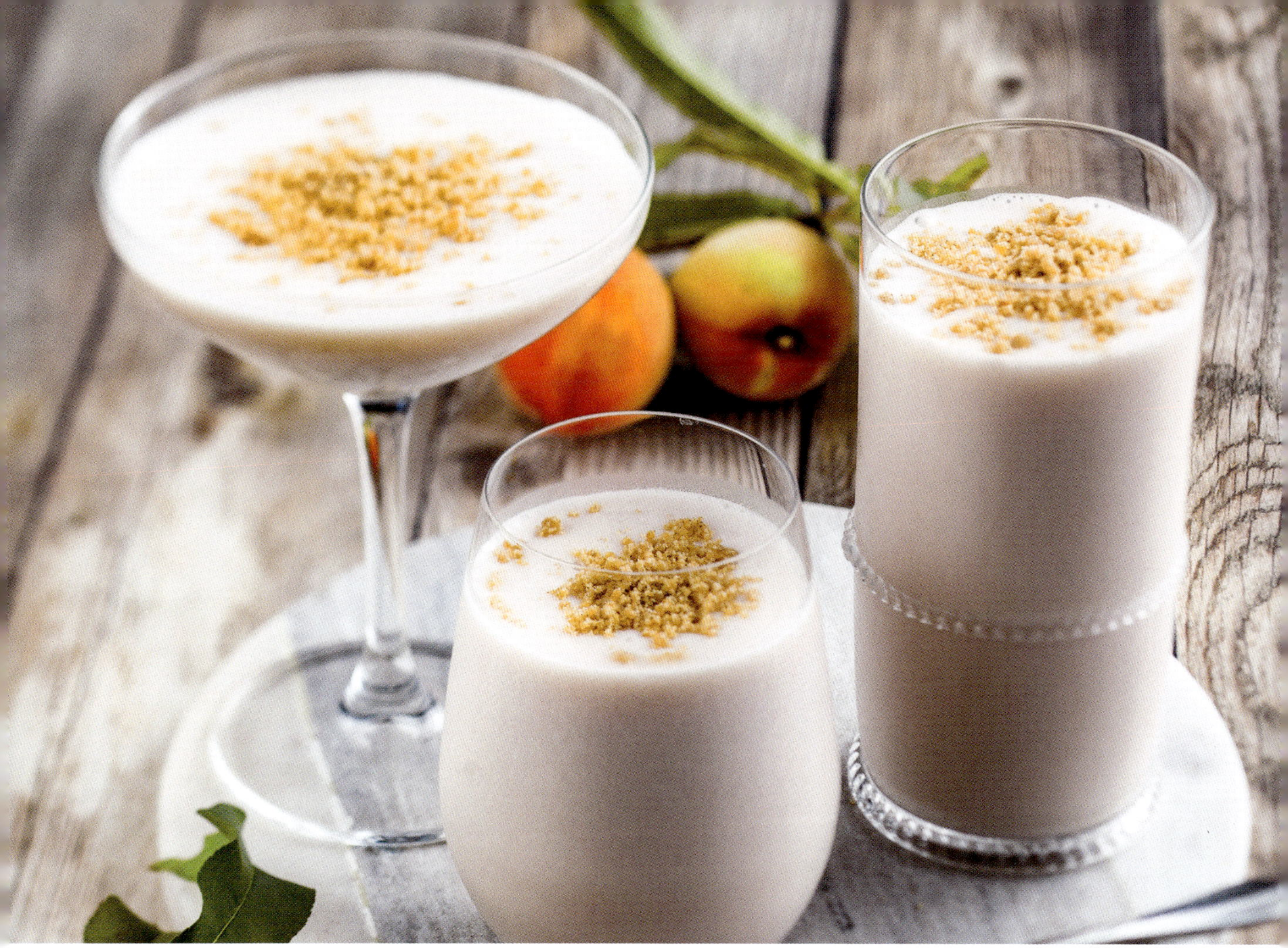

HONEY-PEACH COBBLER FREEZE

FESTIVAL DEBUT: 2018 · HONEY BEE-STRO OUTDOOR KITCHEN

Perfect for peach season. For a grown-up version, add 1 ¼ ounces blueberry vodka.

SERVES 2

FROM THE WALT DISNEY WORLD RESORT

2 cups diced fresh peaches, peeled

1 ½ tablespoons honey

2 cups frozen vanilla yogurt

½ cup milk

½ cup granola, for topping

Blend peaches, honey, frozen yogurt, and milk in blender until smooth. Pour into 2 tall glasses and garnish with granola.

BLACK CHERRY BOURBON HOT CHOCOLATE

REMEMBERED FROM DISNEY'S HOLLYWOOD STUDIOS

Warm up and get in the holiday spirit with this easy libation.

SERVES 1

FROM THE WALT DISNEY WORLD RESORT

Mix together hot chocolate powder with hot water (or warm milk). Add toasted marshmallow syrup and bourbon. Stir together, and top with whipped cream and a cherry.

1 package of hot chocolate powder mix

5 ounces hot water (or warm milk)

½ ounce toasted marshmallow syrup

1 ¼ ounces black cherry bourbon

2 ounces whipped cream, for garnish

1 maraschino cherry, for garnish

ACROSS DISNEY'S HOLLYWOOD STUDIOS, SEASONALLY

PEANUT BUTTER & JELLY MILKSHAKE

REMEMBERED FROM 50'S PRIME TIME CAFÉ

This is Pam's all-time favorite at the Walt Disney World Resort, and it has been on the menu at 50's Prime Time Café since the restaurant debuted in 1989. These four ingredients will take you back to your childhood.

SERVES 1

FROM THE WALT DISNEY WORLD RESORT

Blend ingredients in a blender until smooth. Add additional peanut butter or jelly, to taste. Top with whipped cream and a cherry.

2 tablespoons peanut butter, plus more to taste

2 tablespoons grape jelly, plus more to taste

2 cups vanilla ice cream

4 tablespoons whole or 2 percent milk

2 ounces whipped cream, for garnish

1 maraschino cherry, for garnish

PUMPKIN MILKSHAKES
WITH ALMOND COOKIES

If you're making milkshakes for adults, bourbon adds panache and punch to this seasonal sweet. The cookies are a crunchy sidenote.

SERVES 4-6

FROM THE WALT DISNEY WORLD RESORT

FOR PUMPKIN ICE CREAM

1 Whisk pumpkin and vanilla in a small bowl until combined. Refrigerate until ready to use.

2 Combine egg yolks, 4 tablespoons brown sugar, ½ cup heavy cream, ginger, cinnamon, salt, and nutmeg in a bowl, whisking until sugar is dissolved, and set aside.

3 Combine remaining 1½ cups heavy cream and ½ cup brown sugar in a medium saucepan. Whisk over medium heat for 5 minutes, until bubbles form around the edge of the pan. Remove from heat. Gradually whisk ½ cup of the warm cream-sugar into the egg mixture until smooth. Then pour entire egg mixture into saucepan with remaining cream-sugar mixture.

4 Cook over medium heat, stirring constantly with a wooden spoon, for 5 minutes, until custard is thick enough to coat the back of the spoon but is not boiling.

5 Strain custard through a fine-mesh strainer into a bowl. Place bowl in an ice bath and stir to cool. Whisk pumpkin mixture into the custard. Cover with plastic wrap, pressing directly onto the top. Refrigerate at least 3 hours.

6 Transfer to an ice cream maker and freeze according to manufacturer's instructions. If desired, add bourbon whiskey during the last minute of churning. Store covered in freezer until ready to serve.

PUMPKIN ICE CREAM

1 cup canned or fresh pumpkin

1 teaspoon vanilla extract

5 large pasteurized egg yolks

¾ cup brown sugar, divided

2 cups heavy cream, divided

½ teaspoon ground ginger

½ teaspoon ground cinnamon

¼ teaspoon salt

⅛ teaspoon ground nutmeg

1 tablespoon bourbon whiskey, if desired for adults

OPPOSITE, RIGHT: Dopey greets a young guest at Story Book Dining at Artist Point with Snow White.

FOR ALMOND COOKIES

1 Preheat oven to 325°F. Cream almond paste and sugar in an electric mixer fitted with a paddle attachment until fluffy.

2 Add egg whites and mix until smooth. Using a 1-inch cookie scoop, place cookie dough on a baking sheet lined with parchment paper. Top with crushed Marcona almonds.

3 Bake for 24 to 25 minutes, until golden brown. Store in an airtight container until ready to serve.

FOR MILKSHAKES

Place Pumpkin Ice Cream and heavy cream in a blender. Blend on medium speed until smooth, adding additional heavy cream if milkshakes are too thick. Then pour into glasses and serve with Almond Cookies.

ALMOND COOKIES

7 ounces (¾ cup) almond paste

1 cup sugar

2 large egg whites

4 tablespoons lightly crushed Marcona almonds

MILKSHAKES

3 cups Pumpkin Ice Cream

1 ½ cups heavy cream, plus more to taste

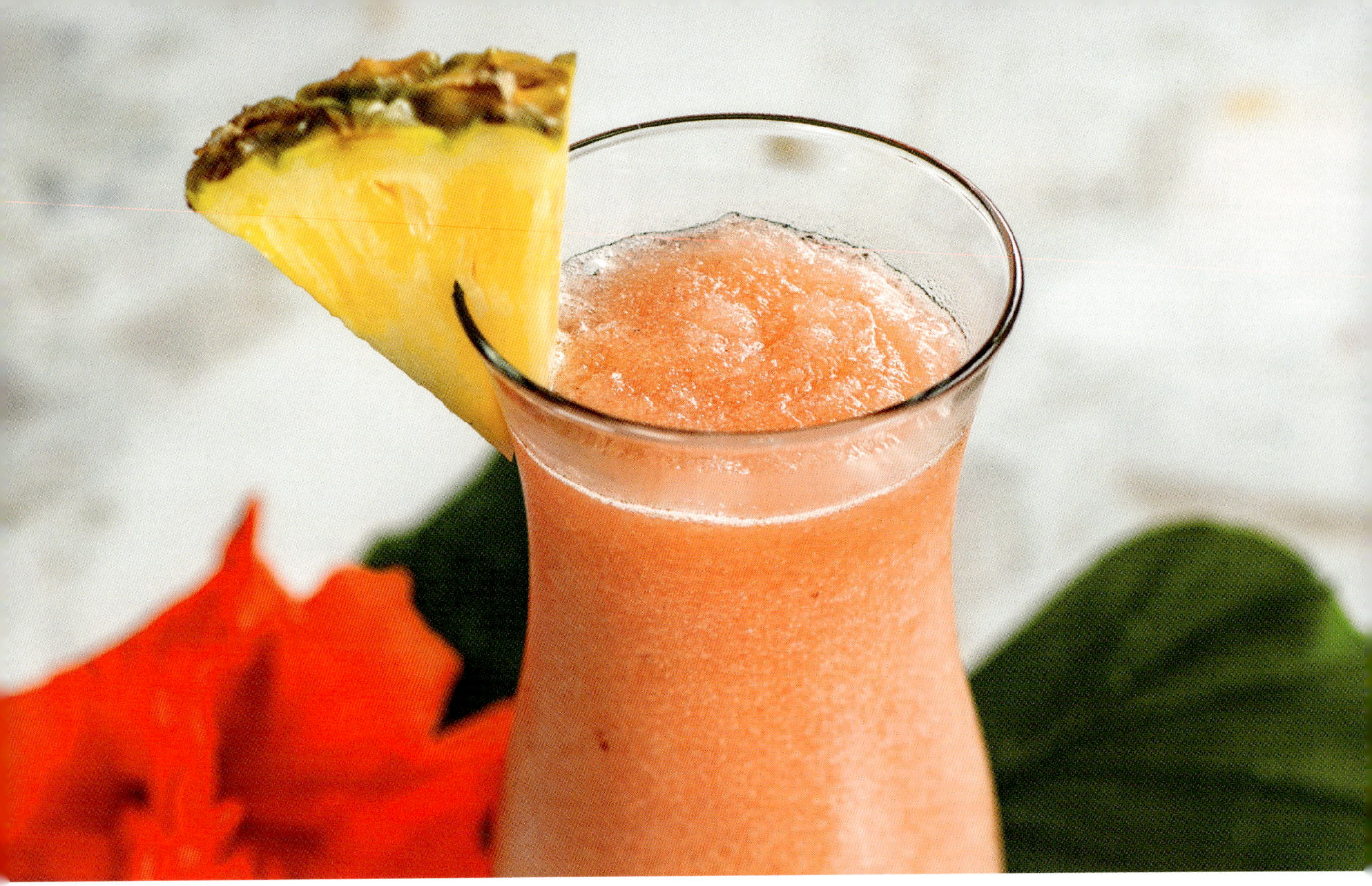

KUNGALOOSH

Disney fans remember this cocktail from the Adventurers Club at Walt Disney World Resort, a concept designed and created by Walt Disney Imagineering in the late 1980s. "Kungaloosh" was the club's official greeting and official beverage. Trader Sam's pays homage with this "IYKYK" cocktail.

SERVES 1

FROM THE WALT DISNEY WORLD RESORT

¾ ounce spiced rum

¾ ounce light rum

½ ounce blackberry brandy

2 ounces strawberry daiquiri mix

2 ounces orange juice

7 ounces crushed ice

Fresh pineapple wedge, for garnish

Put all ingredients in a blender and mix well. Serve in a tall glass, and garnish with a pineapple wedge.

SOUL CANDY

This recipe first appeared in 2006 in the very first Delicious Disney cookbook. We definitely consider it a drink to soothe one's soul.

SERVES 1

FROM THE WALT DISNEY WORLD RESORT

Mix vodka, both liqueurs, and cappuccino in a warm 12-ounce coffee glass. Garnish with freshly whipped cream and white and dark chocolate shavings.

½ ounce Dutch chocolate vodka

¾ ounce white chocolate liqueur

¾ ounce dark chocolate liqueur

4 ounces cappuccino

Freshly whipped cream, for serving

White and dark chocolate shavings, for garnish

INDEX OF DESSERT RECIPES & SOURCES

Recipes

Sources

PHOTOGRAPHIC INDEX

CHAPTER ONE
Cookies & Bars

2–5
MEYER LEMON MACARONS
WITH BLUEBERRY PRESERVES &
HOMEMADE BUTTERCREAM

6–7
SNICKERDOODLE COOKIES
WITH SNICKERS® BAR PIECES

8–10
PEANUT BUTTER
BROWNIES

11
MADELEINES

12
S'MORES

13
DISNEY'S RIVIERA RESORT
SIGNATURE COOKIE

14–15
PIZZELLE CANNOLI

16–17
COOKIES & CREAM
BONBONS

18
PLANT-BASED CHOCOLATE
CHIP COOKIE FRIES

19
S'MORES COOKIES

20–21
SALTED CARAMEL
MAGIC BAR BLONDIE

22–23
WHOLE WHEAT CHOCOLATE
CHIP COOKIES

CHAPTER TWO
Pies, Tarts & Crisps

26–27
STRAWBERRY TWISTS

28–29
CHOCOLATE MUD
PIE-O-RAMA

30–31
MILK CHOCOLATE–
ALMOND TARTS

32–33
BOURBON-CHIPOTLE
CHOCOLATE WHOOPIE PIES

34–35
KUMQUAT MINI PIES

36–37
BLUEBERRY-ALMOND
TARTS

38–39

SPICED CHOCOLATE TART

40–41

CHOCOLATE-
HAZELNUT TARTS

42–43

PEANUT BUTTER, BANANA
& APPLEWOOD-SMOKED
CANDIED BACON TREAT

44–45

APPLE PIE

46–47

GLUTEN-FREE
KĪLAUEA TORTE

48–49

CHOCOLATE-CRUSTED
KEY LIME PIE

50–51

MASCARPONE-
AMARETTO TART

52–53

PEANUT BUTTER PIE

54–55

PINEAPPLE-COCONUT
COBBLER

CHAPTER
THREE
Cakes

58–59

LEMON BUMBLEBEE
CUPCAKES

60–61

LEMON TEA CAKE,
CELEBRATING DISNEY100

62–63

TIRAMISU

64–65

WARM APPLE-BUTTER
CAKE

66–67

CHOCOLATE TRUFFLE
CAKES WITH GANACHE

68–69

TRIPLE CHOCOLATE
CUPCAKES

70–71

ALMOND-SWEET
CORN CAKE

72–73

GREEK YOGURT–
VANILLA CAKE

74–75

PISTACHIO-CARDAMOM
CAKES WITH CHOCOLATE-
COCONUT CREAM

76–77

OLIVE OIL CAKE
WITH LEMON CURD

78–79

ROCKY ROAD CAKE

80–81

AVOCADO CUSTARD
CAKES

82–84

CAFÉ CON LECHE CHOUX

85–86

WARM CHOCOLATE CAKE
WITH MOLTEN RASPBERRY-
CARAMEL CENTER

87–89
CHOCOLATE CREAM
COOKIE CUPCAKES

90–92
CHOCOLATE–PEANUT
BUTTER PRETZEL CAKE

93–95
PLANT-BASED PEANUT
& BANANA TORTE

96–97
PEANUT BUTTER &
JELLY CUPCAKES

98–99
PINEAPPLE CUPCAKES,
INSPIRED BY DOLE WHIP®

100
BANANAS FOSTER
ANGEL FOOD CAKE
WITH VANILLA ICE CREAM

101
MOIST APPLE CAKE

CHAPTER FOUR
Shortcakes & Cheesecakes

104–106
CRÈME FRAÎCHE
CHEESECAKE

107–109
STRAWBERRY-RHUBARB
SHORTCAKE

110–111
VANILLA BEAN-YOGURT
CHEESECAKE

112–113
BLUEBERRY-LIME
CHEESECAKE ROLL

114–115
CHEESECAKE
WITH PASSION FRUIT CURD

116–118
MAPLE-BOURBON
CHEESECAKE

119–121
GLUTEN-FRIENDLY LEMON
MERINGUE CHEESECAKE
(NO SUGAR ADDED)

122–123
STILTON CHEESECAKE

124–125
PLANT-BASED COFFEE &
CASHEW CHEESECAKE

126–127
STRAWBERRY SHORTCAKE
WITH LEMON CORN BREAD

CHAPTER FIVE
Bread, Transformed

130–131
BANANA SPLIT
MONTE CRISTO

132–133
COOKIES & CREAM
BREAD PUDDING

134–135
ORANGE-CRANBERRY
BREAD PUDDING WITH WARM
ORANGE-VANILLA SAUCE

136–137
PLANT-BASED
BANANA BREAD
WITH WARM MIXED-BERRY COMPOTE

138–139
PRETZEL BREAD PUDDING
WITH WARM VANILLA SAUCE

140–141

BANANA BREAD PUDDING
WITH VANILLA SAUCE

142–143

ORANGE-CRANBERRY
MUFFINS

144–145

HOUSE-MADE DONUTS

146–147

PLANT-BASED
LAVENDER DONUTS

148–149

GLUTEN-FRIENDLY
BEIGNETS

150–151

PIÑA COLADA BREAD
PUDDING

152–153

MALASADAS

CHAPTER SIX
Creamy & Frozen Confections

156–158

DARTH BY CHOCOLATE

160–162

COCONUT-MANGO POSSET
(TAPIOCA)

163–165

COCONUT-LIME SEMIFREDDO
WITH STRAWBERRY-CITRUS SOUP

166–167

WHITE CHOCOLATE–JASMINE
TEA MOUSSE *WITH LEMON-
LIME CURD & HONEY-OAT CRISP*

168–169

ESPRESSO-CARAMEL
CREAM

170–171

AVOCADO PUDDING
(POTTED CHOCOLATE)

172–173

LEMON CUSTARD VERRINE
WITH BLUEBERRY COMPOTE

174–175

WARM CHOCOLATE PUDDING
WITH IRISH CREAM CUSTARD SAUCE

176–177

PEANUT BUTTER–WHITE
CHOCOLATE MOUSSE

178–179

BANANA-ALMOND SOFT-
SERVE SUNDAE *WITH FRESH
BERRIES & CRUNCHY CHOCOLATE OATS*

180–181

CHOCOLATE PICANTE

182–183

DECONSTRUCTED PAVLOVA

184–185

PLANT-BASED GUAVA
MOUSSE ON A SUGAR COOKIE

186–187

BANANA EGG ROLLS

188–190

PASSION FRUIT–
COCONUT PARFAIT

191

MAPLE CRÈME BRÛLÈE

192–194

COCONUT–KEY LIME SUNDAE

195–197

PISTACHIO MOUSSE
WITH LEMON CURD & COFFEE-HAZELNUT CUSTARD

198–199

PANNA "CARPA"

200–201

ROASTED WHITE CHOCOLATE BUDINO

202–203

RASPBERRY GELATO
(DAIRY-FREE)

204–205

HAUPIA
WITH MANGO COMPOTE

CHAPTER SEVEN
Drinks

208

DOUBLE PEAR MARTINI

209

CALPICO® CONCENTRATE YOGURT-STRAWBERRY SWIRL SAKE

210

IRISH STOUT & IRISH CREAM MILKSHAKE

211

HONEY-PEACH COBBLER FREEZE

212

BLACK CHERRY BOURBON HOT CHOCOLATE

213

PEANUT BUTTER & JELLY MILKSHAKE

214–215

PUMPKIN MILKSHAKES
WITH ALMOND COOKIES

216

KUNGALOOSH

217

SOUL CANDY

ACKNOWLEDGMENTS

Karen McClintock gets my first and most important thank-you, as always. Gratitude to Katie Wilson for both testing recipes and her amazing proofreading, one of the most important jobs in creating a cookbook. Jennifer Eastwood, Catalina Castro, and Lindsay Broderick, thank you for making these books come to life with all your behind-the-scenes work, attention to detail, and TLC.

—Pam Brandon

THIS BOOK'S PRODUCERS WOULD LIKE TO SPECIALLY THANK Becky Ballentine, Alyce Diamandis, Katie Farmand, Michele Fortier, Shelby Grasser, Kiran Jeffery, Aileen Kutaka, Mark LaVine, Renee Leask, Ryan March, Karen McClintock, Wendy Meyers, Frank Moreno, Kent Morikawa, David Nguyen, Nikki Nguyen, Chris Ostrander, David Roark, Stacy Salazar, Whitney Simmons, Karlos Siqueiros, Annie Skogsbergh, Matt Stroshane, Lindsay Swantek, Kimi Thompson, Janice Thomson, Cayla Ward, Katie Wilson, Jennifer Woods, and Juleen Woods.

ALSO THANK YOU TO THOSE AT DISNEY PUBLISHING: Nancee Adams, Jennifer Black, Christine Choi, Monique Diman-Riley, Jennifer Flagg, Kelly Forsythe, Susan Gerber, Alison Giordano, Daneen Goodwin, Tyra Harris, Winnie Ho, Jackson Kaplan, Vicki Korlishin, Kaitie Leary, Meredith Lisbin, Warren Meislin, Scott Piehl, Rachel Rivera, Zan Schneider, Alexandra Serrano, Fanny Sheffield, Dina Sherman, Megan Speer-Levi, Jenny Spring, Pat Van Note, Lynn Waggoner, Jessie Ward, and Rudy Zamora.

BIBLIOGRAPHY & SOURCES

Brandon, Pam; and the Disney Chefs, with commemorative contributions by Marcy Carriker Smothers and essays by the Staff of the Walt Disney Archives. *Delicious Disney: Disneyland: Recipes & Stories from The Happiest Place on Earth*. Los Angeles • New York: Disney Editions, 2023.

Brandon, Pam; and Marcy Carriker Smothers and the Disney Chefs. *Delicious Disney: Walt Disney World: Recipes & Stories from The Most Magical Place on Earth*. Los Angeles • New York: Disney Editions, 2021.

Brandon, Pam; and the Disney Chefs. *The Official Disney Parks Celebration Cookbook: 101 Festival Recipes from the Delicious Disney Vault*. Los Angeles • New York: Disney Editions, 2024.

____. *The Official Disney Parks Cookbook: 101 Magical Recipes from the Delicious Disney Vault*. Los Angeles • New York: Disney Editions, 2022.

____. *Delicious Disney: The Fresh Edition*. Los Angeles • New York: Disney Editions, 2019.

____. *Disney Festivals Cookbook: 50 New Recipes, 6 Fabulous Festivals*. Lake Buena Vista, Florida • Anaheim, California: The Walt Disney Company, 2018.

____. *Disney Food and Wine Festivals Coast to Coast Cookbook— Disney California Adventure & EPCOT*. Lake Buena Vista, Florida • Anaheim, California: The Walt Disney Company, 2017.

____. *The Best of EPCOT Festivals Cookbook*. Lake Buena Vista, Florida • Anaheim, California: The Walt Disney Company, 2016.

____. *Delicious Disney: Sweet Treats*. Los Angeles • New York: Disney Editions, 2016.

____. *EPCOT International Food & Wine Festival [2015]: Recipes & Stories Celebrating 20 Years*. Lake Buena Vista, Florida • Anaheim, California: The Walt Disney Company, 2015.

____. *A Cooking Safari with Mickey: Recipes from Disney's Animal Kingdom Theme Park and Disney's Animal Kingdom Lodge*. Los Angeles • New York: Disney Editions, 2015.

____. *A Taste of EPCOT: Festival Food from Around the Globe Cookbook*. Lake Buena Vista, Florida • Anaheim, California: The Walt Disney Company, 2014.

____. *Kitchen Magic with Mickey: Favorite Recipes from the Disney Parks and Cruise Ships*. Los Angeles • New York: Disney Editions, 2014.

____. *EPCOT International Food & Wine Festival [2013] Cookbook: Taste Your Way Around the World*. Lake Buena Vista, Florida • Anaheim, California: The Walt Disney Company, 2013.

____. *EPCOT International Food & Wine Festival [2012] Cookbook: Taste Your Way Around the World*. Lake Buena Vista, Florida • Anaheim, California: The Walt Disney Company, 2012.

____. *Delicious Disney: Holidays*. New York: Disney Editions, 2012.

____. *EPCOT International Food & Wine Festival [2011] Cookbook: Passport to a World of Flavors*. Lake Buena Vista, Florida • Anaheim, California: The Walt Disney Company, 2011.

____. *Delicious Disney: Just for Kids*. New York: Disney Editions, 2011.

____. *EPCOT International Food & Wine Festival [2010] Cookbook: Celebrating 15 Years of Delicious Discoveries*. Lake Buena Vista, Florida • Anaheim, California: The Walt Disney Company, 2010.

____. *Chef Mickey: Treasures from the Vault & Delicious New Favorites*. New York: Disney Editions, 2010.

____. *EPCOT International Food & Wine Festival [2009] Cookbook: 50 Most Requested Recipes of the EPCOT International Food & Wine Festival*. Lake Buena Vista, Florida • Anaheim, California: The Walt Disney Company, 2009.

____. *EPCOT International Food & Wine Festival [2008] Cookbook: 25 Select Festival Favorite Recipes from Past and Present*. Lake Buena Vista, Florida • Anaheim, California: The Walt Disney Company, 2008.

____. *Delicious Disney: Desserts*. New York: Disney Editions, 2008.

____. *Delicious Disney*. New York: Disney Editions, 2006.

____. *Cooking with Mickey and the Disney Chefs: Recipes from Walt Disney World Resort, Disneyland Resort, and Disney Cruise Line*. New York: Disney Editions, 2004.

____. *Cooking with Mickey and the Chefs of Walt Disney World Resort*. New York: Hyperion, 1998.

Disney Chefs. *Mickey's Gourmet Cookbook: The Most Popular Recipes from Walt Disney World and Disneyland*. New York: Hyperion, 1994.

____. *Cooking with Mickey—Gourmet Mickey Cookbook: The Most Requested Recipes from Walt Disney World and Disneyland, Volume II*. Lake Buena Vista, Florida • Anaheim, California: The Walt Disney Company, 1991.

____. *Cooking with Mickey Around Our World: The MOST Requested Recipes from Walt Disney World and Disneyland*. Lake Buena Vista, Florida • Anaheim, California: The Walt Disney Company, 1986.

Smith, Dave; and Steven Vagnini. *Disney A to Z: The Official Encyclopedia, Sixth Edition*. Los Angeles • New York: Disney Editions, 2023.

IMAGE CREDITS

All images in this book courtesy **Yellow Shoes Marketing Resource Center**, with exception of the photos by **Jennifer Eastwood** on pages 62, 63 (bottom), and 159.

MORE RECIPES FROM THE
DELICIOUS
DISNEY
VAULT

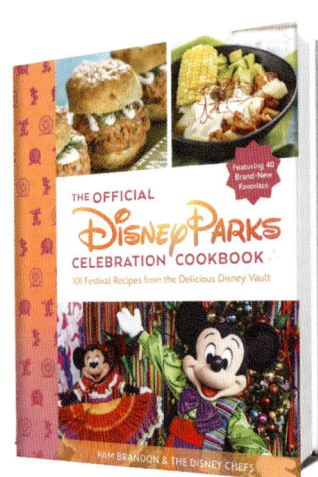
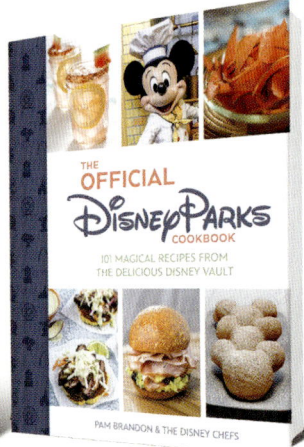

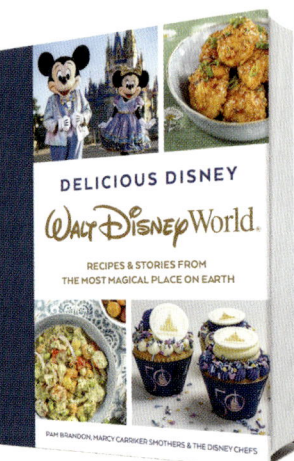

For more information, visit Books.Disney.com/series/Delicious-Disney

DISNEP EDITIONS